BEYOND THE WOMAN QUESTION

Beyond the Woman Question

Reconstructing Gendered Identities in Early India

SNIGDHA SINGH
SHATARUPA BHATTACHARYA
SHWETANSHU BHUSHAN
TARA SHEEMAR

with an Introduction by
KUMKUM ROY

PRIMUS BOOKS

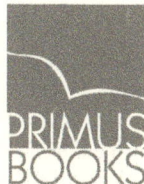

PRIMUS BOOKS
An imprint of Ratna Sagar P. Ltd.
Virat Bhavan
Mukherjee Nagar Commercial Complex
Delhi 110 009

Offices at
CHENNAI LUCKNOW
AGRA AHMEDABAD BENGALURU COIMBATORE DEHRADUN GUWAHATI
HYDERABAD JAIPUR JALANDHAR KANPUR KOCHI KOLKATA MADURAI
MUMBAI PATNA RANCHI VARANASI

First published 2018

ISBN: 978-93-84092-77-1 (hardback)
ISBN: 978-93-84092-78-8 (POD)
ISBN: 978-93-84092-79-5 (e-book)

Published by Primus Books

Laser typeset by Mithu Karmakar
mithu.karma@gmail.com

Printed and bound in India by
Replika Press Pvt. Ltd.

To

Our Friends
Families
and
Fellow Travellers

Contents

List of Tables ix
List of Plates and Figures x
Acknowledgements xi

Introduction
KUMKUM ROY 1

PART I: ENGRAVED IDENTITIES

1. Exploring the Question of Gender at an Early *Stūpa:* Inscriptions and Images
SNIGDHA SINGH 21

2. Gender, *Dāna* and Epigraphs: Access to Resources in Early Medieval Central India
SHATARUPA BHATTACHARYA 63

PART II: NORMS AND NARRATIVES

3. Ensuring the Arrival of Sons: Birth *Saṃskāras* in the Gṛhyasūtras
SHWETANSHU BHUSHAN 103

4. Re-viewing Elite Sexuality: Erotic Love, Adultery, and Chastity in the *Kathāsaritsāgara*
TARA SHEEMAR 124

Notes on Authors 167
Index 169

List of Tables

1.1 Indicating Individual and Collective Donations from the Inscriptions at Bharhut 26
1.2 Indicating Identity based on Religion from the Inscriptions at Bharhut 28
1.3 Indicating Identity based on Gender Difference of Lay Donors from the Inscriptions at Bharhut 29
1.4 Indicating Identities based on Places of Residence from the Inscriptions at Bharhut 31
1.5 Indicating Identities based on Kinship Ties from the Inscriptions at Bharhut 35
1.6 Indicating Identities based on the Occupations of the Donors from Bharhut 37
1.7 Indicating the Donations Made at Bharhut 40

2.1 Gendered Distribution of Grants 70

List of Plates and Figures

PLATES

1.1 Disciples listening to discourse 56
1.2 *Apsarās* and musicians 56
1.3 Ajātaśatru with courtiers 57
1.4 Ajātaśatru's procession with women attendants 57
1.5 Cāpa Devā's pillar gift 58
1.6 Occupations of *gahapatnī* and maid-servant/labourer 58
1.7 Female soldier 58
1.8 Merchants 59
1.9 Soldier 59
1.10 Sirimā *devatā* 59
1.11 Suciloma yakṣa 60
1.12 Queen adorning herself 60
1.13 Prasenajit, south gate pillar 60
1.14 Sudarśanā *yakṣinī* 61
1.15 Cakavāka, king of *nāgas* 61
1.16 Prasenajit, south gate pillar with portrayal of *nāga* and *nāgins* 61
1.17 Medallion, purchase of Jetavana and bullock-cart 62

FIGURES

2.1 Ratio of the Vākāṭaka Gifts 72
2.2 Gendered Distribution of the Vākāṭaka Grants 74
2.3 Ratio of the Kalacuri Gifts 77
2.4 Gendered Distribution of the Kalacuri Grants 80
2.5 Ratio of the Candella Gifts 83
2.6 Gendered Distribution of Candella Grants 86
2.7 Changing Access to Resources 90

Acknowledgements

WE HAVE WORKED TOGETHER on this volume, a process that was often enjoyable, sometimes tedious and even frustrating, and occasionally exciting. We would not have been able to see it through without one another.

We have benefited from institutional support, from the Centre for Historical Studies, Jawaharlal Nehru University, New Delhi, and especially from the generosity of the faculty members of the Ancient Unit, evident in both formal and informal interaction over the years. We are thankful to our colleagues and students at the Centre for Historical Studies, at Miranda House, Lady Shri Ram College, and Janki Devi Memorial College.

We have drawn on the resources of several institutions—the American Institute of Indian Studies, Gurgaon; the Archaeological Survey of India, Delhi; the Indian Council of Historical Research, Delhi; and the libraries of Delhi University and Jawaharlal Nehru University, including the Centre for Advanced Study Library of the Centre for Historical Studies, and would like to thank the staff of all these institutions for their support.

Finally, we have relied on, and tested the patience of our friends and families. It is to them, and to our fellow travellers that this volume is dedicated.

Introduction

Kumkum Roy

THE TURN OF THE TWENTIETH century and the first decade of the twenty-first have witnessed a sustained interest in engendering history. This has been somewhat uneven, more or less fruitful, lively, engaged, challenging and demanding. How do we visualize the present moment in terms of our locations within academic spaces, our dialogues with mainstream disciplines such as history, and the research that is possible within the discipline? These are some of the questions we will explore before we turn to the often tentative but rich interventions that have been made through their research by four scholars (young and not so young) in the last decade. We explore how far their research has been shaped or even constrained by the 'woman question' and the ways in which they have attempted to move beyond that. The extent to which they have been successful, as well as the possible paths ahead are for readers and other researchers to assess.

The Resilience of the Woman Question

Through the seventies, eighties and nineties of the twentieth century, feminist scholars within history and other disciplines analysed, attempted to understand and offered critiques of the 'woman question' that loomed large in our understanding of ancient Indian history. Some of the earliest and most incisive critiques were offered by Uma Chakravarti, whose writings[1] generated widespread debate and discussion, apart from being disseminated widely. And yet, in the twenty-first century, the 'woman question' seems to be as alive and kicking as it was in the nineteenth century. Here, I turn briefly to the contents and contexts of the woman question as it emerged in the nineteenth century and focus on just one example of how it has resurfaced in the twenty-first, highlighting, in the process, its problems.

The woman question acquired significance in the colonial context. Briefly, part of the strategy of the British colonial authorities in India rested on creating an understanding that they were shouldering the 'white man's burden' of civilizing the 'barbarous' Indians. One of the ways of constructing this image of the 'barbarian' or 'uncivilized' East was by focusing on what was designated as the status of women. This, the colonial authorities argued, was abysmally low—widows were either condemned to burn on the funeral pyres of their husbands to prove that they were virtuous sati, or live lives of ignominy, indignity and dire poverty. They were denied access to education, child marriage was rampant, and they had no access to property.

Understandably, these formulations generated a range of responses. On the one hand were reformers who implicitly and explicitly accepted the validity of the colonial critique and attempted to redress what was seen as a situation of social injustice. Others chose a more defensive route, evident, for instance, in the text of A.S. Altekar[2] that has remained the most accessible work on women in ancient India throughout the twentieth century, and promises to thrive in the twenty-first century as well.

To summarize Altekar's now classic and influential position—he argued that while the position of women in the nineteenth and twentieth centuries was admittedly deplorable, this had not always been so. Instead, there had been a glorious past, identified as the Vedic age, when there were women seers, when women had access to education, performed Vedic rituals, and took an active role in public life. What is more, the evils of sati, child marriage and enforced widowhood were all absent in this projected golden age.

What, then, led to the degeneration that Altekar observed around him? His answers were fairly simple—this had to do with the dilution of the 'pure' Aryan blood through contact with indigenous śūdra women, to 'foreign' invasions, especially but not only by Islamic people, and to the growth of ascetic traditions such as Buddhism, and, to a lesser extent, Jainism, that valorized renunciation as opposed to the model of the householder on which the Vedic tradition rested.

As Chakravarti[3] and I[4] have pointed out elsewhere, these formulations were highly problematic. Chakravarti drew attention to the fact that the category of woman was by no means homogeneous, and that there was a need to understand why servile women whose presence is evident in Vedic literature were ignored in the image of the past that was created. This image, clearly, resonated with the concerns of middle-class, upper-caste Hindu, often Western educated, men (and to some extent women). To generalize and universalize it into an image of the Indian woman was anachronistic and simplistic to say the least.

It is also evident that the focus on a set of markers of status often prevented engagement with other issues—with relations of production and reproduction, for instance, and, at another level, with the ways in which texts such as Vedic literature were often used to constitute meanings.

In other words, the Altekarian paradigm assumed status as a given, rather than as something that could be actively constituted, consolidated and even challenged through a variety of strategies. So, in spite of its apparent dynamism, the Altekarian model provides us with a static, unchanging picture of the past.

At another level, the causes that Altekar identified as being responsible for the decline in the status of women, have proved troubling, to say the least. Chakravarti pointed out their implicit and explicit racism and communalism. Also, it was sadly ironic that Altekar found it fit to dismiss those very traditions that more or less grudgingly conceded, created and sustained alternative spaces for women outside the confines of the household.

One would have thought that with such critiques available and circulating in the public domain for at least two decades and more, the Altekarian paradigm would be laid to rest. However, these expectations have been belied, in a rather spectacular way, by a volume that forms part of a series intended to provide a comprehensive survey of Indian history.[5] While we focus more closely on a handful of essays from this volume, it is useful to remember that the ideas expressed by the authors are illustrative rather than exceptional, and that the Altekarian paradigm continues to inform middle-class and upper-caste perceptions, especially amongst those with access to higher education. It has also been reincarnated in a variety of ways in the Western academia.

But to return to our example. In the introduction to *Women in Ancient India*, Shubhada Joshi informs us that Indian traditions consist of a threefold division—Vedic, Sramanic and Tantric. To state the obvious, this threefold classification ignores a whole range of other traditions, both within what is commonly understood as Hinduism and otherwise. The tradition of Bhakti or Puranic Hinduism, for instance, finds no space within this formulation. Nor is there room for Islam, Sikhism or Christianity, to name a few obvious and glaring omissions. Second, and more fundamental, it alerts us to the understanding that Indian and Hindu are regarded as synonymous—once again asserting a commonsensical position whose dangerous political implications cannot be overestimated. Finally, in arguing for a division of Indian history in terms of religious traditions, it pushes us back, almost insidiously, into the traditions of communal historiography that have been critiqued for decades by secular historians. It is also a reminder that the construction of communal and gendered identities are almost inextricably interwoven, and that we ignore these connections at our peril.

Given this perspective, it is not surprising that Joshi assures us that: 'All the three articles are based mainly on *Ṛgveda*, the oldest source of ancient

Indian culture and are in agreement that the position of Vedic women at home and in society was that of respect and dignity, based on equality, harmony, obligation and love towards women.'[6]

Note, once again, the way in which the *Ṛgveda* is automatically equated with the oldest evidence of ancient Indian culture. This ignores the complex mosaic of human existence in the subcontinent that has been painstakingly reconstructed by archaeologists. Many of these traces of human existence, including the Harappan civilization, are prior to the composition and compilation of the *Ṛgveda.* There is also evidence of contemporary, non-Vedic cultures. Given this complexity, asserting the monolithic priority and authority of the *Ṛgveda* is inaccurate to say the least. Second, as mentioned earlier, the women mentioned in the *Ṛgveda* are by no means homogeneous and, therefore, it becomes important for us to specify which women we are talking about, rather than make sweeping generalizations, no matter how comforting these may be.

This refusal to engage with diversity and the attempt to create a monolithic image of the Indian woman is evident in the contribution by Mishra[7] as well. He states: 'This is the reason why woman is ideally regarded as goddess (*Devī*) and in the Indian tradition the name of a woman is suffixed by the appellation '*Devī*' (meaning goddess).'

Once again, the almost glib adoption of the strategy of deification becomes a means for not engaging with unsettling questions of diversity, change, and disruption. Thus, gendered identities are robbed of their critical potential.

Joshi goes on to enlighten us about the causes of the decline of the status of women.[8] Once again, this has a depressingly familiar ring. We are told:

> The major blow from Islam has its long lasting impact on the old Indic culture. It was a major political upheaval. Whenever there are political upheavals, invasions, revolutions, etc, women become the first victims. They are raped, killed, enslaved, as a symbol of victory of the rulers and symbol of the defeat of the ṛuled. The old Indic culture was no exception. The status of women suffered considerably. The freedom of women was encroached upon severely, and they were enslaved in the purdah system.

The historical inaccuracy of this formulation has been pointed out earlier. One can just reiterate that the early and early medieval epigraphic record is replete with inscriptions where 'Hindu'/Brahmanical rulers proclaim their martial exploits in terms of leaving widows behind and/or marrying women from the lineages of those whom they defeated. And, as is well known, veiling, never a universal practice, has a complex, complicated history that cannot be reduced to or explained simply in terms of religious categories.

Joshi also reiterates the idea that Sanskrit was synonymous with the best, implying that its decline was symptomatic of a widespread degeneration: 'The rise of regional languages and increased importance of foreign languages like Persian and Arabic especially in the royal courts, gave a setback to the importance of Sanskrit during the medieval period.'[9]

Once again, as Pollock,[10] amongst others, has made amply evident, histories of languages and literary traditions are complex. To reduce these to a neat hierarchy, and to equate the rise of regional languages with a decline in the status of women, is not particularly useful.

Elsewhere, Joshi[11] goes on to lament the emergence of traditions that no longer regarded the household as the central point of reference. These were associated with the growth of ascetic traditions. Once again, the argument is that the 'decline' of the household was symptomatic of the decline in the status of women.

At the risk of repetition, we need to remind ourselves that the ascetic traditions in fact opened up spaces for some women. Also, the relationship between the ascetic and the householder was often one of complicated symbiosis rather than outright hostility.[12]

If Joshi asserts the validity of the Altekarian paradigm and reiterates its formulations unquestioningly, Sugavaneswaran's[13] approach to the Vedic material is somewhat disingenuous. He cites the familiar verse from the Vedic marriage hymn which wishes that the bride would be the empress of the household, without exploring the implications of imperial authority within the domestic framework. More importantly, he points out that the Vedic hymns do not mention child marriage, they do not prohibit *sagotra* marriages, they do not contain any prohibition of inter-caste marriages, and they contain no indications of domestic violence. All these silences are then used to argue that this was, indeed, an idyllic age. What is ignored in the process is a simple, almost commonsensical precaution expected of academic practitioners—the need to remember that absence of evidence is not necessarily evidence of absence. In this particular instance, Sugavaneswaran assiduously avoids engaging with any discussion on questions of genre. Given that the *Ṛgveda* generally consists of mantras or prayers addressed to a range of gods and goddesses, would one expect to find mention of prescriptions and prohibitions about issues of marriage, for instance, in such a text?

The ability of the Altekarian model to survive well beyond the colonial/nationalist framework in which it originated is significant. Clearly, while much has changed with globalization and liberalization, some ideas continue to resonate and are revived in these times of rapid transition. These include the idea of a monolithic Indian woman, who can then be treated as a site for the constant and the stable, increasingly idealized in an ephemeral present. The lure of this image, with its promise of durability, is so strong that critiques are simply ignored as it is reiterated and reinforced time and again. In the process, opportunities for engaging with the complexities and inconsistencies of both past and present are obliterated.

Emerging Alternatives: Households, Courts, Cities, and Cultural Practices

While the dominant model seems to resound through the decades with remarkable persistence, feminist historians have worked their way through and against the model to enrich our understanding of the past. Here, once again, I discuss writings that are illustrative of these possibilities rather than attempt a comprehensive survey. The focus will be on the painstaking research of Jaya Tyagi,[14] Shonaleeka Kaul,[15] Devika Rangachari[16] and Shalini Shah,[17] all of which appeared during the last decade and have opened up ways of revisioning the past, and of engaging with textual traditions in complex and innovative ways.

All these scholars are acutely sensitive to the contexts in which the texts that we treat as sources were produced. Tyagi's focus is the Gṛhyasūtras, manuals relating to domestic rituals, centred on the *gṛha* or household, produced by and possibly for brāhmaṇas, composed in terse Sanskrit prose, and consisting of prescriptions and prohibitions, dating to the mid-first millennium BCE and somewhat later. While they point to the codification of a range of popular practices, and implicitly and often explicitly create space for rituals that were practised by women, the process of generating the texts was clearly under the control of upper-caste men.

Kaul draws primarily on the Sanskrit *kāvya* tradition that flourished during the first millennium CE, produced and perhaps consumed within an urban milieu, primarily but not solely by elite men. Rangachari taps many of the same resources, but with a different set of questions, and also analyses inscriptions that are more securely dated and localized, pertaining to some of the major early medieval dynasties. Shah, too, delves into the *kāvyas*, but also draws on several diverse *śāstras*, including medical and philosophical treatises, as also, inevitably, the *Kāma Sūtra.* All these scholars explore how the 'sources' themselves are implicated in the constitution of gendered identities in a variety of ways.

Most of these scholars are also aware that the very process of textualization, especially in Sanskrit, was gendered and skewed in favour of the upper castes/classes. Tyagi,[18] for instance, points out that women were excluded from routine access to Vedic learning and states: 'The texts were written by men, exclusively for men, and are representations of what the authors believed women should be.' Similarly, Rangachari[19] points out that the texts under consideration were 'composed by a literate male elite largely associated with the court'. As such, attempts to reconstruct the lives of ordinary men and women are often difficult. At the same time, these scholars use a variety of strategies to highlight the ways in which men and women, within the limited, visible social worlds represented in the texts, were differentiated, and explore the significance of such differences. In doing so, they move away from the static, changeless world of the woman question where 'the woman' can be isolated, dissected and deified in a rarefied, decontextualized and ahistorical, if not anti-historical, world.

Tyagi, for instance, is explicit that she is concerned with the domestic rituals as codified within the Brahmanical tradition, which she conceptualizes as a means of socialization into the beliefs and practices that were central to Brahmanism. What is more, she locates this process of codification within the *varṇa/jāti* framework. Thus, gender and caste categories are viewed as intertwined rather than isolated, and the Brahmanical or brahmanized household, too, is contextualized within a wider community.

Clearly, the engagement with these texts allows for fresh questions. Do we accept all prescriptions and prohibitions at face value? Do we engage with them more critically? How do we engage with the process whereby certain texts were canonized, both in the ancient tradition of Sanskrit aesthetics and in modern recoveries of these texts and traditions? While immediate answers may elude us, such engagements are likely to prove more fruitful than the rhetorical reiterations of the glories of the Vedic age.

At another level, what is also worth highlighting is the way in which these scholars gender spaces that are often taken for granted in gender-blind scholarship. In Tyagi's account, for instance, the quotidian household emerges as a locus of constructing and sedimenting gendered identities. Kaul draws attention to other, more visible, spaces, most notably the city, and the ways in which representations of urban space are gendered. Rangachari, on the other hand, given her concern with women who are visible in the political domain as understood conventionally, focuses on the royal court. The working out of differentiated spaces, which cannot be collapsed into one another to create a flat socio-scape, is perhaps one of the most fascinating aspects of the work of these scholars.

The ways in which these scholars handle the textual and epigraphic material is by no means uniform. Kaul works with the notion that the Sanskrit *kāvya* is not concerned with literal truths, and explores the possibility that it represents archetypes of a range of men and women in extremely sophisticated ways. Rangachari, on the other hand, is often preoccupied with a more literal reading of the texts, and tends to classify the women characters in particular, in terms of whether they are represented as offering resistance to patriarchal institutions and practices or conform to them. Thus, for her, the figure of Vāsavadattā, often depicted as a jealous queen in a polygynous household within the genre of drama, becomes a figure of resistance, whereas the Vāsavadattās who acquiesce in the king's dalliance are regarded as models of subservience. While more nuanced readings are possible, we may note that Rangachari draws attention to the fact that the 'same' character could be represented in diverse ways. In other words, the Sanskrit *kāvya* tradition was by no means homogeneous.

What is also interesting, although not entirely unproblematic, is the ways in which these scholars attempt to build up a case for women as active agents in history, within the limits of the material that they grapple with. One catches a glimpse of this in Kaul's almost wistful recall of the *abhisārikā*, the woman who ventures beyond the confines of domesticity for a nocturnal tryst with her lover, whom Kaul contrasts with the *kulastrī*, the woman within her home or family, and the *gaṇikā* or the courtesan. Kaul suggests that the *abhisārikā* represents a figure who exercised choice in matters of sexuality and emotion, whereas both the *kulastrī* and the *gaṇikā* were visualized as being constrained, in different ways, by the institutions within which they were located. Once again, whether we agree with Kaul's reading or not, what is significant is that women no longer remain an undifferentiated category—even the identities of elite women, we notice, could be constituted in a variety of ways.

If Kaul empathizes with the *abhisārikā*, Shah, in turn, attempts to elicit a difference between *prema* and *śṛṅgāra* in her reading of Sanskrit *kāvya*. The former, according to her, represents a more emotional understanding of love, whereas the latter is closer to a physical erotic representation. She uses this classification to valorize the compositions of Bhavabhūti and Jayadeva. Once again, we may disagree with Shah's classification, but it is useful in drawing attention to the fact that representations of love within the Sanskrit *kāvya* tradition were by no means uniform, in spite of the existence of codes of poetics.

Shah also draws attention to texts that focus centrally on the courtesan, such as Dāmodaragupta's *Kuṭṭanīmātā* and Kṣemendra's *Samayamātṛikā*. She analyses these to move beyond the framing of the sex worker as a victim to discuss strategies of survival and access to and control over material and cultural resources within a matrilineal household structure that would have been anomalous within the prevailing ideals of patriarchal kinship. In doing so she creates the space for engaging with the ambivalence regarding courtesanal traditions, and for a degree of autonomy for women sex workers. Once again, these arguments are useful in destabilizing the notion of a monolithic Indian woman.

Sometimes, the scholarly enterprise veers towards the nostalgic. Shah, for instance, attempts to recover the voices of women from *kāvya*, listening carefully to what she considers 'authentic' expressions of women's erotic emotions. In the case of Rangachari, this becomes a quest, at times overzealous, for women as agents. She finds these, somewhat expectedly and predictably, in women who make grants that were recorded in inscriptions, but also, and more surprisingly, in literary traditions. Some of these insights are interesting. For instance, she explores the figure of the maid in Sanskrit *kāvya*, a woman who was ostensibly of low status, but often acted as a go-between for elite men and women. The maids are almost invariably represented as autonomous, wise/clever, and resourceful.

Yet, literary representations are not always amenable to a literal reading. Note, for instance, Rangachari's almost exuberant celebration of the description of Yaśovatī:[20]

> Yaśovatī's pride in her position as Prabhākaravardhana's chief queen and of having borne the heirs to the throne is palpably evident. She calls herself the 'lioness mate of a great spirit . . . daughter, spouse, mother of heroes . . .' She further refers to having won 'the honourable fillet of chief-queen . . .' upon whose head 'have the subservient wives of countless feudatories poured coronation water', who 'has been fanned by chowries waved by captive wives of foes.' (HC V.186)

One notices here that Rangachari virtually loses sight of the authorial intervention of Bāṇabhaṭṭa, the writer, who created this image of the queen for the consumption of a specific audience. At the same time, one notices a certain impatience with women whom she finds passive or coy, who are represented as appendages or simply ornamental.

At another level, most of these scholars engage with the specific ways in which relations of gender were constituted, and patriarchal institutions and practices consolidated. These run through as significant strands in the work of Tyagi and Shah, for instance, even as they work with very different historical milieus. Shah, for example, draws attention to the strategies for controlling the reproductive power of women, documented in a variety of textual traditions. Tyagi broadens the discussion substantially, to include access to, control over and the use of a range of material resources such as animals, food, land as well as offspring, besides inclusion in or exclusion from the social relations constituted by gift exchange. What these investigations achieve, effectively, is to sensitize us to the quotidian, non-spectacular ways in which relations of power could be constituted. Tyagi also engages with the implications of Brahmanical practices and precepts for the non-brahman majority and argues that these may have been influential.

What these investigations also reveal is that a wide range of strategies of communication related to gender as well as other issues was deployed in early/early medieval contexts. These included ritualization, on the one hand, of daily domestic practices, as well as of rites of passage. They also included codification of the norms associated with the court, which were often aestheticized, leading to a situation where cultural practices constituted relations of power and hierarchy in complex ways. These strategies of communication both co-existed, may have been in competition with one another, and could have reinforced messages as well.

More recently, Tyagi[21] has investigated the Puranic traditions, to argue for women's participation in the process whereby these were consolidated. This participation is envisaged in terms of both contestation and compliance, and is located within a context of engagement with alternative religious traditions and cultural practices. Some of these ideas resonate with those of the contributors to this volume.

Further Possibilities

The contributors to this volume move away from some of the earlier preoccupations even as they derive many insights from previous scholarship. Excerpted from or inspired by their doctoral research, in terms of themes and methodology, each of the contributions to this volume is part of a larger argument that the authors develop elsewhere.

Each of the contributors opens up a distinct temporal and spatial area for investigation. Shwetanshu Bhushan's essay on the *saṃskāras* related to birth, for instance, deals with rituals that were codified in the second half of the first millennium BCE, in the mid-Ganga valley. Tara Sheemar's analysis of the representation of sexual relations in the *Kathāsaritsāgara* is located in twelfth-century Kashmir. Snigdha Singh focuses on inscriptions and sculptures from the early historic site of Bharhut in central India. These relate to the end of the first millennium BCE/beginning of the first millennium CE. Finally, Shatarupa Bhattacharya analyses inscriptions pertaining to three major lineages, the Vākāṭakas, Kalacuris and Candellas, all ruling over parts of central India, in an attempt to trace long-term changes from the fifth century CE to the twelfth century CE. Thus, these studies allow us to ground gender relations in specific contexts, and implicitly provide a critique to the commonsensical tendency to reduce gender relations in early India to global trends of a decline from a glorious past.

If the spaces and times explored by the contributors are different, so are the materials they open up as sources. For instance, both Singh and Bhattacharya use epigraphic material, even as the former juxtaposes this with visual representations. However, the inscriptions that Singh analyses are brief, if not almost cryptic, while most of those studied by Bhattacharya are far more complex, elaborate documents. So, even as both attempt to understand how women (and men) were represented, it is evident that they address this question by looking at very different genres of inscriptions. Similarly, while both Bhushan and Sheemar study texts, each one focuses on a different genre. The texts Bhushan investigates are concerned with codifying ritual prescriptions, while Sheemar explores the rich narrative of the *Kathāsaritsāgara*, arguing that even as it never explicitly critiques the normative Brahmanical order, it provides evidence for visualizing alternatives. There are variations in language as well: Singh's texts are in Prakrit, while Bhattacharya, Bhushan and Sheemar study materials in Sanskrit.

A general methodological trajectory explored by most of these scholars is that questions of gender necessarily, though not only involve a comparison between men and women. The first essay, by Singh, explores this possibility through an examination of inscriptions and images from early historic Bharhut.

Apart from using inscriptional material, both Singh and Bhattacharya share a common concern with the ways in which the cultural practice of *dāna* or gift-giving was deployed to construct social identities. The contexts within which they locate the practice are distinct: Singh's focus is on the early Buddhist tradition, whereas Bhattacharya is concerned with multiple religious traditions within the early medieval context, and with a more differentiated set of patrons/matrons, for whom the secular and the sacred intersect in complex ways. In each of these studies the links between donors and donees is explored, as are the material and spiritual transactions that constitute the act of giving and receiving gifts.

Related to this is a concern with questions of identity formation. None of the authors assume identities as a given. Instead, they draw attention to the ways in which it is constituted for (and by?) women and men in a variety of contexts. For example, Singh lists a set of criteria that could have been used as markers of identity by women and men who made grants to the Buddhist sangha and provided the resources that went into the making and embellishment of the *stūpa* at Bharhut. She then analyses how these were used. Implicit in the discussion is the way in which gender identities were implicated in material transactions. Bhattacharya also consistently compares the ways in which men and women are described in the inscriptions she studies, carefully noting similarities and differences within hierarchies amongst elite men and women.

Singh also focuses on visual markers of gender identity deployed in sculpture. What emerges is that the visual and the inscriptional evidence occasionally coincide, but often differ. This brings up interesting questions about audiences/spectators, and the significance of the written word juxtaposed with striking visual representations. What emerges, then, is a certain multi-vocality around gendered identities, evident at this single site.

Identities are also a preoccupation within the second set of essays. Bhushan discusses attitudes towards potential and real children as well as towards parenthood, as revealed in ritual literature, whereas Sheemar explores the ways in which expressions of sexuality were implicated in sociopolitical hierarchies and were often used to represent these.

Both Singh, in her discussion on visual material, and Sheemar, in her analysis of a complex narrative, take into consideration non-human figures as well. These occasionally reiterate the concerns of the human world in spectacular and dramatic ways; and they provide alternative visions as well. In drawing them into the framework of historical analysis, the authors attempt to investigate the different ways in which gender relations were imagined and visualized.

Another common preoccupation in this set of essays is with the category of elite, which is both deployed and problematized, not necessarily uniformly. Consider, for instance, the essay by Bhattacharya, which opens up a fairly well-known corpus of inscriptions from early medieval central India. Most, though not all, of the inscriptions are votive, and deal with a variety of grants made to a range of religious institutions/traditions/individuals whose religious identities were considered significant. Given their character, the inscriptions provide access to a relatively limited social category, which Bhattacharya identifies as the elite. This is, in a sense, inevitable; the very ability to deploy resources for such activities would have been confined to the affluent. Also, the use of Sanskrit, and access to those with skills of literacy, as well as to relatively imperishable writing materials such as copper and stone, would have been the privilege of a limited few. However, even within these limitations, it is possible to disaggregate different trends, and to track these through the centuries in terms of gender. Bhattacharya enriches this possibility by distinguishing at least two strands within the broad category of elite—the royal and the non-royal—and pursues a comparative analysis through her data.

The inscriptions that Bhattacharya focuses on have been the staple of constructing our understanding of the early medieval, and have been drawn on to argue both for and against the model of Indian feudalism. They have been read as proof of decentralization as well as indications of the emergence of new regional polities, based on distinctive sociocultural formations. Bhattacharya's exercise is a useful reminder that these frameworks do not exhaust the potential richness of the epigraphic material. She attempts to reflect on gift-giving, especially land grants, in early medieval inscriptions, to explore how these were used to constitute gendered identities amongst other things. She contextualizes her discussion in terms of the general significance of gifts and gift-giving, and the ways in which this changed over time.

Focusing on some of the major dynasties of early medieval central India, the Vākāṭakas, Kalacuris and Candellas, Bhattacharya uses strategies of comparison, highlighting the similarities and differences between women and men donors. Comparisons are made in terms of the numbers of grants, the kinds of gifts that were made, as well as the social significance of these. Bhattacharya also examines variations related to the occasions on which gifts were made and the ostensible motives that were stated.

It is evident that these inscriptions have much more to tell us—they can be contextualized in a variety of ways, and it is to be hoped that future scholarship will be directed to exploring the wealth of material that they contain to yield other insights. What, for instance, was the impact of such grants on ordinary men and women who lived in the region? How did elite interventions shape their lives? Can we read the inscriptions against the grain to recover some traces of these contexts, at once invisible and yet omnipresent?

In the second part of this volume, Shwetanshu Bhushan revisits the early Brahmanical compilations of domestic ritual practices, the Gṛhyasūtras. Compiled from the mid-first millennium BCE onwards, these texts, in Sanskrit prose, represent an attempt to codify routine ritual practices. Bhushan focuses on a handful of these—prenatal and postnatal rituals. She suggests that these were significant occasions, used to constitute the ideal relations between husband and wife, with or without the intervention of the priest, and also to distinguish between the girl and the boy child. What emerges from her descriptions of these rituals is that gender differences were not regarded as natural or given; rather they were carefully constructed through rituals, using a variety of substances, different chants, invoking gods and goddesses, to ensure that men and women, boys and girls, learnt their place within the social order.

The question of the extent to which these rituals were 'really' practised remains a tangled one, perhaps unanswerable at the moment. Nonetheless, the fact of codification is in itself significant, and worthy of exploration and understanding. These possibilities are opened up by Bhushan's discussion. She points out how some provisions were varṇa-specific, for example, and thus far from universal. In fact, while rites of passage can have certain universal qualities, Bhushan demonstrates how the specific ways in which these were codified in the Gṛhyasūtras implicated them in the construction and reinforcement of a differentiated gender order.

While Bhushan's focus is on normative texts, Tara Sheemar draws attention to an entirely different genre, narrative poetry, located in a distinct context, early medieval Kashmir. Through her discussion on the

Kathāsaritsāgara, literally the ocean of stories, she explores how the text constitutes masculinities and femininities in a variety of ways, examining, in particular, how these intersect with issues of caste and class.

Sheemar situates the text in terms of language, genre, authorship, and audience. She then proceeds to analyse the significance of the characters and the narratives, acknowledging, like Bhattacharya, the preoccupation with elites, even as the text explores an array of diverse scenarios. Sheemar problematizes the category of elite, which allows her to read the text in interesting ways.

In her analysis, Sheemar highlights the treatment of premarital relationships, which, contrary to the normative tradition, were not viewed with disfavour as long as they culminated in 'respectable' unions. Thus, spaces were notionally opened up within the normative framework. At the same time, she explores how kingship is invoked, and occasionally subverted, in recognizing sexual and social relations. She also draws attention to the ways in which kinship relations and other social ties are reworked in constituting sexual unions.

Sheemar illustrates how love was constructed and rendered available within certain social situations rather than being construed as a universal or natural phenomenon. Class and caste are critical to this analysis. At the same time, circumventions are accommodated through a variety of strategies. In drawing attention to these, Sheemar opens up possibilities of viewing the erotic as socially constituted and fluid.

While Bhushan discusses ritual codes, Sheemar focuses on the centrality of the *gāndharva* union, by mutual choice, in the narrative, and its many implications. She points out that while it was explored as a possibility, it could be considered less binding than more *śāstric* forms of union. She then goes on to explore narratives of sexual unions within marriage, relatively scarce though they are. Variations, including polygyny, are both discussed and contextualized. Sheemar argues that, by and large, it served as a marker for royalty. Also analysed are narratives of adultery, and the extent to which these corroborate or contest normative ideals. In contrast to the adulterous woman, whose narrative potential seems to have been exploited to the full, depictions of chaste women are relatively rare, as Sheemar points out. Nevertheless, where developed, they conform closely to Brahmanical norms, which are occasionally reinforced by being attributed to women narrators.

Several questions remain. One of these is whether our existing vocabulary, both academic and otherwise, can capture the complexities of gender relations. We can see attempts to push towards new categories. Singh, for example, adopts Findly's suggestion of matronage to focus on individuated women donors whose presence is significant at the site she explores.

Also, while the essays succeed in shifting the focus from women to gender relations, the authors work within a binary framework of men and women. Recent scholarship has emphasized the need to move towards a more complex understanding, and to engage with gender as a more fluid category. While the sources the authors explore can lend themselves to such an understanding, this potential is only partially explored in the present exercise.

The other, and in a sense more fundamental, set of issues relate to the extent to which texts, sculpture and inscriptions can allow insights into the lives of ordinary people. Are there ways of moving beyond the intricacies and intrigues of the elite, no matter how sophisticated our analysis? Or are we inescapably caught in a situation where the preoccupations of the elite will refract our research? If this set of essays can generate further thinking, critique and even contestation of the categories with which we operate, consciously and often unconsciously, it will have served its purpose.

NOTES

1. Uma Chakravarti, 'Beyond the Altekarian Paradigm: Towards a New Understanding of Gender Relations in Early Indian History', in *Women in Early Indian Societies,* ed. Kumkum Roy, New Delhi: Manohar, 1999, pp. 72–80, 'Whatever Happened to the Vedic *Dasi?* Orientalism, Nationalism and a Script for the Past' and 'Conceptualizing Brahmanical Patriarchy in Early India: Gender, Caste, Class and State', both in Uma Chakravarti, *Everyday Lives, Everyday Histories: Beyond the Kings and Brahmanas of 'Ancient' India*, New Delhi: Tulika Books, 2006, pp. 3–38 and pp. 138–55, respectively.
2. A.S. Altekar, *The Position of Women in Hindu Civilisation: From Prehistoric Times to the Present Day*, repr., 3rd edn., New Delhi: Motilal Banarsidass, 1991 (1st edn. 1938).
3. Chakravarti, 'Beyond the Altekarian Paradigm'.
4. Kumkum Roy, 'Where Women are Worshipped, there the Gods Rejoice: The Mirage of the Ancestress of the Hindu Woman', in *Women and the Hindu Right*, ed. Tanika Sarkar and Urvashi Butalia, New Delhi: Kali for Women, 1995, pp. 11–28.
5. Bhuvan Chandel, in association with Shubhada Joshi, ed., *Women in Ancient and Medieval India* (*History of Science, Philosophy and Culture in Indian Civilization*), vol. IX, pt. 2, Delhi: PHISPC and Centre for Studies in Civilizations, 2009.
6. Shubhada Joshi, 'Introduction', *Women in Ancient and Medieval India*, p. xxiv.
7. Kamalakar Mishra, 'Position of Woman in Tantra (Śaiva-Śākta Tradition)' *Women in Ancient and Medieval India*, ed. Chandel, in association with Joshi, p. 97.
8. Ibid., p. xxviii.
9. Ibid., p. xxx.
10. Sheldon Pollock, *The Language of the Gods in the World of Men: Sanskrit, Power and Culture in Premodern India*, New Delhi: Permanent Black, 2007.

11. Shubhada Joshi, 'The Vedic Woman', *Women in Ancient and Medieval India*, ed. Chandel, in association with Shubhada Joshi, p. 57.
12. See, for instance, Uma Chakravarti, 'Renouncer and Householder in Early Buddhism', in *Everyday Lives, Everyday Histories: Beyond the Kings and Brahmanas of Ancient India*, New Delhi: Tulika Books, 2006.
13. A.V. Sugavaneswaran, 'Women in the Vedic Age Gender Problems—Status and Role', *Women in Ancient and Medieval India*, ed. Chandel, in association with Shubhada Joshi, pp. 3–30.
14. Jaya Tyagi, *Engendering the Early Household: Brahmanical Precepts in the Early Grhyasutras, Middle of the First Millennium BCE,* New Delhi: Orient Longman, 2008.
15. Shonaleeka Kaul, *Imagining the Urban: Sanskrit and the City in Early India*, New Delhi: Permanent Black, 2010.
16. Devika Rangachari, *Invisible Women, Visible Histories: Gender, Society and Polity in North India (Seventh to Twelfth Century AD)*, New Delhi: Manohar, 2009.
17. Shalini Shah, *Love, Eroticism and Female Sexuality in Classical Sanskrit Literature, Seventh–Thirteenth Centuries*, New Delhi: Manohar, 2009.
18. Tyagi, *Engendering the Early Household*, p. 1.
19. Rangachari, *Invisible Women, Visible Histories*, p. 13.
20. Ibid., p. 233.
21. Jaya Tyagi, *Contestation and Compliance: Retrieving Women's 'Agency' from Puranic Traditions*, New Delhi: Oxford University Press, 2014.

REFERENCES

Ali, Daud, *Courtly Culture and Political Life in Early Medieval India,* Cambridge: Cambridge University Press, 2006.

Altekar, A.S., *The Position of Women in Hindu Civilisation: From Prehistoric Times to the Present Day,* New Delhi, Motilal Banarsidass, 1991 (repr., 3rd edn., first edn. 1938).

Chakravarti, Uma, 'Beyond the Altekarian Paradigm: Towards a New Understanding of Gender Relations in Early Indian History', *Women in Early Indian Societies*, ed. Kumkum Roy, New Delhi: Manohar, 1999, pp. 72–80.

———, *Everyday Lives, Everyday Histories: Beyond the Kings and Brahmanas of 'Ancient' India,* New Delhi: Tulika Books, 2006.

Chandel, Bhuvan, in association with Shubhada Joshi, eds., *Women in Ancient and Medieval India* (*History of Science, Philosophy and Culture in Indian Civilization*), vol. IX, part 2, Delhi: PHISPC and Centre for Studies in Civilizations, 2009.

Findly, E.B., *Dāna: Giving and Getting in Pali Buddhism*, Delhi: Motilal Banarsidas, 2003.

Joshi, Shubhada, 'Introduction', in *Women in Ancient and Medieval India,* ed. Bhuvan Chandel in association with Shubhada Joshi, 2009, pp. xxiii–xxxii.

———, 'The Vedic Woman', in *Women in Ancient and Medieval India*, ed. Bhuvan Chandel in association with Shubhada Joshi, 2009, pp. 43–59.

Kaul, Shonaleeka, *Imagining the Urban: Sanskrit and the City in Early India*, New Delhi: Permanent Black, 2010.

Mishra, Kamalakar, 'Position of Woman in Tantra (Śaiva-Śākta Tradition)', in *Women in Ancient and Medieval India*, ed. Bhuvan Chandel in association with Shubhada Joshi, Delhi: PHISPC and Centre for Studies in Civilizations, 2009, pp. 95–115.

Pollock, Sheldon, *The Language of the Gods in the World of Men: Sanskrit, Power and Culture in Premodern India*, New Delhi: Permanent Black, 2007.

Rangachari, Devika, *Invisible Women, Visible Histories: Gender, Society and Polity in North India (Seventh to Twelfth Century AD)*, New Delhi: Manohar, 2009.

Roy, Kumkum, '"Where Women are Worshipped, there the Gods Rejoice": The Mirage of the Ancestress of the Hindu Woman', in *Women and the Hindu Right*, ed. Tanika Sarkar and Urvashi Butalia, New Delhi: Kali for Women, 1995, pp. 11–28.

Shah, Shalini, *Love, Eroticism and Female Sexuality in Classical Sanskrit Literature, Seventh–Thirteenth Centuries*, New Delhi: Manohar, 2009.

Sugavaneswaran, A.V., 'Women in the Vedic Age Gender Problems—Status and Role', in *Women in Ancient and Medieval India*, ed. Bhuvan Chandel in association with Shubhada Joshi, 2009, pp. 3–30.

Tyagi, Jaya, *Engendering the Early Household: Brahmanical Precepts in the Early Grhyasutras, Middle of the First Millennium BCE*, New Delhi: Orient Longman, 2008.

———, *Contestation and Compliance: Retrieving Women's 'Agency' from Puranic Traditions*, New Delhi: Oxford University Press, 2014.

PART ONE

Engraved Identities

1

Exploring the Question of Gender at an Early *Stūpa*: Inscriptions and Images

Snigdha Singh

I ATTEMPT TO LOCATE GENDER identity with the help of votive inscriptions from a 'sacred place', in this case a *stūpa* at Bharhut, located at the northern end of the long narrow valley of Mahiyar, in central India. Its location was important as it connected Ujjain and Bhilsa to Pāṭaliputra, Kauśāmbī and Śrāvastī.[1] The strategic location and easy accessibility may have been the reason why a large number of donors came to Bharhut to make donations that were recorded.

The time frame explored in this chapter is from the second century BCE to the first century BCE (the early historic period), envisaged as a period of urbanism, accompanied by the formation of a number of new monarchies or chieftainships. The aggressive and expansive character of early Indian urbanism[2] can be witnessed during this period. This includes a number of changes, such as the opening up of new regions to trade and agriculture and the introduction of currency, which facilitated daily transactions and promoted long-distance trade. Knowledge of pottery, iron technology, and other crafts spread to the peripheral areas and paved the way for the rise of a large number of towns.

It was during this period that we witness donations being made in large numbers. What is interesting is the absence of references to varṇa affiliations in the ways in which donors are identified. Instead, there is a preference for using other occupational categories. Amongst other things, this indicates that prosperity was not restricted to the elite, but had percolated to a wide range of occupational groups. What is also noteworthy is that gift-giving was now part of a wider set of cultural, social and economic practices. Even small gifts could be acknowledged, and renunciatory traditions, such as Buddhism, encouraged gift-giving as a mode whereby the laity could acquire merit; at the same time, the sangha could be sustained. Thus, many people were able to make donations within their means. Sculpture also portrays people from all walks of life. Thus, to a certain extent, we can notice parallels between inscriptions and visual representations.

This period is also characterized by the increasing visibility of women, both as donors and as members of renunciatory orders. Part of this may have been the outcome of the belief that salvation could be achieved through renunciation,[3] even if this was not an easy option open to women. For men, a desire to escape from the bonds of the world was recognized as a major reason for the transition to homelessness, but this was not as strong for women. Despite these hurdles, we find that women succeeded in becoming *bhikkhunīs* and left a lasting record of self-expression.[4]

It was in this context that the concept and method of *dāna* underwent change. There is ample evidence to show that *dāna* was pivotal to the social, economic and political fabric. *Dāna* was governed by its own rules and requirements that kept changing with time. Gift-making is never a one-way process. It entails reciprocation. All gifts though in theory voluntary, disinterested and spontaneous are in fact obligatory and interested.[5]

That *dāna* was meant to be made out of surplus wealth is effectively borne out by the Dharmasūtras, which categorically uphold that *dāna* must be made in such a way as not to cause detriment to one's family. The same idea was later repeated by Manu.[6] Further, gift-giving has been seen largely in the context of religious rituals and the associated symbolism. The earliest references to *dāna* as a distinct function in society come from the *dāna-stuti* hymns of the *Ṛgveda,* in praise of those who made generous gifts. It served a magico-religious function where the gift was symbolic of communion with the supernatural.[7] In the later Vedic period, the notion of *dāna* underwent change as it became a conduit of deliberate exchange. Therefore, gift-giving in the Vedic context not only presupposed possession of excessive bounty by the donor but it was also expected to win fame and prestige for him.

In the post-Vedic period, Buddhism and Jainism stressed on *dāna* as it was essential for the survival of the sangha. The sangha was solely dependent on the *bhikṣā* given by the laity. In return, the sangha was expected to provide merit or preach the Buddhist ethics. The exchange of *dāna* for merit is common to Buddhism and Jainism. Thus, the notion of exchange remains central, but in return for tangible wealth the donor acquires merit. *Dāna* was expected to bring greater prosperity for the donor. Gift-making also served as the chief means of acquiring social status.[8] In the post-Mauryan period, we witness a change in the mode of gift-making. Now there is evidence of votive records of gifts of images, pillars, etc. They also constitute a reliable source of information regarding new categories of gift items.

However, increasingly, *dāna* came to connote gifts to a religion or a religious community with a focus on the purity and the good intention of the giver.[9] *Dāna* became a doctrine that governed the redistribution of goods from the increasingly wealthy to the voluntarily impoverished. Thus *dāna* was a vital institution whereby a layman/laywoman gave alms to an ascetic and gained merit through that action.

Another significant change was the rise of the individual, which was reflected in the method of gift-giving. Thus *dāna* shifts away from the valuation of traditional duty and obligation to a greater celebration of individual choice.[10] It is in this scenario that we find women portraying themselves as individual entities. Second, gift-giving was meritorious under all circumstances and at the same time gave the donor an opportunity to invest in the future.[11] Moreover, giving was the most strategic form of merit making because it provided public prestige or status[12] along with visibility and even an identity to the donor who could be remembered for posterity.

It is in this context that we find a new autonomy for women in matters of *dāna*, reflecting a wider involvement in economic matters. Women took the initiative and appeared as individual agents in the process of making donations, which were essential for the monastic order. Their contribution as individual donors was publicly recognized. What is more, they were regarded as individuals and not as an extension of the family. Thus matronage needs to be differentiated from patronage.[13]

The *stūpa* was frequented by men and women who came to make donations and earn merit for themselves or their near and dear ones through *dāna*. We can identify the donors, their contributions, and also the purpose of the donations from the votive inscriptions. We will also examine the sculptures on pillars, crossbars, coping-stones, etc., to see if there is a similarity between the inscriptions and sculpture or whether the picture is different. We will first analyse the inscriptions and then discuss the sculptures at Bharhut.

The inscriptions found at Bharhut are the earliest to be recorded in a substantial number. They are very brief, written in prose, in Prakrit, in the Brahmi script of about the second century BCE.[14] The dates of the inscriptions are based on palaeographic evidence.[15] The language of the gateway and railing inscriptions is a form of Prakrit that differs from the Prakrit of the inscriptions of Aśoka. Palaeographically, railing inscriptions can be dated to the late second century BCE (150–125 BCE), while the gateway appears to be erected later around 80–50 BCE.[16] In its shortest and most common form the inscription mentions the name of the donor, with the genitive-case termination, followed by the word *dānam*. Despite their brevity the inscriptions throw light on the name of the donor, place of residence, occupation, etc. For our study it is important to see how donors identify themselves.

From these epigraphic records we get to know about the identity of the donor, the nature of the gift, her/his religious faith, etc. The inscriptions also give us information about a wide range of people and a picture of the workings of society at large as our knowledge is not confined to activities of kings or nobles or of men and women of the higher varṇas. Importantly, they help by recording specific and concrete events, which make them extremely valuable. They throw light on members of the monastic order as well as laywomen and men. These records allow us to catch a glimpse of women's lives, and the roles of *bhikkhunīs* and laywomen in society.

At the same time, there are limitations to the usefulness of this epigraphic source. For instance, several inscriptions are fragmentary and so we are unable to read the entire text, while some are damaged.

It was during this period that stone was used for the first time in the construction of the architectural parts of the *stūpa* (unlike the Mauryan times), attesting to an experiment with material and an attempt to create enduring representations for posterity. The earliest surviving dates for art, especially visual narratives in stone is from the second century BCE when the Buddha was not directly portrayed; his presence was indicated by symbols such as his sandals, horse, the tree under which he meditated, etc., as is evident at Bharhut and Sanchi.

I will explore the different markers of identity used by men and women as revealed by the votive inscriptions found at the *stūpa* of Bharhut, which was a focus of ritualized devotion. In a sense, the *stūpa* was symbolic of Bharhut's strategic geographical location, and control over economic resources, representing its importance as an urban centre that attracted donors from different areas.

The votive inscriptions have been inscribed on the architectural parts of the *stūpa*. The donations recorded may have been given or dedicated in fulfilment of a vow or pledge, which is generally not stated explicitly. They may also symbolize a wish or desire.

Individual donors made most of the donations for their spiritual welfare except one where the parents are expected to benefit.[17] All the donations at Bharhut are made to the Buddhist institution. The Buddhist tradition emphasized individualism; the individual was primarily responsible for his spiritual destiny without the help of any intermediaries.[18] A layman/

woman could make spiritual progress even by making small donations. Importantly, in the Buddhist *bhikṣā* relationship there was a shift from household obligation to individual patronage.[19] So, instead of obligatory hospitality there was the possibility of voluntary patronage/matronage.

Initially, *dāna* given to the *bhikkhus* and *bhikkhunīs* consisted of food and clothing. Later, with the growth of more complex economic networks and with the institutionalization of life in the sangha, the nature of donations underwent change. We find donations of architectural features such as crossbars, coping-stones, pillars, and gateways that were now made in stone. The donors got their names inscribed on these artifacts in the hope of earning merit.

The effort here would be to examine the markers of identity used by the donors. I focus on the construction of the identities based on these markers and analyse the importance of these in relation to the formation of gender identities. I will focus first on the markers used by donors who designated through religion and the lay donors to highlight the criteria that were important for the *bhikkhunīs* and *bhikkhus* on the one hand, and for laywomen and men on the other. This will be extended to other categories of women and men. An examination of the inscriptions found at the site indicates that there were several markers. These include donors who designate through religion as well as lay donors. Within both categories we take into account whether the donation was made individually, jointly (when two people got together) or collectively (more than two people), the practice of identifying the donor in terms of place of residence, kinship ties, occupation, and gifts given. We will then draw attention to the picture that emerges through a consideration of each of these categories.

As stated earlier we will also examine the sculptures at Bharhut. Our concern would be to examine if there is a similarity with the picture that emerges from the inscriptions or is there a divergence. Second, I will also try to see if there is a difference in the portrayal of men and women in terms of attire, posture, ornaments, tattoo, etc. Is there a difference in the portrayal of royalty and ordinary people? Do the inscriptions match with the sculptural representations? In other words, do the latter portray the donors?

Overview

There are 193 inscriptions that were engraved (Table 1.1) on gateways, pillars, coping-stones, and rails. Of these, seventy-eight were not votive. The votive inscriptions include gifts of three gateway pillars (henceforth G) called *toraṇas*, of which one was given by a king and the other two by unidentified donors. Twenty-two inscriptions are found on coping-stones (henceforth C) but only two of these are votive inscriptions. A hundred inscriptions are found on pillars (henceforth P) out of which forty-four are votive. Sixty-six inscriptions were found on rails (henceforth R) out of which sixty-four are votive.

When we examine the non-votive inscriptions we find that most of them are either names of *Jātaka* tales[20] or labels or titles of the sculptured scenes above which they are placed.[21] These short records are invaluable as they enable us to identify the different scenes to which they are attached with certainty. This enables us to differentiate different classes of people with confidence, and ascertain what legends were current and most popular at that time.[22] Bharhut marks the first organized attempt to evolve a popular iconography and the site attests to a rich sculptural heritage.

Individuals made 111 donations in all, including sixty-six by men and forty-five by women. There is no evidence of joint donations. A single donation was made collectively by a *nigama* from Karahakaṭa.[23] This is the only gift made by a guild. Three gifts were made by unidentified donors.[24]

TABLE 1.1: Indicating Individual and Collective Donations from the Inscriptions at Bharhut

Total	*Not votive*	*Unidentified*	*Individual*	*Collective*
193	78	03	111 (66 m., 45 w)	01 (1 cm.)

NOTE: Collective refers to donations made by more than two persons, m stands for men, w stands for women, cm stands for collective men

SOURCE: 191 from Cunningham and two inscriptions from Luders' list, nos. 882 and 883.

Respected *Bhikkhus* and Marginalized *Bhikkhunīs*

Here we examine the donors who designated through religion. We find that there were twenty-two donations made by men who designated through religion, out of which one was by a pupil.[25] The *atevāsin* mentioned his name along with that of his teacher (Table 1.2).

Monks made the other donations and were recognized only by their ecclesiastical titles. All of them mentioned their personal names. The ecclesiastical title of *aya* (*ārya*), 'the venerable', was adopted by monks in eight inscriptions.[26] There are five donations where donors were referred to as *bhadanta*[27] (the reverend).[28] There are two instances when the epithet *bhānaka* was used.[29] In two instances, both the epithet *bhānaka* and *bhadanta* were used.[30] Barua[31] understands the term *bhānaka* as the reciter of the sacred texts. According to him, they rehearsed, memorized, and orally handed down the traditions of the Buddhists. The schools of such *bhānakas,* as appears from the accounts of Buddhaghoṣa, arose soon after the demise of the Buddha. The institution of these bodies of reciters survived till the time of the construction of the railing at Bharhut, which means that the Buddhist texts were not committed to writing at that time. Sircar[32] also interprets the word *bhānaka* as reciter of sacred texts. We find that in three different instances monks used two or even four different epithets. For example, in one instance a *bhikkhu* used the epithet of *aya, bhadanta*, *bhānaka*, and *navakarmika.*[33]

Significantly, we do not find a single instance of women using any of these epithets, not even that of *bhānaka.* Does this mean that the oral tradition was more accessible to monks than to nuns? Second, we also wonder whether the task of handing down the tradition orally was the prerogative of men. Does this not point out to a similarity with the Brahmanical traditions where the texts were handed down orally by men from one generation to the other, denying women access to this sacred domain? If this is the case then we can suggest that functions within the sangha were sharply gendered.

There are other adjectives that were used exclusively by monks. These include *navakarmika*, which according to Cunningham,[34] must have been a title but, according to Luders,[35] it could mean 'overseer of works'. Maybe Luders presumes that *aya* Isipālita[36] supervised the architectural work at Bharhut. Thapar also refers to *navakarmika* as the builder when she says that monks took on a supervisory role in the construction of the monument, which may gradually have included the more technical aspects of architecture and sculpture.[37] Barua says that there were monks who bore epithets like *navakarmika*, a sangha-functionary, whose business was to supervise the construction of a new Buddhist edifice or monument.[38] What is likely is that the donor who used four epithets, *bhadanta*, *aya* (reverend), *bhānaka* (reciter), and *navakarmika* (supervisor of construction), may have been the ecclesiastic who supervised the entire construction and decoration of the *stūpa.*[39]

There are other references to epithets like *satupadana*,[40] one 'who has abandoned attachment'.[41] In another inscription[42] there is mention of the *sūtrāntika,* a student of the *sūtrāntas*,[43] that is, one who is well versed in the *sūtras*. The word *bhatudesaka* was interpreted 'as distributor of food'.[44] There were some among the laity who were employed as sangha-functionaries in a monastery whose business was to distribute food.[45] According to Findly,[46] the most important official for food was probably the *bhatudesaka* or supervisor of food distribution, or supervisor of meals; like the assigner of bowls, the *bhatudesaka* was chosen by the sangha. Thus, it is likely that he was a member of the sangha. The epithet of *pañcanekāyā*[47] indicated one who knows the five *nikāyas.*[48] None of these epithets occur for nuns. This indicates that they did not find space in these important functions of the sangha.

When we analyse the epithets used by monks we find a number of inscriptions wherein the monks used multiple epithets. This phenomenon has no parallel in the case of nuns. In fact, we hardly get evidence of even a single epithet being used by nuns. This may indicate that nuns did not have access to specialized learning. It was these skills acquired by the monks that enabled them to acquire status that is reflected in the use of these epithets.

There were sixteen donations made by women who designated through religion and in all except one,[49] which is a fragmentary inscription, they mentioned their personal names. In seven of the inscriptions the nuns mentioned their place of residence and in one the epithet *aya* was used.[50] Thus, when we study the references to nuns, the first thing that strikes us is that they were referred to as *bhikkhunīs* unlike the monks, who were not referred to as *bhikkhus* even once. The other striking feature is that there is only one instance where Cunningham reads a title *aya* for a nun[51] whereas Luders[52] regards it as a name, *ayama*. If it was a title, as suggested by Cunningham, then this would be the only instance of its kind. We do not find any mention of *atevāsinī*/pupils for nuns but there is one instance for monks. There is also no mention of *upāsakas* (male lay worshippers) or *upāsikās* (female lay worshippers) who figure at sites like Sanchi, Mathura, etc.

In the sculptures of Bharhut we find very few portrayals of *bhikkhunīs* and *bhikkhus*. In Plate 1.1 we find a male ascetic giving a discourse to a female and male pupils. This finds a parallel with the inscriptions where monks mention female pupils but not vice versa. What is interesting is that men and women renouncers feature in only two panels, and even then not in the typical robes or with the shaven head that would mark their Buddhist affiliation. The visual record, thus, presents a contrast to the inscriptions that throw light on the *bhikkhunīs* and *bhikkhus.*

TABLE 1.2: Indicating Identity based on Religion from the Inscriptions at Bharhut

Religious Donors	*Single*
Men	22 (22SD)
Women	16 (1SD)

NOTE: Information available only from individual donors unless indicated otherwise. SD stands for special designation; Base total for men = 66; Base total for women = 45; Total base for donors = 115.

Laymen and Laywomen

There are forty-four donations made by laymen wherein we find they mentioned their personal names (Table 1.3). On the other hand, we find twenty-nine donations by laywomen. Like the laymen, all the laywomen also mentioned their personal names.

While laymen made more donations than laywomen, we do not find any difference in the way the donations have been recorded. In sculpture, likewise, we find portrayals of both men and women, with some differences. While most sculptures represent women and men within the same space, there are exceptions. For example, there is a sculpture[53] where in one scene we find a woman peeping from a hole, which could be a window, and two men are talking outside. On the same coping-stone we find another depiction where a man and women together listen to the sermon being given by a *bhikkhu.* Here both men and women are sharing the same space. This is one of the few sculptures that depict different spaces being accorded to women.[54]

All the donors, irrespective of gender, identify themselves by their personal names. Thus, personal names were carved in stone and permanently placed in close proximity to a sacred object. He/she may have got the privilege of having his/her name permanently in the presence of the *stūpa* of the Buddha, which, it has been suggested, is more than the symbol of the Buddha, it is the Buddha himself.[55] The personal name is the essential characteristic of a person's identity that cannot be interchanged and represents inherent participation; maybe this led the donors to get their names engraved on the donations. If it is true that when a person's name is present then a person is present, then we must begin to suspect that having one's name carved in stone and permanently placed near a powerful religious 'object' must have placed the person there as well[56] regardless of whether that person was otherwise occupied, absent, dead, male or female. And this, according to Schopen, is the purpose behind the early donative inscriptions. Thus, one can say that all the donors wanted was to mark their presence in close proximity to another more powerful presence.

TABLE 1.3: Indicating Identity based on Gender Difference of Lay Donors from the Inscriptions at Bharhut

Lay Donors	*Single*
Men	44
Women	29

NOTE: Information available only from individual donors unless indicated otherwise. Base total for men = 66; Base total for laywomen = 45; Total base for donors = 115.

Journeying to Bharhut

When we examine the places mentioned by men and women we find that the number of places associated with men who designated through religion was really meagre. We find only six inscriptions[57] where monks mentioned their place of residence. In contrast, nuns mentioned places of residence more frequently, in nine instances.[58] Thus, this is another difference between *bhikkhus* and *bhikkhunīs* (Table 1.4). We may suggest that place of residence was not an important marker of identity for monks. Second, it could be possible that more nuns mentioned places as a marker of identity than monks because the latter were not stationary, unlike the nuns, and therefore, place as a marker of identity would have held less importance for them than for the nuns.

There are fifteen instances of laymen mentioning places of residence,[59] while laywomen did so in sixteen cases.[60] There is one instance when a guild mentioned a place.[61] This shows that proportionately more laywomen mentioned their place of residence than laymen. Yet the difference is relatively insignificant.

Another aspect which needs to be highlighted, is that we find six places associated with monks, each mentioned only once, while nuns mentioned nine different places. Moragiri[62] was the only place mentioned by both monks and nuns and also by a layman and two laywomen. This may indicate that the *vihāras* of nuns could be in different places or that the catchment area of nuns was different. The catchment area was the area that was served by the monastic complex at Bharhut. Monks and nuns might have recruited disciples in the sangha from different areas. In turn, people from this region were drawn towards Bharhut as most of the place names seem to be the names of villages or towns around Vidiśā.

Of the fifteen places mentioned individually by laymen, four of the donors mentioned Karahakaṭa. The place was mentioned once by a *nigama*[63] while individual male donors mentioned it thrice.[64] According to Luders, any name that ends with *kaṭa* probably goes back to Sanskrit *kaṭaka* in the sense of circle, valley or camp.[65] Most probably it was modern Karhad, in the district of Satara, Maharashtra. This indicates that laymen donors travelled to far off places to make donations. It also provides evidence on the networks of communication, for Bharhut was on the trade route. Most of the other places mentioned by laymen have been mentioned once and most of these places were in present-day central India.

Laywomen have mentioned sixteen different places, as stated above. The place most frequently mentioned is Purikā, mentioned four times;[66] Pāṭalīputra and Moragiri have been mentioned twice. The places that have been identified are Nāsika, Pāṭalīputra, and Nandinagara (Nander), which may be in present-day Uttar Pradesh.[67] The other places have not been identified till date.

Two laywomen mentioned that they were inhabitants of Pāṭalīputra[68] and also stated that they belonged to Kauṇḍinya, the name of a *gotra*.[69] We also find a man who identified himself as coming from Pāṭalīputra.

TABLE 1.4: Indicating Identities based on Places of Residence from the Inscriptions at Bharhut

Place names	*Religious Men*	*Religious Women*	*Laymen*	*Laywomen*
Asitamasā	–	–	1	–
Bhogavadhana	1	–	–	–
Bhojakaṭaka	–	1	1	–
Bibikāna	–	–	2	–
Cakulana	–	–	1	–
Cikulani	1	–	–	–
Cūdathīlikā	–	2	–	1
Dabhinika	–	1	–	–
Golā	–	–	–	1
Karahakaṭa	–	–	4 (1 cssm)	–
Kākandi	–	1	–	–
Kujatidakhi	1	–	–	–
Moragiri	1	1	1	2
Nagarika	–	1	–	–
Nandinagara	1	–	–	1
Nāsika	–	–	–	1
Pandelaka	–	–	1	–
Parakatika	–	–	–	1
Pāṭalīputra	–	–	1	2
Purikā	–	–	1	4
Rākutiya	1	–	–	–
Sirīsapadā	–	–	–	1
Vidiśā	–	1	2	2
Venukagrāma	–	1	–	–

NOTE: Information available only from individual donors unless indicated otherwise. The numerals indicate the number of times the places have been mentioned. Base total for religious men = 22; Base total for religious women = 16; Base total for laymen = 45 (1 collective); Base total for laywomen = 29; Base total for donors = 115.

Is it then possible to assume that all the three donors came together from Pāṭalīputra to record their donations? Or, if they all belonged to the same family, maybe the man escorted the women who wanted to make their donations personally.

When we examine places of residence mentioned by men and women donors we find that there are more instances of identified places mentioned by men. Unfortunately, many places mentioned by women have not been identified. Second, on the basis of the identified places we can say that as far as men were concerned their places of residence were mostly towns, but women came from both towns and villages. Third, there were more instances of women coming from the same place while the men came from different places.

We can suggest that for both laywomen and laymen place was an important marker of identity. However, it was more important for women who designated through religion than for men in the same category. Thus, place as a marker of identity seemed to be important for laywomen, laymen and *bhikkhunīs* at Bharhut.

Kinship Ties: Wife, Mother, and Sons

Kinship ties are not mentioned very often in these inscriptions, yet it is evident that they were more important for women than for men (Table 1.5). There was a difference in the way men and women identified themselves through kinship ties. Only two kinship ties were mentioned by laywomen (Table 1.5). Four donors identified themselves as *bhāriyā*[70] (wife). In both the pillar inscriptions the donors mentioned their name and place of residence. As one of the rail inscriptions is fragmentary, we are unable to make out the name of the donor,[71] while in the other rail inscription we find the name of the laywomen being mentioned. All the four donors mentioned the name of their husbands. It is possible that their husbands were known in that locality. In one instance, the donor, wife of King Dhanabhūti, belonged to a royal family.[72] Here only one term, *bhāriyā*, was used to indicate the status of women as wives.

Two of the donors belonged to famous towns, Vidiśā[73] and Nāsika.[74] It is assumed by Barua that as the husband of the first donor, Cāpa Devā, was called Revatimitra, he may have belonged to the royal family of Vidiśā, possibly that of the Śuṅga ruler, Agnimitra.[75] Barua associated the first donation with the royal family because there is evidence of the donation of the gateway and rails by the royal family at Bharhut, as mentioned earlier. Thus, amongst the laywomen, two donors seem to have been connected to the royal household. However, no sculptural portrayals of them have been found. The same holds true for King Dhanabhūti, who gifted the gateway. Instead, as seen in Plates 1.3 and 1.4, we find a portrayal of King Ajātaśatru who did not make a single donation at the site. The pillar gifted by Cāpa Devā is remarkable (Plate 1.5). This is discussed later.

There is a rare instance in one of the inscriptions[76] where the donor is referred to as the descendant of Kauṇḍinya, according to Cunningham.[77] She identified herself by her personal name and as belonging to Pāṭaliputra. We find laywomen mentioning their *gotra* names along with their personal names as in the case of King Dhanabhūti, discussed later. In one of the inscriptions, Luders refers to a nun being the daughter of Mahāmukhi[78] but Cunningham just mentions the word Mahāmukhi[79] maybe trying to suggest it was a title. According to Barua,[80] Mahāmukhi was a great local headman. If we take into account the suggestion of Cunningham and the interpretation by Barua then we may assume that the nun was the daughter of a local village headman of Dabhinika. But as the term for daughter is not mentioned in the inscription, and given the uncertainties of interpretation I have not included it in Table 1.5. Unfortunately, the place Dabhinika has also not been identified till date.

The evidence about the genealogy of Dhanabhūti,[81] who was the king of Srughana, is unusual. From the inscription on the *toraṇa* we get to know the kinship ties of the donor who only mentioned his maternal ties for three generations. He mentioned the names of his mother, grandmother, and great-grandmother. According to Cunningham,[82] Dhanabhūti mentioned in the Mathura inscription[83] is of the same family as the person mentioned at Bharhut. We can trace the genealogy of the family for more than two generations through the Mathura inscription. Dhanabhūti of Mathura was Dhanabhūti II and the grandson of Dhanabhūti I of Bharhut. According to the inscription at Bharhut, the donation was made by Dhanabhūti, born of the queen of the Vācchi and son of Aga Rājā, born of the queen of the Goti and the grandson of King Visa-Deva, born of the queen of the Gāgī. These are the main markers of identity used by the donor besides his occupation, that of a king. Thus we have evidence of metronymics being used for at least three generations. The fact that many of the metronymics were derived from *gotra* names is significant. It suggests that women did not change their *gotra* name after marriage. In other words, they did not practice *gotrāntara* or giving up the father's *gotra* and adopting that of the husband, recommended after marriage according to the Dharmaśāstras.

This feature of using the name of the mother based on her *gotra*, that is metronymics, according to Trautmann,[84] was formed on the basis of *gotra* names of ṛsis known among brāhmaṇas and they were exclusively patrilineal. The feminine name could be a personal name or a derivative of a place name or a *gotra* name which was applied to brāhmaṇas or to a brāhmaṇa who converted to Buddhism. Therefore, it could be derived from the name of ṛṣis and was a method by which the family lineage could be traced. The suggestion of Trautmann does not seem very convincing as the evidence of sons using *gotra* names does not apply to brāhmaṇas alone but to people belonging to other social categories as well. The other point of view is of R.S. Sharma[85] who says that metronymics were common even among ordinary folk. Matrilineal inheritance could be a possible explanation for metronymics. A different viewpoint is that the use of metronymics probably indicates the survival of a substratum of a matrilineal system, despite the fact that the social pattern advocated by the *smṛtikāras* had come into vogue and was widely respected.[86] Even in a patriarchal society we may find sons and daughters mentioning their mother's name, indicating that it is not a monolithic structure but incorporated variations that may have been the result of a changing complex society. The use of metronymics also suggests that a patrilineal system of identification was by no means the only prevalent means of identification.[87]

Overall, we find more kinship ties being mentioned on the rail inscriptions by laywomen than on the pillars. The most important kinship tie that we find from the rails is that of the mother (*mātā*). In all the four instances[88] the women were mothers of laymen donors. In two inscriptions the mothers mentioned their personal names[89] but none of the donors mentioned their place of residence. Thus, their position within the kinship network appears as their most important marker of identity.

The only kinship identity mentioned by laymen is that of son (*putra*) which occurs four times. We find that two of the donors mentioned the name of the mother rather than the father (Siriya-*putra*).[90] As mentioned earlier, a donor described himself as grandson (*pauta*). There are two instances of sons mentioning the mother's name instead of the father and one instance where the name of the grandmother instead of the grandfather has been mentioned. It may suggest that the patrilineal kinship structure was not as monolithic or universal as presumed. There is one inscription where the donation was given on account of the donor's father and mother.[91] This is the only instance where we find a wish for the transference of merit accrued by making a grant.

Thus, if we examine identities based on kinship, we find that they held a relatively more important place for laywomen in comparison to laymen. The terms mentioned by women were wife and mother; we do not find the corresponding kinship terms of husband and father being mentioned by men. The only kinship identity mentioned by laymen was that of son, but the corresponding kinship identity of daughter does not find a mention here. This goes to show that marital ties were of importance for laywomen but not to the same extent for laymen at Bharhut. For men and women who designated through religion, kinship ties do not seem to be a marker of identity as neither category mentioned any kinship ties.

As far as sculptural representation is concerned, we find the portrayal of the wife in Plate 1.6, scene A and B and that of the mother in Plate 1.6, scene C. We do not find any sculptural portrayal of a son alone, but a son and daughter are depicted in Plate 1.6, scene C.

TABLE 1.5: Indicating Identities based on Kinship Ties from the Inscriptions at Bharhut

Kinship Ties	*Son*	*Mother*	*Wife*	*Grandson*
Laymen	5	–	–	1
Laywomen	–	4	4	–

NOTE: Information available only from individual donors unless indicated otherwise. The numerals indicate the number of times the kinship ties have been mentioned. Base total for laymen = 44; Base total for laywomen = 29; Base total of donors = 115.

Occupation as Identity: Portrayals in Inscriptions and Sculpture

Occupational identity does not seem important for women donors. From the inscriptions, we do not find a single instance where women mention their occupation or even their husbands' or sons' occupation. However, we do find a few men donors (only five in all, refer to Table 1.6) who mentioned their occupations. The occupations mentioned are *gahapati* (householder),[92] *aśvavārika* (horseman),[93] two from the royal family, a *kumāra* (prince)[94] and a *rājā* (king).[95] We also find a *rūpakāra* (sculptor)[96] which may be a unique example of patronage when the craftsmen who worked on the object of patronage were themselves the patrons.[97] However, in this particular case, we do not know whether the sculptor sculpted the gift himself. We also find the term *nigama* (guild)[98] of Karahakaṭa mentioned, which has not been tabulated, but points to the association of craftsmen/merchants of a single occupation. I have assumed that laymen were associated with the *nigama* as we do not have a single instance of women being part of the activities of the *nigama*.[99] From the evidence gathered from different geographical regions it seems that women were excluded from the *nigama*.

As stated earlier, we find mention of very few occupations and none associated with women. But when we examine the sculptures from Bharhut the evidence is different. We find quite a few occupations in which women were also involved. For example, in Plate 1.4, we find women were mounted on the elephant as attendants of King Ajātaśatru's royal procession. The female attendants were carrying elephant goads; this is the only weapon that they seem to be carrying. In Plate 1.7 we find a woman soldier mounted on a horse. These two sculptures tell us that women were trained to ride horses and elephants, which, according to the textual references, were meant for the *āryaputra*, the son of a nobleman. Even if one argues that these were exceptions, these cannot be overlooked.

The other occupations depicted are of a woman cutting corn (Plate 1.6) while the plant is depicted on the right side of the panel in Plate 1.6. We find the representation of a *gahapatnī* and a female servant who is helping her mistress in Plate 1.6, scene B. Only the *gahapati* was mentioned in inscriptions; there is no mention of the *gahapatnī*. According to Roy,[100] these occupations were not integrated in the larger picture. It is possible that these occupations are not mentioned in the inscriptions because of this reason. As these occupations do not find any mention in the written documents one wonders whether they were being left out on purpose as they did not fit the norms or it is *only* an oversight.

For men we find the occupations of shepherd,[101] and of merchants in a ship, to be swallowed by a marine monster,[102] being depicted on the sculptural panel. There is a depiction of merchants in the above-mentioned panel and also in Plate 1.8 where there are four men, two seated and two standing. The two who are seated wear the usual costumes of the Bharhut figures, but the two who are standing wear peculiar flat caps on their heads, apparently ornamented with feathers and broad collars of large leaves round their necks. According to Cunningham, these are foreign merchants who seem to be in conversation regarding the price of *chauri* tails and tusks.[103]

There is evidence of a soldier in Plate 1.9, which is very well preserved. According to Mitra,[104] the sculpture represents a foreigner. His head is bare with short curly hair, he wears a tunic and boots, and in his right hand he carries a broad sword, sheathed in a scabbard, which is suspended from the left shoulder by a long flat belt. He, unlike the woman soldier, is not depicted on horseback. However an inscription mentions a male donor using the marker of a horseman for the construction of his identity. There are also other occupations like a royal relic-bearer on an elephant (Plate 1.5), and another man depicted on horseback. There is also a depiction of courtiers, but only men are portrayed on the panel (Plate 1.3). We also find the portrayal of men as musicians and women as dancers (Plate 1.2).

Interestingly, King Ajātaśatru has been portrayed in the sculptural panel (on the western gate, Plates 1.3 and 1.4) while King Prasenajit has been mentioned on the south gate panel (Plate 1.13), but no donations were attributed to them. On the other hand, there are no sculptures or panels depicting or mentioning King Dhanabhūti who had donated a gateway (*toraṇa*).

When we examine occupation as a marker of identity we find it is important only for men, whether laymen or those designated by religion. We find monks using different epithets and a few laymen mentioned their occupation. On the other hand, for women, lay or *bhikkhunīs*, occupation was not an important marker of identity. There is a sharp difference between the inscriptions and sculptural representations here.

TABLE 1.6: Indicating Identities based on the Occupations of the Donors from Bharhut

Occupations	*Laymen*
King (*rājā*)	1
Prince (*kumāra*)	1
Sculptor (*rūpakāra*)	1
Householder (*gahapati*)	1
Horseman (*aśvavārika*)	1

NOTE: Information available only from individual donors unless indicated otherwise. Base total for laymen = 44; Total base of donors = 115.

Displaying Devotion: Elite Women and Learned Monks

There were four different gifts that were made by donors at Bharhut. These were architectural forms that adorn the *stūpa*—pillars, rails, and coping-stones—while the fourth was the gateway. There are three separate gateways and if there are three then there must have been four, as the four corner pillars of the rails found at the four cardinal points show that there were four openings.[105] The pillars (*stambha*) are all monoliths and each pillar bears just one votive inscription recording the gift of an individual donor. The pillars are all sculpted or ornamented. In not a single instance is a pillar recorded to be the gift of one donor and the sculpture that of another. Rails are also called *sūci* or 'needle', serving to stitch together the pillars by being fitted into their mortises or eyelet holes. Each rail, like the pillar, has a votive inscription and here also the rail and the sculpture on it were given by the same donor. Coping-stones (*uṣnīśa*) are architectural features that helped to bond the top of the pillars together. The copings were round on the top and provided enough space on the two vertical sides for the carving of decorative motifs and narrative scenes that became a pleasing feature of *stūpa* sculpture.[106]

Three *toraṇas* (gateways)[107] were donated out of which one was donated by King Dhanabhūti[108] for spiritual benefit. Two *toraṇas* were gifted by unidentified donors.[109]

There are forty-four pillars that were gifted, out of which fourteen were given by monks and an *atevāsin,* nine by nuns, thirteen by laymen, and eight by laywomen (Table 1.7). If we examine the number of donations made by *bhikkhunīs* and laywomen, we find *bhikkhunīs* making more donations than laywomen but the difference is not significant. The difference is significant if we compare it on gender lines; we find men make more donations of pillars than women.

The first pillar of the inner railing, which was the gift of Cāpa Devā, appears to be the largest and heaviest amongst the pillars. It is richly carved (Plate 1.5) on two adjacent faces with a rider on an elephant carrying a relic-casket and a horseman carrying a *garuḍa* banner.[110] If we examine this sculpture carefully we find the elephant in the middle is much larger than those on his two sides, and appears to be a state elephant. The rider mounted on his shoulders has greater dignity than others, and appears to be a king as the leader of the procession. This royal personage carries a relic-casket, placing it on the elephant's head and holding it carefully in his embrace. This casket may really be a small cylindrical box with a handled lid.[111] Thus, the representation is one of a scene of arrival of the royal procession on the site of the mound in which the casket was to be deposited. This was probably designed to remind the visitor or pilgrim of how the relic was brought over to Bharhut and what really constituted the sacredness and importance of the place. The name of the king who came at the head of the procession is not mentioned. The horseman on the inner face of the first pillar must have followed these elephants, bearing a standard which appears to be a small pillar-shaped rod with a flying angel, borne on its capital, and carrying a large piece of garland. This standard is evidently a *garuḍadhvaja*, the human-shaped flying angel, representing the mythical bird *garuḍa.*[112] According to Barua,[113] Cāpa Devā's husband Revatimitra was a member of the royal family of Vidiśā and may have been connected with Agnimitra, the powerful Śuṅga viceroy stationed there.

Seven other pillars were given by laywomen, out of whom only one described herself as a wife. All the pillars here are very well sculpted and there is no significant difference in the sculpture on the pillars given by male or female donors.

There were nine pillars donated by *bhikkhunīs.* In one of the inscriptions a *bhikkhunī* used the title *ayā.*[114] It has been suggested by Dehejia[115] that the railing pillar, carved on one side with the sensuous figure of Sirimā *devatā* and on the reverse with Suciloma *yakṣa*, was the gift of a *bhikkhunī* to whom funds for commissioning an entire sculpted pillar were available

(Plates 1.10–1.11). It is possible that this is the same *bhikkhunī* who used the special epithet. It is possible that some of the donors emerged as significant patrons and may have had a major say in the way pillars were sculpted or narratives portrayed.

As far as the pillars donated by men are concerned, these are generally similar to those given by women. An exception can be seen in the pillar gifted by a sangha official with four titles[116] (*aya, bhadanta, bhānaka*, and *navakarmika*). He may have gifted all six narrative panels on the pillar and as a *navakarmika*, he may have been the ecclesiastic who supervised the entire construction and decoration of the Bharhut *stūpa*.[117]

There are two donations made of a coping-stone (refer to Table 1.7), of which one was a collective donation made by a guild. This guild hailed from the town or market place of Karahakaṭa. The placement of the record indicates that the guild donated a single sculpted narrative and not the entire length of coping. A monk with the epithet *aya* made the other donation of the coping length. We do not find women donors giving coping-stones. Economically, it may not have been feasible for women to give a sculpted coping-stone individually.

If we try to see whether there was any difference in the emphasis on the narratives we find that all the donors chose narratives according to their wishes. In fact, we do not find a running theme in the sculpted pillars at Bharhut.[118]

Sixty-six donations of rails were made, out of which seven were made by *bhikkhus*, seven by *bhikkhunīs*, thirty by laymen, twenty-one by laywomen, and one by an unidentified donor (Table 1.7). We find that there is no difference in the number of donations made by *bhikkhus* and *bhikkhunīs*, nor do we find any difference in the kind of donations made by them. When we examine the donations made by laymen and laywomen, we find more donations made by laymen than laywomen (Table 1.7). Though there is a difference in the number of donations, this is not glaring. Second, there is no difference in the placing or the kind of rails that were given by men or women. Third, we also do not find any difference in the way the donations have been recorded.

Thus, we see that the laity and the ecclesiastics together with a member from the royal family were involved in the erection of the railing that encircled the *stūpa*. But we find that lay donors made more donations of the rails. There is no difference in the rails that were given by the laity or clergy or by men or women. There is an absence of a thematic programme;[119] instead, individual gifts became part of the railing as and when the donations were received. It thus seems that a lack of a sculptural programme went hand in hand with the collective nature of early Buddhist patronage.

What is remarkable is that there is really no disparity that can be witnessed between religious or lay donors. The other aspect that we notice is that at Bharhut, there were more men than women donors but the aspect of matronage was significant. The relationship between the laity and renunciant petitioner can be traced back to the Vedic traditions where the householder's wife gave food to the renunciant. The renunciant was dependent on the household to procure his food and clothing. Once the renunciant came to the door of the house it was obligatory for the housewife to give food, as hospitality was regarded to be one of the most important functions of the housemistress. Therefore, it was expected that she would welcome the *atithi* who came to the door. Thus, her *dāna* was obligatory and not voluntary. Second, the *dāna* was not in her individual capacity but on behalf of the household itself.

Later on there is a shift in the Buddhist tradition, from collective to individual patronage. Now, in addition to the routine things like food and clothing, we find *dāna* changed to architectural parts of the *stūpa*, as we find at sites such as Bharhut. The everyday gifts were essential and significant for the Buddhist sangha and continued, but there was no record keeping of this *dāna* unlike the architectural parts of the *stūpa.* Thus, we see a paradigm shift from obligatory hospitality to voluntary patronage. But the Buddhist encounter remained an encounter with the woman of the household. Thus, with the formal pattern from the *brahmacārin* model, this patronage is, again, a form of matronage.[120]

TABLE 1.7: Indicating the Donations Made at Bharhut

Donors	*Rails*	*Pillars*	*Coping-stones*	*Gateways*
Individual Religious Men	7	14	1	–
Individual Religious Women	7	9	–	–
Individual Laymen	30	13	–	1
Collective Same Sex	–	–	1	–
Individual Laywomen	21	8	–	–
Unidentified Donor	1	–	–	2

NOTE: Information available only from individual donors unless indicated otherwise. Base total for pillars = 44; Base total for rails = 66; Base total for coping-stone = 2; Base of gateway pillars = 3; Base total of gifts = 115.

When we examine the donations made at Bharhut, we find that more donations were made by *bhikkhus* than by *bhikkhunīs.* But the difference was not large. Importantly, the difference was not so much in the number of donations or in the way donations were made but in the way the donors were identified. We find different epithets used by *bhikkhus*, and quite a few used multiple epithets. The case is not the same for the *bhikkhunīs*. Thus, the sangha and its functions seem to be gendered in the early *stūpa* as the power of knowledge along with the privilege to disseminate knowledge remained with the *bhikkhus* and not with the *bhikkhunīs*. Here we see a similarity with the Brahmanical tradition.

Neither the *bhikkhus* nor the *bhikkhunīs* mentioned any kinship ties. Both mentioned places of residence, though we find more evidence of places of residence being mentioned by *bhikkhunīs* than *bhikkhus*. *Bhikkhunīs* also travelled from a distance to make *dāna* and attain spiritual merit. In all likelihood *bhikkhunīs*, unlike *bhikkhus*, came from urban centres or villages that were known; maybe that is the reason why *bhikkhunīs* used place names as a marker of identity.

As far as the gifts are concerned, we find that the *bhikkhus* made more donations of pillars than *bhikkhunīs*. With regard to donation of rails, there was no difference in their contributions. We are not sure whether the difference in resources required to install pillars/railings may account for this variation. It is also possible that pillars were independent structures, unlike railings, and the initiative for erecting them may have been somewhat more easily accessible to monks than to nuns. The placement and size of pillars were probably part of the planning of the structure, where monks may have had a greater say than nuns.

Comparing laymen and laywomen we find that the number of donations made by laymen is more than laywomen. Overall, more donations were made by lay donors than by ecclesiastics at Bharhut. Here we would also like to see if markers of identity were the same for the laymen and *bhikkhus* on the one hand and laywomen and the *bhikkhunīs* on the other or if there is a change in the way they use different markers of identity.

Place names as a marker of identity was important for both laymen and laywomen. The place of residence was also important for *bhikkhunīs*, but not for *bhikkhus*. Relatively more places mentioned by laymen have been identified in comparison with those mentioned by laywomen. This could mean that laymen came from important urban or trading centres. On the other hand, laywomen came from places which were not important urban or market centres, as is evident from the fact that many of these are not identified. However this did not deter them from reaching Bharhut, getting their donations recorded and mentioning the place they came from.

There are more instances of places being mentioned in the pillar inscriptions than in the rail inscriptions. Laymen mention more places on the pillar inscriptions. Even though the number of places mentioned by women is fewer, for the pillar inscriptions we find that a few of the places are well-known sites. This may indicate that people who installed pillars came from important places, including urban centres. It is possible that these donors enjoyed an influential position or had a say in the planning of the structure.

Kinship, as a marker of identity, does not seem to have been very important at Bharhut. If we examine kinship terms used we find that more women mentioned such ties than men, but the difference is marginal. The two kinship positions of importance were that of mother, especially of a son, and wife. Two kinship terms were also mentioned by men, namely, son and grandson. Thus, kinship ties, as markers of identity, were more important for women than men. We do not find any kind of kinship ties mentioned by either *bhikkhus* or *bhikkhunīs*. Place as a marker of identity seems to have been more important than kinship ties for them.

Occupation as a marker of identity was not significant at Bharhut, where only four occupations have been mentioned. We do not have a single instance of laywomen mentioning an occupation.

If we compare the donations of rails and pillars made by laywomen we find more donations of rails than pillars. The picture is the same for laymen. (This comparison has been made by examining the number of donations made of rails and pillars by men and women.) When we analyse the donations made by men and women who designate through religion the picture is different, because we find more *bhikkhus* and *bhikkhunīs* making donations of pillars than of rails. Thus, we find more donations of pillars made by ecclesiastics than lay donors.

When we examine the donations along gender lines we find more laymen and *bhikkhus* making donations of pillars than *bhikkhunīs* and laywomen. As far as the rails are concerned we find that laymen made the maximum number of donations, followed by laywomen, while *bhikkhus* and *bhikkhunīs* made the same number of donations. Thus, the donation of pillars seems to be the prerogative of men. While there is a marked difference between men and women as far as the donations of pillars are concerned, the difference is not as sharp in the case of rails.

It is in relation to the donations of rails that we find a large number of laywomen donors. One wonders whether the resources needed for rails were less than that for pillars. This may explain why laywomen found it easier to donate rails rather than pillars. It is possible that there were major patrons like the monk, who used the epithet of *navakarmika*, Cāpa Devā, who was connected to the royal household, and Nāgarakhitā, wife of King Dhanabhūti, who may have been instrumental in mobilizing resources for the construction of pillars and rails at Bharhut. One may assume this also because the two most elaborate pillars found at Bharhut are those donated by Cāpa Devā and the *bhikkhu*. Though there is no visible difference in the donation of the rail of Nāgarakhitā and those of the other donors, it is possible that Nāgarakhitā may have helped in collecting resources. There is evidence of only three donations made by donors who were associated with the royal household, while people of humble occupations made the rest of the donations. It is on this premise that we speak of the collective patronage of ordinary people and elite women along with respected *bhikkhus*. The *bhikkhus* and *bhikkhunīs* who are visible at Bharhut may have also acted as spiritual guides in explaining the edifying stories to those who came to pay homage to the Buddha's relics.[121]

With two exceptions, the inscriptions do not tell us about the intentions of the vast majority of donors in making gifts. A donor in a rail inscription[122] mentioned that the gifts were for the benefit of his parents. Another donor, King Dhanabhūti, who gifted a gateway[123] made the donation for spiritual benefit. We do not find this kind of evidence in the pillar inscriptions. According to Schopen,[124] the doctrine of the transference of merit is associated with the Theravāda school, which may be represented in these practices.

Overall, we find a large number of women donors (39 per cent), thereby attesting to the fact that women had funds at their disposal that they could utilize for religious grants. Thus, women were active participants in the religious practice and not mere spectators. By getting the *dāna* recorded women made themselves visible and also occupied space in the public sphere. Women appear as singular agents for disposing wealth, apart from the men of their family (who may also have been donors), thus allowing for an identity that is tied to individual action.[125]

Women identified themselves by their personal name, which shows that they wanted to be remembered for posterity in their own right. Second, as mentioned earlier the *stūpa* is seen as more than a symbol of the Buddha, it is the Buddha himself.[126] According to Konow[127] also, 'The name makes him present', and therefore, it has been suggested that when a person's name is present, the person is present. Thus, if one's name is carved in stone and permanently placed near a powerful religious 'object' then the person is there as well[128] and this could have been the purpose behind the early inscriptions at Bharhut and Sanchi when seen from the point of view of the donor. Schopen[129] rightly argued that names were the essential characteristic of identity; names are substitutes for physical presence. Names were inscribed because donors wished to leave their presence, through their names, in close proximity to the sacred presence of the Buddha contained within his relics. Another belief is that 'a person lives in heaven as long as her/his name is remembered on earth'.[130] Thus, what is evident is that in the case of personal identity we do not find a gender difference emerging, whether we take the case of the monastic order or the laity. Women could be placed close to the Buddha in their own right and could also be remembered for posterity in their own right. It also shows that the personal name of women, lay or *bhikkhunīs*, was an essential characteristic of their identity.

When we examine the evidence from Bharhut we find that a difference emerges between men and women in the way they identify themselves. The *bhikkhus* use ecclesiastical titles whereas the *bhikkhunīs* use place of residence as a marker of identity. Neither the *bhikkhus* nor the *bhikkhunīs* use kinship as a marker of identity. Place of residence and kinship terms as markers of identity have been used more frequently by laywomen than laymen but the difference is marginal. Occupation as a marker of identity was used only by laymen. Thus, occupational identity for the laity and epithets for the *bhikkhus* emerge as the overarching markers of difference between men and women. In terms of place and kinship ties as markers of identity the evidence is fragmented. With regard to gifts, there is a clear demarcation as pillars seem to be the prerogative of male donors while rails were gifted by both men and women.

Visual Representations

We will now examine the portrayal of men and women on rail-pillars, pillars, coping-stones, etc., at Bharhut, posing the following question: Does the sculptural representation at Bharhut correspond with the evidence available from inscriptions?

When we examine the variety of sculptures at Bharhut we are struck by the range of themes taken from historical/narrative scenes like Prasenajit and Ajātaśatru going to take blessings from the Buddha, the portrayal of Rāma, Sītā and Lakṣmaṇa, numerous portrayals from the *Jātaka* stories, etc. Having said this, as mentioned earlier, there appears to be a big gap between the inscriptions and sculptures found at Bharhut. I will try to illustrate this.

In the inscriptions there were a number of donations made by monks and nuns but in the sculptures there are very few instances. Plate 1.1 depicts a monk giving a discourse to female and male pupils. The hierarchy seems evident in the depiction of the sitting plan. The sculpture is also revealing to an extent that we find the same kind of hierarchy within the inscriptions, where the monks are referred to by their epithets like *bhānaka, bhadanta*, etc., while the nuns are only addressed as *bhikkhunīs.* Second, even in inscriptions we find an *atevāsin* attached to a *bhikkhu* and none for the *bhikkhunīs.* Third, in the representation of the *Jātaka* stories we find quite a few depictions of *bhikkhus* but virtually none of *bhikkhunīs.* In Plate 1.1 we find the monk addressing disciples from the monastic world or laity. This space is evidently gendered as we only find *bhikkhus* giving discourse but never the *bhikkhunīs*.

The two royal personages mentioned or portrayed are Prasenajit and Ajātaśatru. Obviously, there were no donations made by them, as they were contemporaries of the Buddha, according to Buddhist tradition. The only donation from the royal household is by Dhanabhūti but there is no sculptural depiction of him. On the left side of the sculptural panel of the railing-pillar depicting Ajātaśatru, we find interesting possibilities for reconstructing gender relations.

Plate 1.2[131] has three panels. On the upper half of the first panel we find the portrayal of the *caitya-cūḍā maṇi* or the representation of the relic of the hair ornament of Siddhārtha or the enshrining of the headdress relic. On the lower half of the panel we find the representation of *apsarās* dancing and singing as if they are rejoicing at the enshrining of the relic.

When we examine the portrayal of *apsarās,* we find they are shown as symbols of sexuality through their postures, scanty clothing, exposure of bosom, playing of different instruments, and creating pleasure through music. However, playing music is not unique to them. We find men playing instruments like the drum, harp, etc. There is an overlap between the category of the courtesan and the *apsarās.* So we find the portrayal of Sirimā, who is the sister of Jīvaka, the physician, and is a courtesan. She has been portrayed on a panel with full ornaments and tattoo on her forehead (Plate 1.10) unlike the other female figures. We find that Sirimā got the epithet of *devatā* as she fed the monks till her last days. What is also noteworthy is that it has been said that she fed the monks and not the nuns. If we study this panel carefully we find space has been accorded to men and women in the lower two panels but not in the upper most part of the panel. There also appears a difference in the portrayal of the elite and semi-divine women vis-à-vis women from everyday lives. Elite and semi-divine women were always portrayed with tattoos and were heavily ornamented unlike the non-elite women.

In the second panel we find Ajātaśatru receiving the blessings of the Buddha, who is represented by footprints. The sculpture shows Ajātaśatru touching the footprint and all around him are men who could either be his courtiers or worshippers of the Buddha. Interestingly, no women are depicted in this scene (Plate 1.3). In the third panel (Plate 1.4) we find Ajātaśatru mounted on an elephant, most likely going to take the blessings of the Buddha. Here we find him with female attendants who carry weapons in their hands. What is evident is that different spaces were visualized distinctly in terms of gendered representations.

There is a distinct difference that we can witness in the second panel. When Ajātaśatru is shown worshipping the footprint of the Buddha, no women are seen in close vicinity, perhaps trying to portray that women were not allowed near the portrayal of the Buddha; but from the inscriptions we know that women visited the *stūpa* and also recorded their donations. The visuals would have been seen by the populace visiting the *stūpa*, but the inscriptions would have been read by very few; therefore, one wonders whether the sculpture would create a different portrayal of gender relations.

We also find the depiction of four scenes from the *Rāmāyaṇa*. Except for these, the rest of the depictions are from the *Jātakas*. We may assume that as the stories of the epics were common, therefore, sculptors portrayed scenes from the *Rāmāyaṇa*. What is interesting is that in one such depiction,[132] we find Rāma and Lakṣmaṇa in conversation, while Sītā is shown enclosed in a circular space as if she is eavesdropping. The portrayal is intriguing as literary representations depict Sītā as present in the public space. However, this visual representation suggests that access to such spaces was gendered; while her husband and brother-in-law could be depicted in the public space without any problem, her presence was circumscribed.

Another scene depicts Rāma, Lakṣmaṇa and Sītā dressed as ascetics, in front of a hermit[133] and listening to the sage. Unlike the previous representation, this space seems to be equally accessible to both men and women. Does this suggest that gender differences were considered insignificant when listening to a discourse by a monk/sage?

There are two medallion busts of queens (Plate 1.12). In the first the queen is shown anointing herself, whereas in the second[134] she is holding a mirror that has a snake hood. A royal couple who stand beside each other is presented in the end face of Prasenajit's pillar (Plate 1.13). The inscribed label 'Kadariki' helps identify the male as king Kadariki of the *Kunāla Jātaka.*[135] Standing beside the king is the queen who has a parrot in her hand, she is heavily ornamented and has tattoo on her cheeks and forehead or *lalāṭika*. Again, as mentioned earlier, we do not find any donations by queens in the inscriptions. Thus, there is a difference between visual and inscriptional representations.

We also find hands held in adoration of four *stūpas* or four thrones[136] and representing a crowd where no gender differentiation can be perceived. But when we compare it to Plate 1.3,[137] we find a different representation. In Plate 1.3 where Ajātaśatru touches the footprint of the Buddha, there are others present, but no women are depicted. Is the difference arising because of the portrayal of the king? Or is it because of the scale of depiction? The depiction of Ajātaśatru is on a panel very visible to the visitor whereas the representation of the four *stūpas* is on a medallion that would not be very discernible to the visitor.

We find tattoos on the cheeks and forehead of women who are *apsarās* or female dancers, queens, *yakṣinī*, *nāgins*, the female soldiers and female attendants. It may be possible that tattoos have ornamental value and were used for women of the elite class or semi-divine women. Tattoos on the forehead could also be *lalāṭika* (forehead piece) or *patripāsyā* (the fastened leaf).[138] Tattoos on cheeks are quite common for women who also indulged in variety. For example the statue of Sirimā *devatā* (Plate 1.10) has a single star or flower on the left cheek, while the queen with the parrot (Plate 1.13) has a sun and moon tattoo on her cheeks but these are never seen on men. Interestingly, tattoos are seen only on the women (Plates 1.10, 1.12, 1.13, 1.14, 1.16) whereas ornaments are common to both men and women.

Amidst the single figures found as parts of the railing pillars are a few examples of female statues. The two statues of *yakṣinī* Candā[139] on the northern gate and *yakṣinī* Sudarśanā on the eastern gate (Plate 1.14) are significant as they have been gifted by the monks. The railing pillar carved on one side with the sensuous figure of Sirimā *devatā* (Plate 1.10) on the south-western gate and on the reverse with Suciloma *yakṣa* (Plate 1.11) was the gift of a nun to whom funds for commissioning an entire sculpted pillar were available.

On the southern gate pillar we also find Culakoka *devatā*[140] along with the king of the *nāgas*, Cakavāka (Plate 1.15) and Suciloma *yakṣa* (Plate 1.11), which were also gifted by the ecclesiastics. A statue of a female mounted on a horse with a staff suggests that she could either be a female attendant or a warrior (Plate 1.7). Thus, visual representations of female figures are as common, if not more common, than those of men.

As stated earlier, the portrayal of kings is a dominant feature while queens are rarely portrayed. The king can be distinguished in sculpture by the mark of the *chatra* (parasol) above his head[141] and generally has a retinue of attendants with him but these features do not appear for queens. This is one indication of the gendered way in which royal figures were represented.

When we examine the sculptures of *nāgas* we find that they are portrayed in full human form, clad as a royal personage, while the *nāgins* are shown as half-human and half-*nāgin* and scantily clad or naked unlike the *nāgas.* There is the depiction of a *Jātaka* story about a *yakṣa* and a *nāga*[142] wherein the *nāga* king is depicted with his five-headed snake canopy along with his *nāga* queen who has only a one-snake canopy over her head, blessing their daughter and the *yakṣa* who becomes their son-in-law. In Plate 1.16 (inner face of the pillar), we find the representation of a *nāga rājā* worshipping the Siris tree (symbol of the first of the last four Buddhas, i.e. Krakuchanda) in full form, distinguishable from men in the same representation by the five-headed snake canopy over his head. Behind the *nāga rājā* is a *nāga* and two *nāgins* who seem half-human as half their body is concealed. This seems to be the norm for representing *nāgas* and *nāgins* in sculpture. What is noteworthy is that these representations are gendered.

There are two portrayals of mercantile occupations in the sculptural depictions at Bharhut. One portrayal shows two boats, which appear like marine monsters along with the travellers/traders.[143] In another instance, Plate 1.8,[144] we find two men sitting on stools, while two men with flat caps are standing. It has been assumed on the basis of their flat caps that they could be merchants from a distant land as they are showing elephant tusks and *chauri* tails of the yak (as mentioned earlier). It is interesting that while we have representations of merchants, none of the donors identify themselves in terms of this occupation. On the other hand, inscriptions record donations made by a sculptor and horseman, but these categories are not depicted. There is evidence of sculptural depiction of a relic-carrier, where a man rides on an elephant and horse respectively (Plate 1.5). There is no mention of them in the inscriptions. It is possible that this was a unique and occasional function performed by some men, and did not constitute a regular occupation. It is also important to note, as mentioned earlier, that Cāpa Devā donated this rail-pillar.

There are a number of other occupations that are suggested by the sculptural representations. The bullock cart (Plate 1.17) indicates the presence of transporters/drivers, there are also labourers who may have unloaded the bullock-cart; there is depiction of a washerman,[145] hunter, archer[146] and a scene of a boar hunt.[147] None of these everyday occupations find any mention in the inscriptions.

The other evidence is of a woman cutting corn (Plate 1.6).[148] On the same panel we find another woman who may be her employer, who is sitting and cooking. The next scene (Plate 1.6 scene B) shows a man, maybe a householder, and his wife eating while a female servant is serving chapattis to them. She may be the corn-cutter of the first scene. In Plate 1.6 we find the portrayal of corn. One aspect that emerges is that women were employed in agriculture and as domestic help. Not surprisingly, these occupations do not find mention in the inscriptions. Nonetheless, it is interesting to note the representation of these women involved in production and food processing. As mentioned earlier, there are depictions of women attendants of the king and of armed women. These visual representations allow us access to categories of women who do not find space in the textual tradition or in epigraphic records. Unfortunately, there is no portrayal of the *navakarmika*, Cāpa Devā and Nāgarakhitā, who were instrumental in mobilizing resources for the construction of the pillar and rails at Bharhut.

Second, we also find a number of portrayals of *Jātaka* stories and scenes from the *Rāmāyaṇa*. These do not figure directly in the votive inscriptions. However, they indicate that these narratives were considered significant, and were, therefore, represented with care.

Thus, when we compare the inscriptions with the sculpture at Bharhut, we find there is a difference in the way in which gender is represented. In sculpture, kings were portrayed with parasols while *nāgas* were depicted with a five-headed canopy and were depicted as men unlike the *nāgins*. We do not find such a sharp difference between men and women in the inscriptions. In fact, there was no difference in the recording or placement of donations made by women and men.

At the same time, we can see that the visual representations covered a larger range of categories, including semi-divine beings and labouring women. We may also note that for visitors or pilgrims it is likely that the sculpture would appear more significant than the small votive inscriptions, which may or may not have been read. Therefore, it is noteworthy that these visual representations, even as they differentiate amongst men and women, also portray both in a variety of contexts, suggesting that gender identities were constructed and preserved in more ways than one.

ACKNOWLEDGEMENTS

My sincere thanks to Professor Ranabir Chakravarti for his suggestion to make a comparative study of inscriptions and sculpture. I also thank Professor R.N. Misra for sharing his unpublished article and Professor Kumkum Roy for reading the drafts of this essay endlessly without complaining. I extend my thanks to Mr Sushil Sharma and the photography archive of AIIS, Gurgaon for the photographs that appear in this book and for the permission to use them.

NOTES

1. A. Cunningham, *The Stupa of Bharhut* (hereafter *SB*), New Delhi: Munshiram Manoharlal, repr. 1998, 1st edn. 1879, p. 1.
2. F.R Allchin, *The Archaeology of Early Historic South Asia: The Emergence of Cities and States*, Cambridge: Cambridge University Press, 1995, p. 332.
3. Uma Chakravarti, 'Rise of Buddhism as Experienced by Women', *Seminar on Women's Life Cycle and Identity*, Faridabad, 1981, pp. 1–9.
4. Ibid.
5. M. Mauss, *The Gift*, tr. Ian Cunnison, London: Routledge, 1954, p. 1.
6. P.V. Kane, *History of Dharmaśāstra*, vol. II, Poona: Bhandarkar Oriental Research Institute, 1968, pp. xi–xii.
7. Romila Thapar, *Ancient Indian Social History: Some Interpretations*, Delhi: Orient Longman, 1978, pp. 110–12.

8. V. Nath, *Dāna: Gift System in Ancient India (c. 600 BC–c.AD 300): A Socio-Economic Perspective*, Delhi: Munshiram Manoharlal, 1987, p. 12.
9. E.B. Findly, *Dāna: Giving and Getting in Pali Buddhism*, Delhi: Motilal Banarsidass, 2003, p. 112.
10. Ibid., pp. 37–8.
11. T. Brekke, 'Contradiction and the Merit of Giving in Indian Religions', *Numen*, vol. 45, no. 3, 1998, pp. 298–320.
12. K. Gutschow, *Being A Buddhist Nun: The Struggle for Enlightenment in the Himalayas*, Massachusetts: Harvard University Press, 2004, p. 89.
13. According to the Oxford dictionary a patron is 'one that supports protects or champions someone or something, such as an institution', and is derived from the root word 'pati', that is male or father. The conventional feminine equivalent of patron is patroness. Findly (2003) coined the term matronage to highlight support given by the mother and thus distinguishes it from patronage.
14. D.C. Sircar, 'Bharhut Inscriptions in Allahabad Museum', *Epigraphia Indica, 1959–60*, vol. 33, 1987, pp. 57–60.
15. Cunningham, *SB*, p. 15.
16. A. Ghosh, *Remains of Bharhut Stupa in the Indian Museum*, Kolkata: Indian Museum, 2006, p. 17.
17. Cunningham, *SB*, no. 29-rails. All inscription numbers refer to Cunningham's *SB*. Two inscriptions (H. Luders, 'A List of Brahmi Inscriptions from the Earliest Times to about A.D. 400 with the Exception of those of Asoka', Appendix to *Epigraphia Indica*, vol. 10, nos. 882 and 883, 1912) have been listed from Luders's list, as they do not find mention in Cunningham's list.
18. R.F. Gombrich, *Theravada Buddhism: A Social History from Ancient Benares to Modern Colombo*, London: Routledge, 1988, p. 72.
19. Findly, *Dāna*, pp. 16–20.
20. Ten on coping stones (hereafter C), seven on pillars (hereafter P) and one on rails (hereafter R).
21. Eight on coping stones, forty-nine on pillars and one on the rails.
22. Cunningham, *SB*, p. 127.
23. Ibid., no. C 16.
24. Ibid., nos. R 65, G 2 and G 3.
25. Ibid., no. P 88.
26. Ibid., nos. P 4, P 5, P 52, P 85, C 1, R 16, R 27, and R 41.
27. Ibid., nos. P 55, P 57, P 80, R 35 and R 43.
28. A.P.B. Mahathera, *Concise Pali-English Dictionary*, Delhi: Motilal Banarsidass, 2002, p. 19.
29. Cunningham, *SB*, nos. P 91 and R 18.
30. Ibid, nos. P 51 and P 77.
31. B.N. Barua, *Barhut* , 3 vols., Patna: Indological Book Corporation, 1934–37, pp. 45–6.
32. Sircar, 'Bharhut Inscriptions in Allahabad Museum', p. 58.
33. Cunningham, *SB*, no. P 62.

34. Ibid., p. 136.
35. H. Luders, 'Brahmi Inscriptions from Bharhut', *Corpus Inscriptionum Indicarum*, vol. II, pt. II, Ootacamund, 1963, p. 3.
36. Cunningham, *SB*, no. P 62.
37. Romila Thapar, 'Patronage and the Community', in *The Powers of Art: Patronage in Indian Culture*, ed. B.S. Miller, Delhi: Oxford University Press, 1992, p. 30.
38. Barua, *Barhut*, p. 45.
39. V. Dehejia, *Discourse in Early Buddhist Art: Visual Narratives of India*, New Delhi: Munshiram Manoharlal, 1997, p. 107.
40. Cunningham, *SB*, no. P 80.
41. Luders, 'Brahmi Inscriptions from Bharhut', p. 3.
42. Cunningham, *SB*, no. P 85.
43. Luders, 'Brahmi Inscriptions from Bharhut', p. 3.
44. Luders, 'A List of Brahmi Inscriptions from the Earliest Times to about A.D. 400 with the Exception of those of Asoka', no. 812.
45. Barua, *Barhut*, p. 45.
46. Findly, *Dāna*, pp. 321–2.
47. Cunningham, *SB*, no. R 52.
48. Luders, 'Brahmi Inscriptions from Bharhut', p. 3.
49. Cunningham, *SB*, no. R 36.
50. Ibid., no. P 100.
51. Ibid.
52. Luders, 'A List of Brahmi Inscriptions from the Earliest Times to about A.D. 400 with the Exception of those of Asoka', p. 81, no. 813.
53. Cunningham, *SB*, Plate XLIV.4.
54. Ibid., Plate XLIV.4.
55. G. Schopen, 'What's in a Name: The Religious Function of the Early Donative Inscriptions', in *Unseen Presence: The Buddha and Sanchi*, ed. V. Dehejia, Mumbai: Marg Publications, 1996, pp. 60–73.
56. Ibid., p. 72.
57. Cunningham, *SB*, nos. P 2, P 77, P 85, P 86, P 91 and R 43.
58. Ibid., nos. P 7, P 9, P 12, P 53, P 67, P 93, P 100, R 3 and R 5.
59. Ibid., nos. P 14, P 17, P 48, P 52, P 56, P 69, P 86, P 95, P 96, P 99 and R 4, R 21, R 46, R 61, and R 62.
60. Ibid., nos. P 1, P 8, P 71, P 73, P 84, P 87, R 2, R 6, R 21, R 22, R 23, R 24, R 37, R 44, R 45, and R 63.
61. Ibid., no. P 16.
62. Ibid., nos. P 95, R 45, and R 84.
63. Ibid., no. C 16.
64. Ibid., no. P 52, P 56, and P 96.
65. Luders, 'Brahmi Inscriptions from Bharhut', p. 7.
66. Cunningham, *SB*, nos. R 22, R 23, R 24, and P 71.
67. Luders, 'Brahmi Inscriptions from Bharhut'1963, p. 9.
68. Cunningham, *SB*, nos. R 2 and P 8.
69. Barua, *Barhut*, p. 123.

70. Cunningham, *SB*, nos. P 1, P 87, R 39 and Luders 1912: no. R 882.
71. Ibid., no. R 39.
72. Luders, 'A List of Brahmi Inscriptions from the Earliest Times to about A.D. 400 with the Exception of those of Asoka', no. R 882.
73. Cunningham, *SB*, no. P 1.
74. Ibid., no. P 87.
75. Ibid., no. P 17.
76. Ibid., no. P 8.
77. Cunningham, *SB*, p. 132.
78. Luders, 'A List of Brahmi Inscriptions from the Earliest Times to about A.D. 400 with the Exception of those of Asoka', p. 69, no. 718.
79. Cunningham, *SB*: no. P 7.
80. Barua, *Barhut*, p. 123.
81. Cunningham, *SB*, no. G 1.
82. Ibid., pp. 129–30.
83. H. Luders and K.L. Janert, eds., *Mathura Inscriptions*, Gottingen: Vandenhoeck and Rupercht, 1961. I have referred to this volume as MI in the text.
84. T.R. Trautmann, *Dravidian Kinship*, New Delhi: Vistaar Publications, 1995, p. 373.
85. R.S. Sharma, *Aspects of Political Ideas and Institutions in Ancient India*, Delhi: Motilal Banarsidass, 1991, p. 282.
86. S. Nagaraju , *Buddhist Architecture of Western India (c250B.C. –c AD300),* Delhi: Agam Kala Prakashan, 1981, p. 32.
87. K. Roy, 'Women and Men Donors at Sanchi: A Study of Inscriptional Evidence', in *Position and Status of Women in Ancient India*, ed. L.K. Tripathi, vol.1, Varanasi: Banares Hindu University, 1988, p. 216.
88. Cunningham, *SB*, nos. R 7, R 23, R 38, and R 45.
89. Ibid., no. R 7 and R 38.
90. Ibid., no. R 59 and G 1.
91. Ibid., no. R 29.
92. Ibid., no. P 14.
93. Ibid., no. P 17.
94. Ibid., no. R 54.
95. Ibid., no. G 1.
96. Ibid., no. R 42.
97. Thapar, 'Patronage and the Community', pp. 19–34.
98. Cunningham, *SB*, no. C 16.
99. I can say this as I have examined inscriptions from the Western Ghats and Mathura from where we have mention of guilds frequently and only men were members of these guilds. Thus women seem to be absent from this economic organization.
100. K. Roy, *The Power of Gender and the Gender of Power: Explorations in Early Indian History*, New Delhi: Oxford University Press, 2010, pp. 195–217.
101. Cunningham, *SB*, Plate XLI, scene 1 and 3.
102. Ibid., Plate XXXIV, scene 2.
103. Ibid., p. 100.

104. D. Mitra, *Buddhist Monuments*, Calcutta: Shishu Sahitya Samsad, repr. 1980, 1st edn., 1971, p. 95.
105. Cunningham, *SB*, p. 128.
106. V.S. Agrawala, *Indian Art (A History of Indian Art from the Earliest Times up to the Third Century A.D.)*, 2nd edn., Varanasi: Prithvi Prakashan, 2003, p. 127.
107. Cunningham, *SB*, nos. G 1, G 2, and G 3.
108. Ibid., no. G 1.
109. Ibid., nos. G 2 and G 3.
110. Dehejia, *Discourse in Early Buddhist Art*, p. 108.
111. Barua, *Barhut*, pp. 14–15.
112. Ibid., p. 15.
113. Ibid., p. 17.
114. Cunningham, *SB,* no. P 100.
115. Dehejia, *Discourse in Early Buddhist Art*, p. 108.
116. Cunningham, *SB,* no. P 62.
117. Dehejia, *Discourse in Early Buddhist Art*, p. 109.
118. Ibid., pp. 108–10.
119. Ibid., p. 109.
120. Findly, *Dāna*, p. 73.
121. Dehejia, *Discourse in Early Buddhist Art Visual Narratives of India*, p. 105.
122. Cunningham, *SB,* no. R 29.
123. Ibid., no. G 1.
124. Schopen, 'What's in a Name: The Religious Function of the Early Donative Inscriptions', pp. 38–41.
125. Findly, *Dāna*, p. 24.
126. Schopen, 'What's in a Name', p. 66.
127. Sten Konow, ed., 'Kharosthi Inscriptions with the Exception of Those of Asoka', *Corpus Inscriptionum Indicarum*, vol. II, pt. 1, Calcutta, 1929, p. 23.
128. Schopen, 'What's in a Name', p. 172.
129. Ibid., xxiv.
130. M. Rao, *Sanchi Sculptures: An Aesthetic and Cultural Study*, New Delhi: Akay Book Corporation, 1994, p. 143.
131. Cunningham, *SB,* Plate XVI.
132. Ibid., Plate XLIV.4.
133. Ibid., Plate XLVI.4.
134. Ibid., Plate XXIV fig. 5.
135. Dehejia, *Discourse in Early Buddhist Art*, p. 88.
136. Cunningham 1998, Plate XXXI:1.
137. Ibid., Plate XVI.
138. Ibid., p. 35.
139. Ibid., Plate XXII fig. 3.
140. Ibid., Plate XXIII fig. 3.
141. R.N. Misra, 'The Popular in a Sacred Universe: Formation of Iconographic Types in Bharhut Panels', Unpublished article, pp. 6–9.
142. Cunningham, *SB*: Plate XVIII.1.
143. Ibid, Plate XXXIV.2.

144. Ibid, Plate XLII.9.
145. Ibid., XXVI.6.
146. Ibid., XXV.1.
147. Ibid., XXXIV.3.
148. Ibid., Plate XL, scene B.

REFERENCES

Agrawala, V.S., *Indian Art (A History of Indian Art from the Earliest Times up to the Third Century A.D.)*, 2nd edn., Varanasi: Prithvi Prakashan, 2003.

Allchin, F.R., *The Archaeology of Early Historic South Asia: The Emergence of Cities and States*, Cambridge: Cambridge University Press, 1995.

Barua, B.M., *Barhut*, 3 vols., Patna: Indological Book Corporation, 1934–7.

Brekke, T. 'Contradiction and the Merit of Giving in Indian Religions', *Numen*, 1998, vol. 45, no. 3, pp. 287–320.

Chakravarti, U., 'Rise of Buddhism as Experienced by Women', *Seminar on Women's Life Cycle and Identity*, Faridabad, 1981, pp. 1–9.

Cunningham, A., *The Stupa of Bharhut*, New Delhi: Munshiram Manoharlal, 1st edn., 1879, repr. 1998.

Dehejia, V., *Discourse in Early Buddhist Art: Visual Narratives of India*, New Delhi: Munshiram Manoharlal, 1997.

Findly, E.B., *Dāna: Giving and Getting in Pali Buddhism*, Delhi: Motilal Banarsidass, 2003.

———, 'The Housemistress at the Door: Vedic and Buddhist Perspectives on the Mendicant Encounter', in *Jewels of Authority: Women and Textual Tradition in Hindu India*, ed. Laurie L. Patton, New Delhi: Oxford University Press, 2002, pp. 13–31.

Ghosh, A., *Remains of Bharhut Stupa in the Indian Museum*, Kolkata: Indian Museum, 1st edn. 1978, repr. 2006.

Gombrich, R.F., *Theravada Buddhism: A Social History from Ancient Benares to Modern Colombo*, London: Routledge, 1988.

Gutschow, K., *Being A Buddhist Nun: The Struggle for Enlightenment in the Himalayas*, Massachusetts: Harvard University Press, 2004.

Kane, P.V., *History of Dharmaśāstra*, vol. II, Poona: Bhandarkar Oriental Research Institute, 1968.

Konow, Sten, ed., Kharosthi Inscriptions with the Exception of Those of Asoka, *Corpus Inscriptionum Indicarum*, vol. II, pt. 1, Calcutta, 1929.

Luders, H., ed., 'Brahmi Inscriptions from Bharhut', *Corpus Inscriptionum Indicarum*, vol. II, pt. II, Ootacamund, 1963.

———, 'A List of Brahmi Inscriptions from the Earliest Times to about A.D. 400 with the Exception of those of Asoka', Appendix to *Epigraphia Indica*, vol. 10, 1912, pp. 1–226.

Mahathera, A.P.B., *Concise Pali-English Dictionary*, Delhi: Motilal Banarsidass, 2002.

Mauss, M., *The Gift*, tr. Ian Cunnison, London: Routledge, 1954.

Misra, R.N., 'The Popular in a Sacred Universe: Formation of Iconographic Types in Bharhut Panels', Unpublished article.

Mitra, D., *Buddhist Monuments*, Calcutta: Shishu Sahitya Samsad, 1st edn., 1971, repr. 1980.

Nagaraju, S., *Buddhist Architecture of Western India (c.250 BC–c. AD 300)*, Delhi: Agam Kala Prakashan, 1981.

Nath, V., *Dāna: Gift System in Ancient India (c.600 BC–c. AD 300): A Socio-Economic Perspective*, Delhi: Munshiram Manoharlal, 1987.

Rao, M., *Sanchi Sculptures: An Aesthetic and Cultural Study*, New Delhi: Akay Book Corporation, 1994.

Roy, K., 'Women and Men Donors at Sanchi: A Study of Inscriptional Evidence', in *Position and Status of Women in Ancient India*, ed. L.K. Tripathi, vol. 1, Varanasi: Banares Hindu University, 1988.

———, *The Power of Gender and the Gender of Power: Explorations in Early Indian History*, New Delhi: Oxford University Press, 2010.

Schopen, G., 'What's in a Name: The Religious Function of the Early Donative Inscriptions', in *Unseen Presence: The Buddha and Sanchi*, ed. V. Dehejia, Mumbai: Marg Publications, 1996, pp. 60–73.

Sharma, R.S., *Aspects of Political Ideas and Institutions in Ancient India*, Delhi: Motilal Banarsidass, 1991 (3rd edn.).

Sircar, D.C., 'Bharhut Inscriptions in Allahabad Museum', *Epigraphia Indica, 1959–60*, vol. 33, 1987.

Thapar, R., *Ancient Indian Social History: Some Interpretations*, Delhi: Orient Longman, 1978.

Thapar, R., 'Patronage and the Community', in *The Powers of Art: Patronage in Indian Culture*, ed. B.S. Miller, Delhi: Oxford University Press, 1992.

Trautmann, T.R., *Dravidian Kinship*, New Delhi: Vistaar Publications, 1995.

PLATE 1.1: Disciples listening to discourse

PLATE 1.2: *Apsarās* and musicians

PLATE 1.3: Ajātaśatru with courtiers

PLATE 1.4: Ajātaśatru's procession with women attendants

PLATE 1.5: Cāpa Devā's pillar gift

PLATE 1.7: Female soldier

PLATE 1.6: Occupations of *gahapatnī* and maid-servant/labourer. (Three scenes—in scene A maid-servant and housemistress cooking, scene B gahapati, *gahapatnī* and maid-servant serving food, scene C father and mother with children)

PLATE 1.8: Merchants

PLATE 1.9: Soldier

PLATE 1.10: Sirimā *devatā*

PLATE 1.11: Suciloma yakṣa

PLATE 1.13: Prasenajit, south gate pillar

PLATE 1.12: Queen adorning herself

PLATE 1.14: Sudarśanā *yakṣinī*

PLATE 1.15: Cakavāka, king of *nāgas*

PLATE 1.16: Prasenajit, south gate pillar with portrayal of *nāga* and *nāgins*

PLATE 1.17: Medallion, purchase of Jetavana and bullock-cart

2

Gender, *Dāna* and Epigraphs: Access to Resources in Early Medieval Central India

Shatarupa Bhattacharya

ACCESS TO RESOURCES HAS always been a pertinent question. Those who can access resources can also access power. Epigraphs show that the identity of an individual is in accordance with his/her access to resources. This question becomes all the more important during the early medieval period when various law-givers were trying to regulate the right to property. In this context, what women could own and whether they could claim the power to alienate property becomes relevant.

Strīdhana has been known as a resource accessible to women. It is described as a movable gift which women received at the time of marriage, and one which, therefore, would never include land. It was mostly restricted to clothes, jewellery, utensils, etc. Women, according to the early Dharmasūtras, did not have access to property in terms of land. Later, women could have a claim to the property, although this was possible only in the absence of a direct male heir, but they did not have the right to alienate it.

Compared to the normative texts, inscriptions portray a different picture as there is evidence of women as donors. Land grant charters are a good source for understanding economic power and gender relations. Giving donations to brāhmaṇas and building temples, wells, gardens, etc., were open to women. The act of *dāna* suggests access to and control over resources. Cynthia Talbot posits that women who acquired political prominence did have some kind of economic power and social prestige.[1] They often had control over significant economic resources either in their own right or as agents of their children. K.K. Shah[2] also opines that the property rights of women in theory did have some substance in reality, especially when the woman happened to be a queen or belonged to the aristocracy. The subject of analysis, however, has been queens/ elite women.

Dynastic epigraphs tell us that access to property was not unknown and that women not only had the right to property but could alienate it as well. In some inscriptions of central India, non-royal women, i.e. women who were outside the royal household, were mentioned as donors. Buddhist and Jain inscriptions mention lay women giving donations. Thus the right to property and the subsequent right to alienate it, seems divergent from what texts of the period ordained. In a way, women did have the right to resources and at the same time, could donate them as well as record their donations, thus participating in the larger practice of identifying themselves within the social processes. The early medieval inscriptions being mostly elite in nature explicitly show access to and alienation of resources by women who had considerable power within the household structure.

The focus of this chapter goes beyond what women had; it attempts to place this in the context of various other grants mentioned in epigraphs. The aim is to understand *dāna* through a gendered perspective during the early medieval period. Gift-making, as a marker of identity during the early medieval period, is well acknowledged. The attempt here is understand how gendered was the practice of giving donations.

Ritual Expiation and Gifts: Formalizing *Dāna* in the Early Medieval Period

Dāna was an act of giving where reciprocation was expected, although not in a literal sense. Manu reiterated that just as *tapas* was the trait of the *Kṛta yuga,* similarly *dāna* was a feature of the *Kali yuga.*[3] *Dāna* was a major social, economic, and religious activity prevalent in ancient societies. The concept of *dāna* had gained prominence from the *Ṛgvedic* period onwards, and by the early medieval period it had became formalized with rules and regulations. It had become a prominent feature in textual sources, especially the Dharmaśāstras and Purāṇas. Vijay Nath posits that the nature of *dāna* reflects the changing modes of production.[4]

The idea of *dāna* is well demonstrated in the epigraphical sources of the early medieval period. Besides containing *praśastis*, recording gifts was the core objective of inscriptions. The list of items that can be given as *dāna* in the early medieval period, according to epigraphical records includes plots of land, villages, wells, gardens, construction of temples etc. It may range from oil for lamps to the installation of the image of the god to villages given to the donee, generally a brāhmaṇa of repute. Land grant records form the majority of inscriptions for this period. That the notion of *dāna* gained prominence in the early medieval period is evident from the spurt of land grants. The study of land grants has assumed a pivotal role in understanding the socio-economic history of the period. Granting land was one of the processes through which new dynasties claimed legitimacy and ritual sanction. Vijay Nath states that the feudal aspect was evident from the term '*mahā*' in the context of *dāna.* It emphasized the magnificent form of gift-giving.[5]

The meaning and the purpose of gift exchange has been a matter of contention among scholars. Marcel Mauss has talked about the reciprocity of gifts as an important aspect of gift-giving.[6] Distinctions are made between a pre-capitalist society and an industrial capitalist society in understanding gift exchange. Scholars have tried to understand the gift from a purely sociological or anthropological aspect. It is well agreed by scholars that the nature of *dānadharma* in its Indian context is different. Here reciprocation has a different meaning and the role of the brāhmaṇa has been emphasized based on the normative texts. However, the inscriptional evidence of the late twelfth century suggests a different scenario. The Candella inscriptions indicate that grants were given to officers and functioned more in terms of payments for services rather than gifts made for religious merit.

Gift-giving was a complicated ritual in the Indian context. The notion of sin incurred in the process of acceptance of the gift and also in terms of appropriate/eligible recipients is more important than the donor or the act itself. The religious nature of gift-giving in the Indian context cannot be understood as the simple giving and receiving of gifts. Axel Michaels compared gift-giving to greeting and how both have been formalized.[7] He further points out how normative texts provide the platform to understand and compare the two. What makes gift-giving more interesting is the relation between the donor and donee. The status of the brāhmaṇa and the concept of purity or impurity of the gift makes *dāna* more complicated. The gift is material while the reciprocation intended or expected is spiritual. As Michaels has shown in his work, altruism has a larger role in the Indian concept of the gift.[8] Thus, the concept of *pratigraha*, i.e. ritual acceptance, becomes important. The normative texts mention conditions such as receiver, receiver's status and qualities, time, place, etc. Thus, gift-giving becomes a formalized religious act.

The nature of *dāna* in the inscriptions follows the norm in most cases. With the grant, the donor identifies himself/herself socially, economically, politically, religiously, and culturally. Thus, mere give and take is not the purpose of the grant. Its relevance as a method of social bonding is explicit. It was a marker of status for both the donor and the recipient as was evident from the *dāna stutis* in the *Ṛgveda*[9] and also the permanent form of recording the gift in later periods. It legitimized the ritual as well as the social position of the individual. It symbolized status and was an investment whose return was expected, although not in a literal sense. Thus, gift-giving had three main characteristics—reciprocity, acquiring social status, and a strong competitive spirit.

Vijay Nath documents three stages in gift-giving; first, the early Vedic offering, i.e. *dāna* and *dakṣiṇā*; second, the gift freely given out of one's surplus to a beggar or mendicant monk from about the fifth century BCE, observed in the Buddhist notion of *dāna*; and, third, the ritualized obligatory gift bestowed out of a sense of moral duty and indebtedness, i.e. *ṛṇa*, from around the third century CE, i.e. *dāna*.[10]

By the period of the Dharmaśāstras, the notion of giving gifts was legalized with rules and regulations. Jaimini (500–200 BCE) mentioned that *dāna* was the transference of one's ownership and should be given according to one's means.[11] *Dāna* was recognized as an important method to cleanse sins. It had to be given with respect and good feelings towards the recipient, otherwise the donor would not get the desired result. *Dāna* by the Dharmaśāstric period was categorized into *iṣṭa* and *pūrta dāna*. The distinction between them was well formed. Spiritual merit that was acquired by giving gifts at the time of a sacrifice was *iṣṭadharma*. The gift that was given outside the sacrificial altar was *pūrta*.[12] Charitable work such as the dedication of wells, tanks, temples, groves, food and also gifts on the occasion of eclipses, on the twelfth day of the month, etc., were *pūrta*.[13] Besides, *dāna* could vary according to one's means and had to be given to a worthy person with pleasure according to Manu.[14] *Dāna* could be performed even by women and śūdras; however, the latter could perform only the *pūrta dharma*.[15]

By the time of the compilation of the Purāṇas, the concept of debt to the forefathers, gods and sages, i.e. *ṛṇa* had gained prominence, along with the belief that the debt could be repaid through *dāna*. Not giving a gift was considered a sin that a householder should avoid.[16] Six distinct constituent elements were referred to in the context of *dāna*—*dātā* (donor), *pratigrahīta* (recipient), *śraddhā,* (appropriate attitude), *deya* (appropriateness of the gift), *tithi* (proper time), and *deśa* (proper place).[17] Axel Michaels[18] points out seven distinct features of *dānadharma*: first, the recipient should be a brāhmaṇa, who should be a *snātaka*, *śrotriya*, i.e. one who knew the Vedas. He should not be a hypocrite or a self-centred brāhmaṇa. Second, *dāna* was to be given in a liberal spirit; only then would the donor get *puṇya* or merit. Third, acceptance of the gift in the proper place and time alone made it a religious offering. Fourth, there was the danger associated with *dāna* in terms of loss of knowledge or *tejas*, which only a worthy recipient could withstand. Thus *dāna* was to be given to a virtuous recipient. Fifth, the proper *dāna* had no material reciprocation, i.e. its benefit was to be religious. Sixth, the transactions were hierarchical and asymmetrical, as the recipient was higher in status than the donor. And, lastly, in times of emergency, *āpad*, brāhmaṇas could accept anything from anybody.

The proper time for gifts was laid down in the Dharmaśāstras.[19] Special stress was laid on the gift given on the first day of the *ayana*, i.e. the passage of the sun to the north or south, eclipse of the sun or moon, new moon day, twelfth day, *saṅkrānti* and other such *tithis*. Generally, gifts were not to be given at night except during an eclipse, marriage, birth of a child, and *saṅkrānti*. With reference to the proper place, there was mention of increase in benefits depending on the place where the gift was made. Gifts given at home yielded ten times as much merit, those in the cow-pen hundred times, at *tīrthas* a thousand times, and infinite times if made near a Śiva-*liṅga*. There was also mention of specific places such as Prayag, Kuruksetra, Puskara, Benaras, forests, and riverbanks. The texts mention the rivers Ganga, Yamuna, Narmada, etc. The benefit of making gifts at such sites was proclaimed as infinite.

The concept of *dāna* was discussed in Buddhist literature as well, but it was different from the Dharmaśāstric view. The notion of giving and receiving was central to the Buddhist doctrine of *dāna*. The relationship between the renunciant and the householder was based on *dāna*. Pali literature referred to *dāna* as *dhammadānam* (gift of spiritual blessing) and *āmisadānam* (gift of temporal blessings).[20] It was used more in the sense of charity/alms rather than ritual gift. Unlike the Dharmaśāstras, Buddhist doctrine was more concerned with the inner transformation for both the donor and the recipient.[21] The discussion on *dāna* was focused more towards householders. There were three ways by which they could gain merit—*dāna*, *śīla*, moral habit, and *bhāvanā*. Of these, *dāna* was considered the best way of gaining merit. According to the Buddhist theory, *dāna* should be given because of *anukampā*, i.e. compassion.[22] In contrast, the *Mahābhārata* mentions desire for merit, fear, profit, free choice, and pity as reason for giving gifts.[23] According to Kalpana Upreti, there were reasons for the glorification of *dāna* in Buddhism. First, the monks were dependent on *dāna* for their survival and, second, for the benefit of society as a whole. The *dukkha* (sorrow) of the poor could be minimized to some extent by regular or occasional *dāna*.[24]

In the present context, we will discuss *dāna* by looking at the epigraphic evidence from central India, focusing on the Vākāṭaka, Kalacuri and

Candella inscriptions. How far the elites, both men and women used grants as a marker of identity will be compared and analysed.

Epigraphs and Evidence: The Changing Perceptions of *Dāna*

Epigraphs present a different context to *dāna*. It was not only important to give gifts but it was equally important to record it. Emphasis was beyond merit and social duty but on access, status and identity both for the donor and the donee. It was a method of claiming legitimization and in a way, an equally important tool to establish social and political hierarchies.

The gift of land was highly valued in early texts. It was important not only to give but also to record it for future kings. According to Yājñavalkya, '. . . the king should issue a permanent edict bearing his signature and the date on a piece of cloth or a copper plate marked at the top with his seal and write down there on the name of his ancestors and of himself, the extent of what is gifted and set out the passages that condemn the resumption of gifts'.[25] The inscriptions issued by kings, queens, and other elite men and women thus adhered to the Dharmaśāstras.

Grants documented in inscriptions can be classified under the following heads—plots of land, villages, resources for the construction of temples, tanks, gardens, etc. Sometimes the grants were combined, i.e. a grant of land along with the construction of a temple and so on. James Heitzman points out that a network of temple donations was a two-way process: on the one hand the local leaders established their links to royalty and on the other the king through these grants legitimized his rule.[26]

Epigraphic records demonstrate the relevance of *dāna* in the early medieval context. The records were replete with land grant donations, generally made to brāhmaṇas. Scholars are divided over the nature and purpose of the land grants in terms of political developments. The medieval era, according to Cynthia Talbot, is a period of progressive change characterized by the extension of agrarian settlement, a rise in the number of religious institutions, expansion in commercial activities, and evolution of political systems and networks.[27] From the Gupta period onwards, villages were given to the donee/s together with the fields and their inhabitants, along with fiscal, administrative and judicial rights, and exemptions from royal interference.

B.D. Chattopadhyaya regards political integration as a counterpoint to the decentralized polity of the feudal model and as a key feature of the early medieval period. It implies the 'transformation of pre-state polities into state polities and thus marked the integration of local polities into structures that transcend the bounds of local polities'.[28] The development was based on a series of processes, for example, the extension of agrarian society through the peasantization of tribal groups, improvement of trading networks, expansion of caste society, the emergence and spatial extension of ruling lineages by the process called kṣatriyization, increasing the hinterland with a network of religious institutions patronized by royalty and land assignments to officials and attempts to centralize administrative functions, particularly revenue collection.[29]

The inscriptions of the early medieval period generally mention the donor, donee, dynastic details and also time, place and purpose of the grant. The stated purpose of most of the grants was accrual of religious merit for the donor and sometimes for her/his parents. In many cases, grants were given for the religious merit of the mother, as in the Patna Museum grants where Pravarasena II of the Vākāṭaka dynasty mentioned that the benefit of the *dāna* was religious merit for his mother, Prabhāvatīguptā; the term used is *mātṛ-bhaṭṭārikā*.[30] The occasion of the grant could be a lunar or solar eclipse or any other special occasion such as victory in a battle or *śrāddha*, etc. Sometimes it was linked with other religious activities such as taking a bath on a certain day or breaking a fast. The records sometimes also mention the prevention of a calamity as in the Amoda Plates of Jājalladeva II,[31] which records that the king was saved from an attack by an alligator. It sometimes mentioned the great deed of a minister during war, e.g. in the Garrā Copperplate inscription of Trailokyavarman, year 1261,[32] which records that the grant is given to the son of the minister who died fighting the Turuṣkas (Turks). Some records do not provide any explicit reason for the grant. Thus, the rationale for the grant could be either worldly or spiritual. What seems important is the right to give and record donations. Only elite men and women, who had access to resources, claimed an identity through these practices.

By observing the percentage of grants by elite men and women, and also the contents of the grants, we can understand the gendered notion of *dāna*. The overall percentage of grants given by women is low but nevertheless it shows that elite women had some control over resources. As the source for the present study is based only on the published epigraphs, it does not represent the entire corpus.

In the Vākāṭaka dynasty we have thirty-four published records of which five documents mention grants by women. In the Kalacuri dynasty, of the total of sixty-four grants, three grants were made by women, which included not just royal women but a non-royal woman as well. There are two joint grants and another record mentions that the grant was in honour of the wife of the donor, a feudatory. In the Candella dynasty, of a total of sixty-eight records, two mention grants by queens. Another record mentions a grant previously made by two queens. The Kālañjar pillar inscription VS 1186[33] mentions a joint donation by a non-royal woman, *mahānācaṇī* Padmāvatī and a man designated as *mahāpratīhāra* Saṅgrāmasiṃha. Besides, there were four memorial sati stones which do not mention any kind of grant and belong to a later period (thirteenth/ fourteenth centuries CE); since they record some information about the period and dynasty, they are included in the list of records.

It is interesting to note that the percentage of grants by kings decreased over time, while the access to resources by men other than the king increased. This increase is not noticed in the case of royal and non-royal elite women. But, at the same time, non-royal elite women who may or may not have administrative positions had access to resources and were using similar methods to claim identity.

TABLE 2.1: Gendered Distribution of Grants

Dynasty	*Percentage of Grants by Kings* (in %)	*Percentage of Grants by Queens* (in %)	*Percentage of Grants by other Elite Men* (in %)	*Percentage of Grants by other Elite Women* (in %)	*Percentage of Joint Grants* (in %)
Vākāṭakas	58.8	11.8	23.5	2.9	2.9
Kalacuris*	39	3.1	45.3	1.6	7.8
Candellas*#	38.2	4.4	42.6	0	1.5

NOTES: *Missing Donor: Kalacuris -2, Candellas -5+4; # Sati stones. These are not counted in the percentage calculation.

In the Kalacuri dynasty there are a number of joint donations. These include donations by the king, queen, prince, ministers, and also feudatories. In the case of the Candellas, one inscription, which mentions some pious work by an elite woman other than the queen, is a joint donation. It is noteworthy that a dancer (*mahānācaṇī*) has recorded benefactions to the deity on a pillar inside the fort of Kālañjar. Another record that needs mention is the Bharat Kala Bhavan Plates of Madanavarman VS 1192, which states that part of the grant was earlier donated by two queens. This multiple grant mentions a grant by the king, a previous grant by the chief priest of *rājñī* Lakhamīdevī, and also a grant by the two queens. (I have counted this grant thrice, as made by the king, priest and by two queens.)[34]

A gendered pattern in terms of giving gifts and also in terms of access to resources can be seen during the early medieval period. Three dynasties ranging over a period of time, i.e. fifth century CE to thirteenth century CE, in central India have been considered for the present study. The notion of *dāna* changes over a period of time. *Dāna* as a symbol of status and a marker of one's position in society also undergoes changes with different political conditions. Non-royal elite men claimed a prominent position over a period of time, especially during turbulent phases, but even during such phases non-royal elite women, as shown by the epigraphic sources, could not claim an important place. At the same time, the composition of the people who could record a grant and what they could record reflect changes over time.

Control over Resources and Royal Prerogative: The Vākāṭaka Grants

In the last quarter of the third century CE, central India saw the emergence of a local power which succeeded the Sātavāhanas, the Vākāṭakas. From a minor ruling dynasty they became a major power by the fourth century CE. The Vākāṭakas claimed to be brāhmaṇas of the Viṣṇuvṛddhi *gotra* and their first king was Vindhyaśakti. The Purāṇas (*Vāyu, Brahmāṇḍa, Viṣṇu*, and *Bhāgavata Purāṇas*) referred to the Vākāṭakas as '*vaideśika nṛpa*'.[35] Pargiter holds them to be 'dynasties of Vidiśā'.[36] But all of the dynasties mentioned in the texts were not linked with Vidisha, Madhya Pradesh, even remotely. According to A.M. Shastri, it probably meant 'kings of various regions'.[37] The place of origin of the Vākāṭakas is debated among scholars.[38]

For the present study, thirty-four published inscriptions of the Vākāṭakas have been considered; of these, two are in fragmentary condition. The Vākāṭakas had two branches: one ruled from Nandivardhana-Padmapura-Pravarapura, mentioned as the Eastern Branch, after Bakker.[39] The other branch ruled from Vatsagulma, and will be treated as the Western Branch. Of the total, twenty-six inscriptions belong to the Eastern Branch and eight to the Vatsagulma/Western Branch. In the Western Branch there were no records of donations by women.

Most of the grants recorded donations by kings, of which sixteen were given by kings of the Eastern Branch. Other elite men include ministers and feudatories of the Vākāṭakas, of which three grants belonged to the Eastern Branch and four to the Vatsagulma/Western Branch. Of grants by queens there were three grants by Prabhāvatīguptā and another by an unnamed queen. The grants by other elite women include one by the daughter of Prabhāvatīguptā. The joint donations, two from the Eastern Branch, mention grants by the king as well as the minister.

In the inscriptions of the Vākāṭaka dynasty (Eastern and Western branches), of the total thirty-four records, sixteen document gifts of villages. Other records mentioned plots of land, temples, lakes, caves, *dharmasthāna*, i.e. place of worship, according to V.V. Mirashi.[40] A.M. Shastri translates the term as court of justice.[41] Villages were granted by the king, whereas the ministers and feudatories gave land, caves, etc. Probably giving villages was a royal prerogative during this period. It is

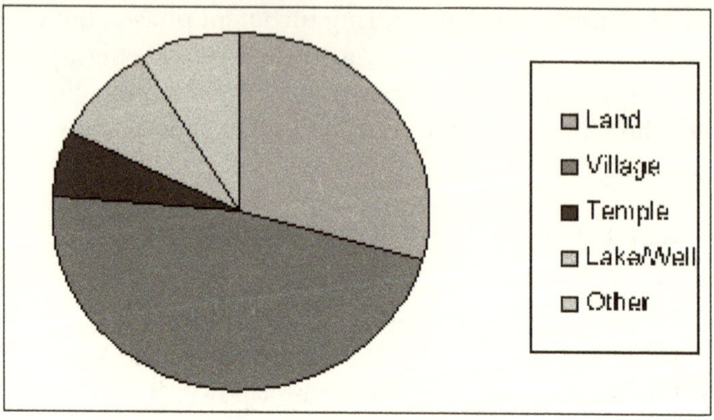

FIGURE 2.1: Ratio of the Vākāṭaka Gifts

also interesting to note that only one record mentioned the construction of a shrine, although many records referred to temples.

Of the grants by kings, most of which were villages, some deserve special attention. For instance, the Wadgaon Plates of Pravarasena II[42] mentioned 400 *nivartanas* (a unit of measurement of land that varied in different periods and localities)[43] given to a brāhmaṇa. The Yavatmal grant of Pravarasena II mentions that the grant was already enjoyed by the recipient.[44] This showed that sometimes the grants were recorded later. The Pandhurna Plates of Pravarasena II record the grant of 2,000 *nivartanas* of land in a village that was granted earlier by Pṛthivīṣena I.[45] The grant was given to several brāhmaṇas whose *gotra* and śākhā were mentioned. This was against the norm as a grant once given was not to be taken back according to the Dharmaśāstras.[46] The Pauni grant of Pravarasena II also referred to land being taken back and 50 *nivartana* given in exchange.[47] The ratio of the various items of gift is represented in Figure 2.1.

Figure 2.1 presents the ratio of grants given. It represents the percentage of each item. Of the total, 29 per cent of the recorded gifts were of land, 47 per cent were of villages, temples accounted for 6 per cent, and lakes/tanks for 9 per cent, and gifts such as caves and *vihāras* and *dharmasthāna* (listed as 'other') accounted for 9 per cent. (Many inscriptions referred to more than one item of donation; therefore these percentages are not related to the number of inscriptions.)

In the case of donations by women, all three grants by Prabhāvatīguptā were of villages. Her records show her unique position in the dynasty. Prabhāvatīguptā issued grants with her own seals, used titles, and recorded the Gupta genealogy which marked out her position as different from that of other Vākāṭaka queens. She gave villages, unlike other queens, which implied her control over land. In the Poona Plates she granted a village to an *ācārya*.[48] The Riddhapur Plates record that she granted a village along with one house-site and four huts of farmers to brāhmaṇas.[49] The Miregaon inscription of Prabhāvatīguptā mentioned the grant of a village to five brāhmaṇas.[50]

The Masoda Plates of Pravarasena II record that land was donated at the request of the *mahādevī* or the chief queen.[51] This grant was similar to those made by Pravarasena II. In this grant it was specially mentioned that the land, i.e. 300 *nivartanas*, which was not previously donated was now being given. It further mentioned twenty-five house-sites. It was divided into two, of which one was given to Mahīpuruṣa[52] who was '*apratigrāhī*', i.e. one who does not accept gifts. The rest of the land was given to nineteen brāhmaṇas. The Ramtek inscription records a donation made by the daughter of Prabhāvatīguptā, Atibhāvatī[53] and mentioned the construction of a temple of Nṛsiṃha, named Prabhāvatīsvāmin, obviously a form of the deity named after her mother, and a tank Sudarśana, literally meaning beautiful. The temple was built in the memory of Prabhāvatīguptā. Cynthia Talbot holds that naming the deity of a new temple after an individual was a method of honouring the person.[54] There are instances of places and deities being named after the king; for instance, the capital Pravarapura and the deity Pravareśvara named after Pravarasena II. But there were very few references to places or deities named after queens. The fact that the deity in this case was named after her would reiterate Prabhāvatīguptā's special position in the dynasty.

In the case of the grants by ministers or others, grants of land were recorded in three inscriptions, while one referred to the grant of a village. Of these the Chammak land grant[55] deserves special notice. It records the grant of 8,000 *nivartanas* of land to a thousand brāhmaṇas of whom only forty-nine were mentioned. The grant was given at the request of some Koṇḍarāja, son of Śatrughnarāja. That Koṇḍarāja could grant such a huge amount of land implied that he had some control over land and resources. At the same time, his political position was not clear, although his using the suffix *rāja* would indicate his claim to an elite status. The Indore Plates mention that part of the grant was already donated.[56] The other half of the grant was made by a merchant Candra after purchasing it. The Pattan Plates record a grant at the request of a certain Nārāyaṇarāja and mention 400 *nivartanas* of land to be used (to support) a charitable feeding house associated with the temple of Mahīpuruṣa.[57] Thus, the donor had specified the purpose of the grant explicitly. The Hisse-Borala inscription mentioned the construction of a lake called Sudarśana.[58] Of the various items of gift, plots of land and villages were most commonly documented in the records of the Vākāṭakas. Other gifts formed a small

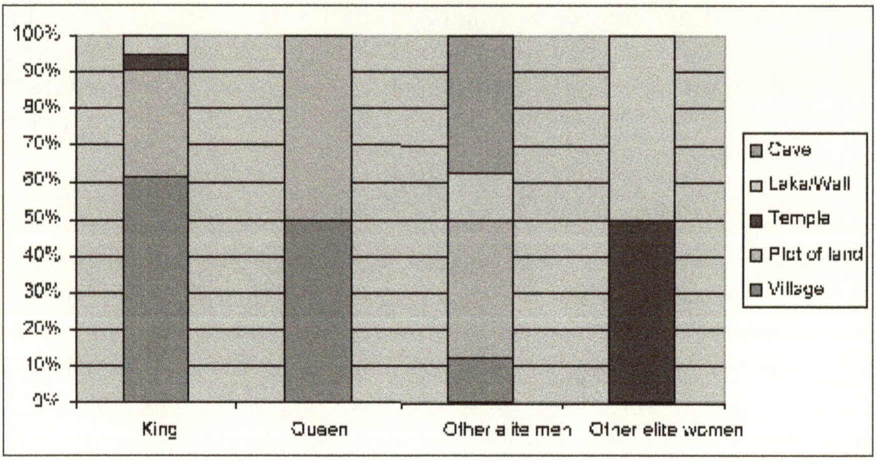

FIGURE 2.2: Gendered Distribution of the Vākāṭaka Grants

proportion. The reason for such documentation could be that the gift of land was regarded as of utmost importance.

Figure 2.2 shows the percentage of items plotted along the lines of gender. As can be observed, kings gave mainly villages and land and even queens gave land. In the case of other elite men, including ministers and feudatories, the donations were largely of plots of land and caves. Thus, while they controlled resources, these were not necessarily identical with those of the rulers. The grants by elite women other than queens, on the other hand (which included the grant by Prabhāvatīguptā's daughter), were primarily of lakes and temples. None of these grants mentioned land. This would indicate that the resources to which elite men and women had access were not identical. This was more visible in the case of non-royal men and women.

The Vākāṭaka inscriptions generally did not mention the occasion on which the gift was made. Of the grant by kings, the Tirodi Plates of Pravarasena II mention that the grant was made on the eleventh day of the month of Māgha from a place called Narattangavāri.[59] According to V.V. Mirashi, the grant was made from a *tīrtha* after a fast on *ṣaṭtilā ekādaśī*, which was believed to be an auspicious day according to the *Padma Purāṇa*.[60] The Wadgaon inscription mentioned that the grant was given on an equinox.[61] The Pandhurna Plates mention that the grant was made for the *tilavācana*, i.e. *śrāddha* in favour of a brāhmaṇa named Somārya.[62]

Of the grants by women, all the grants of Prabhāvatīguptā were given after the observance of the fast on *ekādaśī*. The Poona and Riddhapur Plates mention fasts on *Prabodhinī ekādaśī* in the month of Kārtika, while the Miregaon Plates mentioned that the grant had been made after breaking the fast in the month of Pauṣa. Observing the fast on *ekādaśī* was considered very pious, especially for widows. Even the Dharmaśāstras mentioned giving gifts on the twelfth day, i.e. after breaking the fast on *ekādaśī*. However, in the case of other grants by elite women, the occasion of the grant is not mentioned.

It is possible that conforming to the Brahmanical pattern was more important for kings and queens who wanted to represent themselves as upholders of tradition. That might be the reason that they mentioned the occasions on which they made grants. Other elite men and women did not follow this pattern or they were not expected to portray themselves as conforming to these norms.

In terms of the desired return of the grant, Vākāṭaka grants followed the Dharmaśāstric norm and mentioned religious merit as the purpose of the gift. Most of the grants mentioned religious merit, life, power, prosperity, and well-being in this world and the next as an objective for donations. The Tirodi and Patna/Balaghat Plates of Pravarasena II mentioned that the merit accrued was also for his mother, *mātṛ-bhaṭṭārikā*.[63] The Mandhal Plates 'A' of Pṛthivīṣeṇa II also mentioned that part of the merit was for his mother, Ājjhikabhaṭṭārikā.[64] The grants by Prabhāvatīguptā mentioned religious merit in this world and the next. Other grants mentioned similar reasons for giving gifts.

The records of ministers and other elite men also reveal a similar pattern. In the Mandhal plates of Pravarasena II one-third of the merit accruing from the grant was for Ājjhikabhaṭṭārikā, the mother of Narendrarāja, probably the prince.[65] The Hisse-Borala inscription mentioned that the grant was made for the welfare of all creatures.[66] The Ajanta cave inscription of Varāhadeva mentioned religious merit for both the mother and father.[67] The Ajanta cave XVII inscription also mentioned that the grant had been made for the welfare of all people.[68] This grant seemed to be made according to the Buddhist concept of *dāna* which was ideally meant for the benefit of all. Both grants mentioned donations of caves to monks. Thus reciprocation of the grant was expected, but in spiritual terms.

Dāna was often used as a means of claiming legitimization. Both elite men and women claimed to patronize religious practices of the time, both Brahmanical and non-Brahmanical. Most of the grants were given to the brāhmaṇas and sometimes, as in the case of non-royal elite men, to non-Brahmanical sects as well. The inscriptions show that women had access to resources. They used similar administrative titles and granted similar exemptions, which would indicate that their status was more or less identical with that of men from a similar background during this period.

Only the royal grants mentioned the place of issue. Also, the occasion of the grants is not mentioned in non-royal inscriptions. The ostensible purpose of the donation was religious merit wherever mentioned. This was in adherence to the Dharmaśāstric norms.

Equitable Access to Resources: The Kalacuri Grants

From a minor power, the Kalacuris gained prominence after the fifth century CE. They established themselves in central India. The Kalacuris, like several other contemporary Rajput dynasties, called themselves Candravaṃśīs and traced their descent from the Haihaya Sahasrārjuna, the son of Kārttavīrya. As B.D. Chattopadhyaya opines, the origin myth of a dynasty was a method of claiming legitimization.[69] Thus, the Kalacuris claiming descent from Soma, Atri, Manu, etc., was a way of claiming legitimization and also a method of proving their long ancestry.

D.R. Bhandarkar talks of the foreign origin of the Kalacuris and refers to the *Viṣṇu Purāṇa* and the *Harivaṃśa* where the Haihayas were said to have taken the help of the Śaka, Yavana, Pārada, and Khaśa tribes, who were all foreigners, to defeat King Bāhu.[70] R.K. Sharma[71] and V.V. Mirashi[72] do not accept this explanation of foreign origin.

The Kalacuris were divided into four royal lineages on the basis of their inscriptions. They were the Kalacuris of Tripuri, Saryupara, Ratnapur, and Raipur. The inscriptions of the Kalacuris of Raipur belong to a period after the fifteenth century CE; therefore, they are not considered for the present study. The inscriptions of the Tripuri branch were found from the eighth century CE onwards. There are a total of sixty-four inscriptions of the Kalacuris that have been used in the present study. Of these, thirty-five records belonged to the Tripuri branch, two records were of the Saryupara branch, and the rest of the twenty-seven belong to the Ratnapur branch.

Out of the total sixty-four Kalacuri inscriptions, records of the construction of temples or images constructed and gifting of villages were most common. Of the total number of gifts that were recorded, land constituted 5 per cent; villages 28 per cent; temples or images 29 per cent; wells or tanks 13 per cent; gardens 10 per cent; and other gifts 15 per cent, which included a granary, some tax given as a gift, etc. It is evident that the items of gifts during this period were somewhat different from those that were recorded in the Vākāṭaka inscriptions.

Figure 2.3 shows the proportion of the gift items mentioned in the records.

Large grants are virtually absent, although gift-giving remained significant. Gifts given could be of a village, or only an image installed, or a *maṇḍapa* constructed, or a granary, or a grove. Another feature of the Kalacuri records was joint donations; it could be the king, queen,

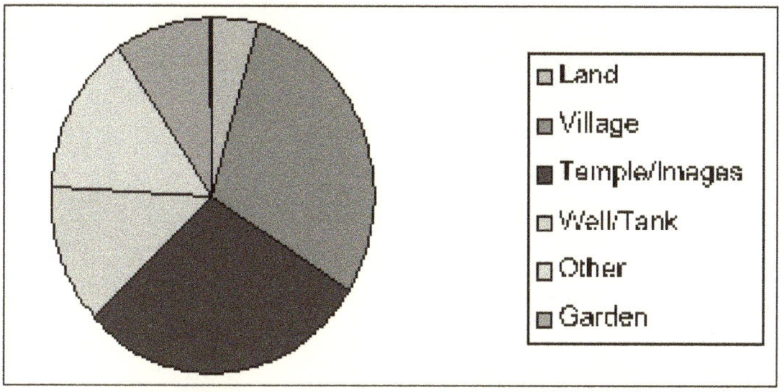

FIGURE 2.3: Ratio of the Kalacuri Gifts

minister, or a feudatory or merchants who made donations that were recorded in one inscription. What is likely is that there were no sharp differences in status amongst these categories. It is also likely that kings used this mechanism to strengthen their ties with people who may have been influential in the locality.

Unlike the Vākāṭaka grants, gifts were not given to *caturvidyā* brāhmaṇas but to Śaiva ascetics and to brāhmaṇas, whose qualifications were not mentioned. Śaivism had developed as the most important religious tradition in this region; while there were references to Vaiṣṇavism and other sects, most of the grants were made to Śaivites.

Some of the grants that deserve special attention are as follows. Of the grants by kings, the Gurgi Stone Inscription of Kokalladeva II mentioned the construction of a temple of Śiva with Umā and Kārtikeya and Gaṇeśa with Sarasvatī on the gate. It also mentioned the grant of a city with citizens along with many villages by King Keyūravarṣa. The grant was given to Śaiva *siddhāntas*. In the Goharwa Plates of Karṇa, the grant of a village to a brāhmaṇa by the king mentions four boundaries and the record cited specifications according to the Dharmaśāstric norms. The grant mentioned the donation along with mango and *madhuka* trees, water, land, pits, barren land, including mines of iron and salt along with woods, meadows, and pastures.[74] Another characteristic feature of the grants was the mention of various public works done by the donor. For instance, the Ratnapur stone inscription of Jājalladeva I, year 866,[75] mentions that the town, i.e. Jājallapura, was established, and monasteries, a garden, grove of mango trees, and a lake were constructed by the king. The inscription also mentions the grant of a village in honour of the installed deity. A cluster of *pāṭala* trees was donated to the monastery. The Pāli stone inscription of Jājalladeva I[76] also mentioned the *kīrti* of the king and referred to repairing the *maṇḍapa* of a Śiva temple.

There were only two records that mentioned grants made exclusively by queens. The Bhera-ghat stone inscription of Narasiṃhadeva[77] mentioned a donation by Alhaṇadevī, the mother of the king. She donated a garden and two rooms to a temple of Śiva referred to as Vaidyanātha. A *maṭha*, a hall of study and the income from two villages were given to the Pāśupata ascetics. The Bhera-ghat Gaurī-Śaṅkara temple inscription of Vijayasiṃha[78] mentioned *mahārajñī* Gosaladevī, but since the inscription is fragmentary the donation is not clear. It was probably related to the construction of a temple.

Unlike the Vākāṭakas, donations made by elite women other than queens were also recorded in the case of the Kalacuris. For instance, the Sarnath stone inscription of Karṇa[79] recorded a gift by Māmakā, wife of Dharmeśvara. She was a follower of Mahāyāna Buddhism and got a copy of the *Aṣtasāhasrīkāprajñā* to be made along with some donation for the recitation of the text. According to the Dharmaśāstras, donating manuscripts, especially of the epics, Purāṇas and Dharmaśāstras, was a prominent gift.[80] It is likely that these ideas were prevalent within other religious traditions as well, as in this case it was a Buddhist text that was to be copied.

A large number of inscriptions referred to donations and various public works by ministers and feudatories. These referred not only to donations by ministers but also their wives. The Rewa stone inscription of Karṇa (Kalacuri) year 812[81] was a *praśasti* of the King Karṇa and his minister Vappulla. The inscription recorded the installation of *liṅgas*. The temple of Viṣṇu, called Śrīvatsa, was built and was surrounded by four small shrines, of which one was of Lakṣmī-Nārāyaṇa. It also recorded the grant of a garden with a hundred mango and other trees. Another five-shrine temple of Śiva known as Vappuleśvara was constructed, where the image of Umā-Maheśvara was donated by Nayanāvalī, wife of Vappulla. The Akaltara stone inscription of Ratnadeva II[82] was again a *praśasti*. It recorded a grant by Vallabharāja, a feudatory, on the outskirts of the town. It mentioned the construction of the temple of Revanta and a tank called Vallabhasāgara. Interestingly, this tank was compared to the *Saugata-mata*, the Buddhist doctrine. It is worth noticing that the tank was named after the minister who had claimed status and honour through this device, which in the earlier period was practised only by the royalty. The Ratnapur stone inscription of Pṛthivīdeva II, year 910,[83] again mentioned donations by Vallabharāja. It recorded one tank excavated at the insistence of his wife Śvetalladevī. This inscription, besides other works, mentioned the donation of a lake called Ratneśvara-sāgara. Another interesting record is the Sheorinārāyaṇa stone inscription of Jājalladeva II, year 919,[84] which referred to a collateral branch of the

Kalacuris. It records donations of Āmaṇadeva II, Vikannadeva, his uncle, and a queen Rāmbhalla. It recorded the gift of a village named Ciñcelī for the expense of incense, lights, and other materials for the temple of Śiva known as 'Candracūḍa'. A temple of Durgā was constructed by his uncle, Vikannadeva. Sarvadeva erected a temple of Śambhu in Sonthiva, and also recorded the donation of a tank and garden. In Pandaratalai, Āmaṇadeva I established a charitable feeding house, an orchard, and a tank. In Patharia, Rājadeva built a temple of Śiva called Purabhida along with the gift of a mango grove and tank. Queen Rāmbhalla had a tank excavated along with the donation of a mango grove in the village Pajaṇī.

The joint donations were given by the king along with the queen and prince or with ministers. The Karitalai stone inscription of Lakṣmaṇarāja II[85] was a joint donation of the king, queen, prince, minister, and some merchants. Villages were given by the King Lakṣmaṇarāja II and Queen Rāhaḍā while Śaṅkaragaṇa III (son and successor) gave two plots of land, of which one consisted of twelve *khaṇḍins*, a land measure.[86] The minister Someśvara recorded the construction of a temple of Viṣṇu. Valleśvara gave a village and a field. Then the record mentioned several taxes donated to the deity. The superintendent of the city and town donated a part of his income of two days to the god along with a jar of corn. The guild '*desi*' gave one and a half times the 1/22nd portion of five spirituous liquors as well as 1/4th of the goods carried in the regions. The chief of the *vagulikas*, i.e. seller of betel leaves, gave fifty leaves while the *payatis* gave another fifty leaves. The whole *maṇḍala* gave alms at four threshing floors. Thus, small traders granted some part of their income in honour of the deity and this was recorded along with the donations made by the elites.

The Bilhari stone inscription of Yuvarājadeva II[87] mentioned the construction of a temple of Śiva called Nauhaleśvara by the queen, Nohalā. Lakṣmaṇarāja II invited the Śaiva ascetic Hṛdayaśiva and gave him a monastery named after Vaidyanātha. King Yuvarājadeva II made it compulsory for the traders and manufacturers to pay tax at the marketplace for the monastery and its occupants. There was also a reference to a fair held in honour of the deity.

The description of the gendered distribution of the grants shows that the king donated all the items mentioned in Figure 2.4. In the grants by queens, temples were more prominent. The gifts by other elite men were very similar to those made by kings. But the proportion of items of gifts was different in each case. The majority of the records by other elite women refer to the construction of tanks.

Figure 2.4 indicates that while both elite men and women resorted to the device of giving gifts, control over resources was gendered. Although women other than the queen could make donations, their access to

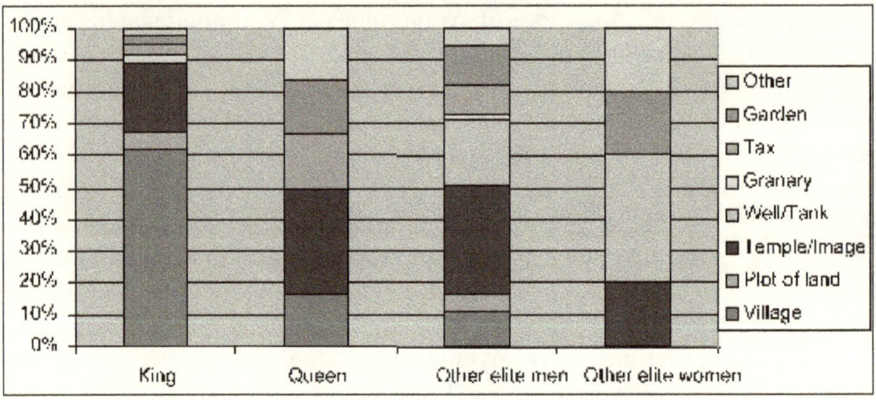

FIGURE 2.4: Gendered Distribution of the Kalacuri Grants

resources was the least. By contrast, other elite men, including ministers and feudatories, accessed various resources and gave a large number of donations. The position of queens was similar, but very few inscriptions mention gifts by them and the range of resources granted was also limited.

Another important aspect was the link between gift-giving and the place chosen to do this. This aspect was not explicit in the case of the Vākāṭakas. Amongst the Kalacuri grants by kings, the Banaras Plates of Karṇa[88] mentioned the *śrāddha* performed at Prayag. Of the places mentioned as sacred in the *Matsya Purāṇa*, Prayag was considered the best for the performance of the *śrāddha*. The Goharwa Plates of Karṇa[89] mentioned that the grant was given after taking a bath in the Ganga at Arghatīrtha. It referred to a *ghāṭ* at Allahabad called Karṇatīrtha. The inscription also records a grant after the performance of the *śrāddha* but details were not specified. Many inscriptions such as the Khairha Plates of Yaśahkarṇa[90] recorded that the gift was given on the occasion of the *uttarāyana saṅkrāntī*. The inscription referred to worship at the temple near the Godavari River. The Kahila Plates of Sodhadeva[91] referred to the *uttarāyana saṅkrāntī* and the donation made after taking a bath in the river Gandaki.

Many of the records mentioned donations made on occasions such as the lunar or solar eclipse. For example, the Bilaigarh Plates of Pṛthivīdeva II,[92] mentioned a grant made on the occasion of a solar eclipse. The Jabalpur Plates of Jayasiṃha[93] mentioned a gift given after a lunar eclipse, subsequent to taking a bath in the river Reva. The Amoda Plates (second set) of Pṛthivīdeva II[94] mentioned the *akṣaya-tritīyā tithi* as the occasion on which the gift was given. The Amoda Plates of Jājalladeva II[95] referred to a donation made after the king was attacked by an alligator. The occasion of the grant was generally on the days mentioned in the Dharmaśāstras as significant for making gifts such as *saṅkrānti*, an eclipse, or *śrāddha*. As noted above, a grant was given when the king was saved from a calamity such as an alligator's attack.

The grants by women do not mention any specific occasion for making donations. In the grants by ministers only some mention the occasion when the grant was made. The Simra stone inscription of Karṇa[96] recorded a commemorative stone erected by Janāda/Janārdana. The Koni stone inscription of Pṛthivīdeva II,[97] which was a *praśasti* of the minister, mentioned a solar eclipse as the occasion on which the king gave land to Puruṣottama, the recipient. The Jabalpur stone inscription of Jayasiṃha[98] referred to donations by Vimalaśiva, and also mentioned a solar eclipse. It also mentioned *tīrthas* such as Gaya, Gokarṇa, and Prabhāsa, where Vimalaśiva paid off his debts to the gods. The Rewa Plates of Jayasiṃha[99] recorded a grant by *mahārāṇaka* Kīrtivarman, a feudatory, probably on the occasion of the *śrāddha* of his father, although the term was not used. Among the joint donations, the Karitalai inscription of Lakṣmaṇarāja II[100] mentioned a lunar eclipse when Śaṅkaragaṇa III gave a grant, while it mentioned a solar eclipse when another village was granted.

Giving was important, but equally relevant was the reciprocation of the grant. The inscriptions generally mentioned the desired return as religious merit, unlike the Purāṇas, which sometimes mentioned worldly returns as well. The stated purpose of donations was religious merit for the donor or whoever else was specified. The Saugor stone inscription of Śaṅkaragaṇadeva I[101] recorded that the grant was for the religious merit of his parents. The Banaras Plates of Karṇa[102] mentioned the welfare of all people as the reason. Other grants by kings mentioned religious merit for parents as an objective. The grants by women do not mention such objectives.

The Bilhari stone inscription of Yuvarājadeva II,[103] a joint donation, mentions that Queen Nohalā built the temple for her religious merit. One of the most fascinating records was the Alha-ghat Stone inscription of Narasiṃhadeva[104] that mentions a grant by *rāṇaka* Chīhula. The purpose of the grant was specified as ensuring that the whole *jātī* of rāut, who lived in Kauśāmbī, would be freed from worldly bondage. It also referred to religious merit, wealth, pleasure, and liberation. The purpose of the grant recorded in the Sheorinārāyaṇa stone inscription of Jājalladeva II[105] was world peace, *maṅgala-jagatām-astu*. The Umariya Plates of Vijayasiṃhadeva[106] recorded a gift by *rāṇaka* Kumārapāla. The religious merit was supposed to accrue to his wife Mokhā. This was probably the only reference to a grant where religious merit was conferred to the wife.

A change from the Vākāṭaka times can be noticed. There was an increase in the number of smaller donations and joint donations. These donations were made jointly by the king, queen, minister, prince, trader, etc. Thus the distinction between royal and non-royal donors was not as sharp as in the earlier period. The larger proportion of donations by ministers and feudatories would suggest a changing political order. Non-royal elite women were making their presence felt through donations, which was not observed during the Vākāṭaka period. This shows that women not only had access to resources, but they also could use donations as a method of claiming status. Women were making independent grants. Although the items they could donate were few, it is significant that they could use the identical administrative processes as other elite sections of society. Queens gave donations to temples or constructed temples. Thus, the grants made by women donors appear to be restricted. By contrast, elite men made a wider range of grants, which included not only land, but temples, wells, gardens, taxes, etc. Thus even non-royal elite men gave a wide range of gifts and claimed a status similar to royal men. They gave donations not just to the non-Brahmanical but also to the Brahmanical traditions, unlike the Vākāṭaka period.

The Kalacuri inscriptions show a gendered pattern in terms of occasion of donations. Women do not mention the occasion on which they gave donations but the Dharmaśāstric practice was followed by the king and frequently by other elite men as well. Elite men mostly mention the solar or lunar eclipse or *saṅkrānti* as the occasion of the donations. In terms of returns from the grant, mostly religious merit is mentioned. Sometimes welfare of the people was mentioned. Women do not mention the returns expected, except in the joint donation where Queen Nohalā mentioned the hope of acquiring religious merit for herself. There is another interesting grant where the donor *rāṇaka* Kumārapāla made a donation with the expectation that religious merit would be gained by his wife. This reflects a change from the earlier period.

Status and Identity through Minor Gifts: The Candellas of Jejākabhukti

The Candellas were one of the dynasties that fought with the Ghaznavids. From a minor power they gradually claimed a stronghold over the Vindhya region. They were famous as rulers of Khajuraho. Their earliest capital was Khajuraho and in many of the inscriptions they are referred to as *khajuravāhaka*. Later they shifted to Mahoba and had a stronghold over Ajayagadh, Panna district, and Kālañjar, Banda district. They had control over Bundelkhand from around the ninth century CE to the thirteenth century CE. They called themselves the rulers of Jejākabhukti or Jejābhuktikā after King Jayaśakti. There is a debate among scholars regarding their status as feudatories. H.V. Trivedi holds that they were feudatories of the Gurjara-Pratihāras and later became independent rulers.[107] Many scholars believe that the Candellas were an aboriginal tribe that came into prominence later. They were not mentioned in the standard list of Rajputs, therefore J.N. Asopa believes them to be brāhmaṇas like many other Rajput clans who later married among royal families.[108] However R.D. Dikshit points out that they were included among the Rajputs in the *Varṇa Ratnākara*, *Pṛthvirāja rāso* and *Kumārapālacarita*.[109] Vincent Smith opines that they originated among the Gonds. K.K. Shah also believes that it is not improbable that the Candellas belonged to a tribal clan and later claimed to be Rajputs.[110] The origin of the Candellas is a matter of debate. According to the legends in the *Mahobākhaṇḍa*, the family descended from the union between Candra and Hemavatī. Hemavatī was the widowed daughter of Hemarāja, the priest of King Indrajit, the Gaharawāra king of Kasi.[111] But inscriptions do not refer to this legend and trace the origin of the Candellas from the sage Atri whose son was the sage Candrātreya and then trace the beginning of the dynasty to its first ruler Nannuka.

Figure 2.5 has been prepared on the basis of the inscriptional records of the Candellas. Figure 2.5 reveals a pattern similar to that of the Kalacuris and shows a wide variety of donations. It includes not just villages and plots of land but also temples, wells, gardens, etc. It shows that the highest percentage (32 per cent) of grants mentioned the construction of temples or the installation of an image. Donation of villages accounts for 25 per cent of the cases while land donations were made in only 7 per cent of the cases.

It is interesting to note that the plots of land donated were measured in terms of the seed that could be sown on the land. The number of grants mentioning construction of tanks and wells are not many. They account

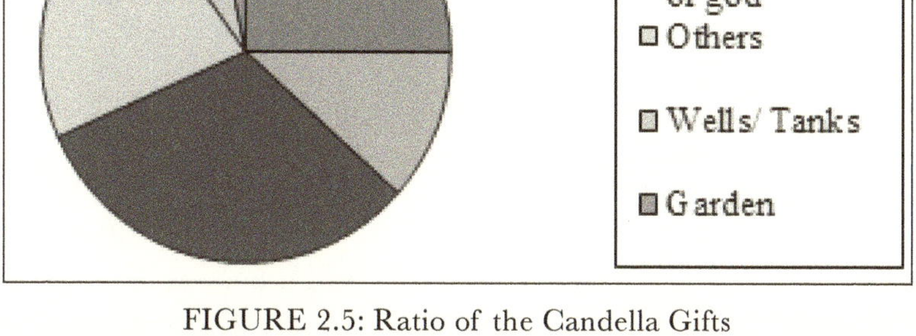

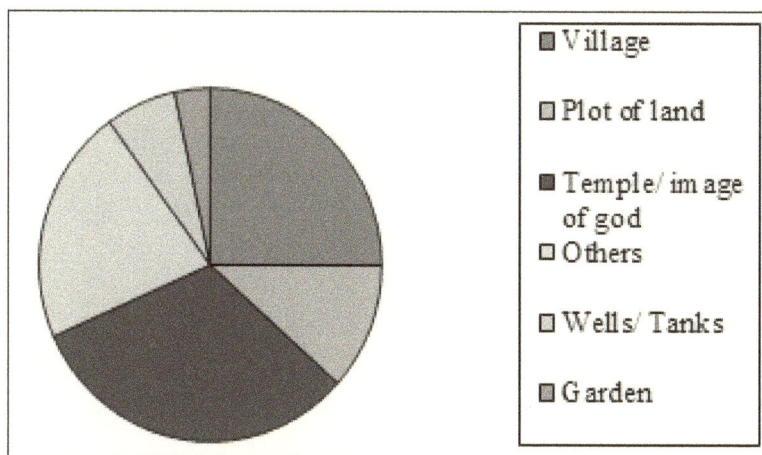

FIGURE 2.5: Ratio of the Candella Gifts

for only 7 per cent of the gifts. As compared to other dynasties the number of gardens given as gifts is few, i.e. 3 per cent. The gardens were granted mostly by the ministers. The last category includes the construction of *maṇḍapa*, composition of a *stotra*, some missing benedictions and also a mortgage deed and other inscriptions, adding up to 13 per cent. Thus, unlike the Vākāṭakas whose records mention only substantial donations, here even minor acts such as the composition of a *stotra* or the construction or repair of a *maṇḍapa* or of a stepwell were also recorded. Land was not the main item gifted; it was more important to build temples or to install images of the deity.

A unique feature of the records is the existence of four *satī* stone inscriptions. These are short records and do not provide much detail and are therefore not counted in Figure 2.5. The Gurha Satī stone inscription VS 1342, i.e. 1286 CE, has not been edited.[112] It mentions the reign of Vāravarman. The Ajayagaḍh Satī stone inscription is also a fragmentary record.[113] It only mentions the date VS 1346, i.e. 1289 CE and the reign of Bhojavarmandeva. Since it was found near a female image it was believed to be a *satī* stone. The Bamhnī Satī stone inscription VS 1365,[114] i.e. 1308 CE, mentions that during the rule of Hammiravarman, Pālhaṇa's wife (*bhāryā*) Malhai immolated herself, and her son Jāme erected the stone to commemorate her death. The last in the list is the Ajayagaḍh Satī stone inscription, VS 1368,[115] i.e. 1311 CE. It mentions the last Candella king Hammiravarman. It mentions that Mene, wife of Bālabhatta, became a *satī*.

Of the earliest grants by a king, Yaśovarman's record mentions the construction of a temple of Viṣṇu, as the enemy of demons.[116] The record mentions that the image was obtained from Herambapāla, king of Kanauj. In addition, it also mentions various expeditions of the king. The Khajuraho stone inscription of Dhaṅgadeva, VS 1059, i.e. 1002 CE, mentions the construction of a temple of Śiva that has two *liṅgas*, one embedded with pearls and other made of stone.[117] It also mentions the grant of other items such as grain, gold, cow, land, etc. The inscription also mentions the grants by previous kings. It mentions that the *liṅga* was worshipped by Yudhiṣṭhira. This record seems to be an attempt to follow the Dharmaśāstric norm of giving *dāna* and also refers to a well-known epic figure. This inscription was later renewed by Jayavarmandeva in VS 1173, i.e. 1117 CE. The Augāsī Copperplate inscription of Madanavarman, VS 1190, i.e. 1134 CE,[118] mentions the donation of a plot of land measured in terms of ten pairs of oxen and 7½ *droṇas* of seed sown. It meant that the land could be ploughed with ten pairs of oxen and would require the above-mentioned quantity of seed. It also informs all the people assembled—*kuṭumbins*, *kāyasthas*, *mahattaras* and others—about the grant. Another grant by King Paramardideva mentions the donation of a plot of land measuring ten *halas*.[119] The Candellas used a different measuring system. The Kālañjar stone inscription of Paramardideva VS 1258,[120] i.e. 1207 CE, records a eulogy of Śiva and Pārvatī. The record mentions that the eulogy was written by the king himself. Thus, the purpose was not to record any donation but to report spectacular deeds such as the composition of verses by the king. The Kālañjar stone inscription of Vīravarman,[121] a fragmentary record, mentions the various pious deeds of the king. He constructed temples, planted gardens, excavated tanks and wells. He also weighed himself against gold and distributed it (*tulāpuruṣadāna*), which was referred to as *svarṇatulāvitaraṇa*. He also performed sacrifices, although the specific sacrifices were not mentioned. He seems to have claimed and legitimized his position by following the traditional norm, and used Dharmaśāstric terminology.

Of the grants by queens, the Kundeshwar Copperplate inscription of the Candella queen Satyabhāmā, year 1060,[122] i.e. 1003 CE, mentions the grant of some portion of land in the village to several brāhmaṇas who belonged to different *śākhā*, *gotra,* and villages. Satyabhāmā was the queen of King Vidyādhara and daughter of *mahārāja* Śri Gopāla (other details are missing). The Ajayagadh rock inscription of the time of Vīravarman[123] mentions the donation of Queen Kalyāṇadevī, wife of Vīravarman. She got a well, named Nirjarakūpa, excavated for travellers and also gave a cup or a water pot and along with it built a hall. The Bhārat Kalā Bhavan Plates of Madanavarman VS 1192,[124] i.e. 1136 CE, mention the grant of land by King Madanavarman. It mentions that part of the land was earlier granted by Nāduka/Nāduki, a priest attached to Queen Lakhamīdevī. Further, the grant also mentions that part of the grant was earlier granted by two queens, *mahārajñī* Vālhaṇadevī and *rājñī* Cāndeladevī with the consent of the king. The original record of the grant of the above-mentioned queens was not found. The same land was re-granted or was exchanged.

There are many records of grants by non-royal elite men that would suggest that, like royal elite men, they had access to resources. The earliest record mentions the planting of seven gardens by a minister, Pāhila, in favour of the temple of Jinanātha.[125] Interestingly, one of the gardens was named Pāhila-vāṭikā and another was named Dhaṅga-vāṭikā. Thus, royal and non-royal elite men claimed similar status. Another inscription, although fragmentary, mentions the founding of a city with a capital.[126] This grant was given by Kanhapa or Kṛnapa, who was the brother of Dhaṅga. The Deogaḍh rock inscription of the time of Kīrtivarman VS 1154, i.e. 1098 CE, mentions the construction of a flight of steps, *ghaṭṭa*, by the king's councillor and chief minister Vatsarāja.[127] Many of the records by non-royal elite men mention the installation of the image of the deity, both Brahmanical as well as non-Brahmanical. The Kālañjar rock inscription of the time of Madanavarman VS 1192, i.e. 1136 CE, mentions the gift of the image of Nṛsiṃha by *ṭhakkura* Narasiṃha.[128] There were many grants that mentioned the installation of the image of a Jain *tīrthaṅkara*. The Horniman Museum image inscription of the time of Madanavarman VS 1208, i.e. 1151 CE, mentions the dedication of the image of Neminātha.[129] The copperplate inscription of Kumārapāladeva VS 1297, i.e. 1239 CE, mentions the donation of a village Rehī in Vadharā by *mahārāṇaka* Kumārapāla.[130] The second part of the grant mentions the portion given to each of the six donees.

The donation by a non-royal woman is a joint donation. It mentions some benefactions to a deity (probably Nīlakaṇṭha, as the record was found on the pillar of the temple) by *mahāpratīhāra* Saṃgrāmasiṃha and *mahānācaṇī* Padmāvatī.[131] It is interesting to note that the dancer was claiming status along with an officer. It does not contain much information about the dynasty/family; even details about the donors are not recorded. But the inscription was found inside the fort of Kālañjar and was dated like the other records, i.e. in Vikrama Samvat.

Figure 2.6 shows the gendered pattern of the Candella grants. As in the case of the Kalacuris, kings grant a variety of gifts and a similar range is seen in the case of other elite men. In the case of women, the range of gifts becomes restricted to smaller items and plots of land as in the case of royal women. As compared to the Kalacuri grants, where other elite women also gave a variety of gifts, this is not seen in the case of the Candellas. The Candella grants seem to indicate that women of the ruling dynasty had relatively limited control over resources in comparison with those of earlier dynasties in the region. This could also be because of the political unrest.

Of grants by the king, the majority of the grants were gifts of villages and plots of land. The king gave a variety of gifts that included a temple and/or an image, a garden, a well/tank and, at the same time, miscellaneous grants for the composition of a *stotra*, for example. The grants by queens

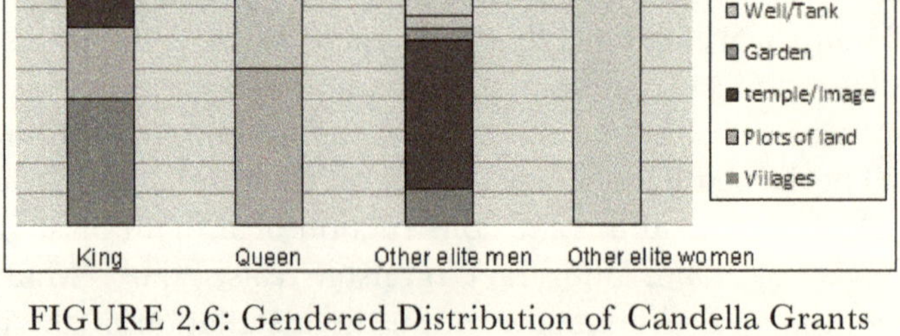

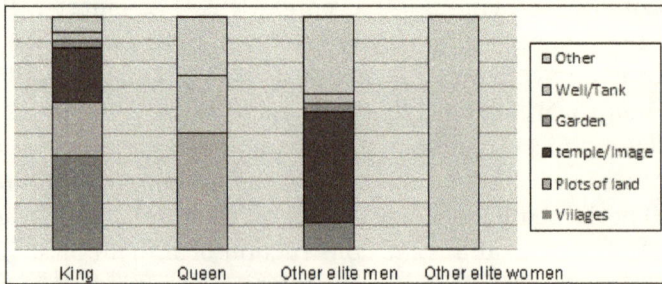

FIGURE 2.6: Gendered Distribution of Candella Grants

included plots of land, tanks, cups for drinking water, etc. The queens did not donate villages. It is likely that their access to resources that could be donated was restricted. Non-royal elite men again made a variety of donations, including villages, temples, tanks, etc. Other elite women gave only minor gifts.

The place from where the grant was made was mentioned in most of the grants made by kings. It was sometimes a temple as in the Khajuraho stone inscription VS 1059, where King Dhaṅga gave a grant and mentioned the place of grant as the temple of Śiva.[132] Thirteen inscriptions mention the grant from the king's camp, for example, the Pachar Copperplate inscription of Paramardideva VS 1233,[133] i.e. 1176 CE, mentions that the grant was issued from the king's camp at Vilāsapura.

Grants by women, both royal and non-royal, do not mention the place from where they were issued, whereas non-royal elite men sometimes mention the place of issue. It could be a temple; for example, the Kālañjar rock inscription of the time of Madanavarman VS 1192, i.e. 1136 CE, mentions the place of the donation as the site of the image of Nṛsiṃha.[134] Another inscription mentions the place of issue as the fort and also mentions the purpose of the gift as some *krīḍā-yuddha* (sham fight).[135] The Ajayagaḍh stone inscription of the time of Paramardideva records the construction of a step-well (*bāuli*), and mentions the road as the place of issue. It also mentions famine (*durbhikṣa*).[136] Non-royal elite men could sometimes mention the place of issue, but it was not common. It thus appears that mention of the place of issue was conventionally a marker of status that was deployed by the king.

In terms of the motive or occasion of the grant, records by women do not mention any except in the case of the Kundeshwar grant of Queen Satyabhāmā where a solar eclipse was mentioned.[137] The *satī* stones explicitly or implicitly mention the occasion of the grants. But no other grant by women or which mentions women refers to any such occasion. Another grant which mentions women is the Nanyaura Copperplate inscription of Devavarmandeva VS 1107, i.e. 1052 CE, which mentions the occasion as the death anniversary of the king's mother, *rājñī* Bhuvanadevī.[138]

The motive of the grant was merit and fame for the king and his parents. Of the total grants by kings, thirteen records mention the occasion during which the grant was made. Many refer to religious merit as the reason for the grant, while some mention a lunar or solar eclipse as the occasion. Unlike the earlier inscriptions (those of the Vākāṭakas and Kalacuris), war and distress was an occasion for giving grants. For example, the Ajayagaḍh rock inscription of the time of Kīrtivarman[139] (undated, probably around the eleventh century) mentions that the donee,

Maheśvara of the Vāstavya family, was granted the village Pipalāhika and was given the authority over the gates of the fort (Ajayagadh) as a gift for his help during the time of distress in Pītādri. The Garrā Copperplate inscription of Trailokyavarman VS 1261,[140] i.e. 1205 CE, mentions that the donee, Sāvanta, son of Pāpe, was given a village as Pāpe was killed in a battle with the Turuṣkas (Turks). The Dahi Copperplate inscription of Vīravarman VS of 1337,[141] i.e. 1280 CE, also mentions that the donee Balabhadra Mallaya was granted the village Dahi as he had defeated many kings. This indicates the changing times and the political instability of the period.

In the case of grants by other elite men, the purpose or occasion of the grants is different. Ten records mention the occasion for grants. Acquiring religious merit for the donor was mentioned in three inscriptions only. The rest mention varied reasons, which also include the writing of a *stotra* besides repairing the temple of Bhaillasvāmin.[142] Another record discussed earlier mentions a sham fight as the occasion of the grant. Another inscription mentions that the *rāuta* Śrī Vīra constructed a step well during famine.[143] The Ahār statue inscription of the time of Paramardideva VS 1237, i.e. 1180 CE, mentions the installation of an image of the Jain *tīrthaṅkara* Śāntinātha.[144] The purpose of the grant was to attain salvation and to pay homage to Vitarāga (details are not provided). In the Ajayagaḍh stone inscription of the time of Paramardin VS 1243, i.e. 1187 CE, the donor *rāuta* Sīhaḍa constructed a platform (*cautrā*) for the use of all the people.[145] The Dhurētī Copperplate inscription of the time of Trailōkyamalla (Kalacuri), year 963, i.e. 1212 CE, records the mortgage (*vitta-bandha*) of a village by a Śaiva ascetic Śāntiśiva in favour of one *rāṇaka* Dharika.[146] It also mentions two paṇḍitas, Viśveśvara and Gaṅgādhara, who made the record and also the various officers who were present. Surprisingly, the record is dated in the Kalacuri year and also uses titles similar to those of the Kalacuris. Trivedi suggests that maybe during this period the Candellas had defeated Vijayasiṃha and occupied the region of Rewa. The Ajayagaḍh stone inscription of the time of Vīravarṁan VS 1325, i.e. 1268 CE, mentions the purpose of the record as the adoration of Abhayadeva of the Vatsa *gotra*, who was an expert in curing horse diseases.[147]

The Candella records were different from the earlier grants in many respects. The number of grants of villages or plots of land seems to have decreased. There is a spurt of minor gifts such as the installation of the image of a deity or grants for composing verses, etc. The donations by kings are comparatively few and the numbers of grants by ministers and feudatories seems to have increased. Grants by elite women are few. Two records mentioned donations by queens, and another inscription mentioned an earlier grant made by two queens. Another feature of the Candella grants was that there was a mention of land brought back or exchanged in lieu of a previous grant. Also, there were many grants that mention not the chivalry of kings but rather that of ministers. It indicates a period of political unrest, especially because of the attack of the Turks. There were also *satī* stones that are altogether a different kind of epigraph. Thus, several changes from the earlier times can be observed.

Examining the grants by elite men, a variety of donations were given, which ranged from larger donations such as land to minor grants like wells, gardens or even for the composition of verses in honour of deities. Non-royal elite men also gave a variety of donations. This may indicate their attempts to claim status, especially in times of political unrest. There are a few records that mention donations by women. One of the records, a joint donation, mentions grants by a dancer along with a minister. Otherwise references to women in the inscriptions are comparatively sparse in comparison to the records of the earlier dynasties.

In terms of the place of issue, grants by kings mention camps in many of the records. Donations by non-royal elite men also sometimes mention the place of issue; in one case it was the road. But records of elite women do not mention the place of issue. In terms of the occasion of the donations, many of the records of kings mention solar or lunar eclipses. One of the records mentions the death anniversary of the king's mother. Many of the records mention distress or a brave act of a minister as the occasion of the grant. The multiple donations in the Bhārat Kalā Bhavan Plates of Madanavarman were made on the occasion of *viṣuvat saṅkrānti* by the king. Non-royal elite men do not mention religious occasions; rather one mentions some sport and another mentions famine. Elite women do not mention any such occasion in their records. Only the Kundeshwar grant of Satyabhāmā mentions a solar eclipse in the month of *śravaṇa*. *Satī* stones also mention the performance of *satī* as the occasion for the record.

The return expected was religious merit, mentioned in some of the grants of the kings. Most of the grants do not mention any explicit purpose for the donation. In the case of non-royal elite men, a few records mention religious merit or fame as the purpose of the grant. Another record mentions homage as the reason for donation. One of the inscriptions mentions mortgage in the record. Another record mentions the donor's ability to treat horses. Again, elite women do not mention any such purpose for granting gifts.

The Issue of Identity: Towards an Epilogue

The epigraphic records mention a variety of items as gifts but as these records belong to the elite section of society, *dāna* as practised by the

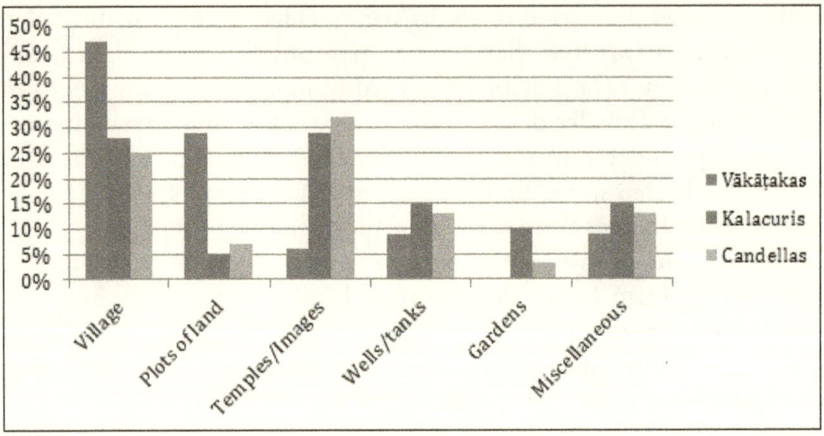

FIGURE 2.7: Changing Access to Resources

masses cannot be gauged. The act of *dāna* was practised as a traditional religious rite that also played the role of strengthening networks between various social groups. The sources indicate the relevance of *dāna* during the early medieval period. What were considered worthy of record were gifts of land, temples, and tanks, etc. Thus, while inscriptions were a means of recording their affiliation, the elite section of society mentioned only gifts that were considered relevant.

There were differences between the Vākāṭaka, Kalacuri, and Candella grants, which can be seen from Figure 2.7, indicating changes over time. In the Vākāṭaka inscriptions, grants of land were most significant, while the Kalacuri records mentioned an extensive variety of gifts including a copy of a text, granary, certain taxes, and sometime fairs organized in honour of the deity, besides the usual grant of land. In the Candella grants, minor gifts were more in number. Thus, it was not only land, constructions of temples and tanks and gardens that were important but small donations were also recorded. By the time of the Kalacuris and the Candellas, gifts of mango groves, and a hundred trees besides gardens were recorded as public works done by the donor. Sometimes inscriptions only mentioned the installation of the image of the deity or verses composed to be the reason of the grant. The trend is towards smaller gifts, which show a changing access to resources.

In terms of the nature of donations, most of the grants of village/s and plots of land were given by the king and sometimes by the queen. Other members of the elite section did not grant villages. Other elite men as well as women gave donations like wells, tanks, gardens, etc. All the dynasties show a gendered pattern in terms of donation.

The Vākāṭaka records mentioned a few donations by queens and ministers and most records mention the king as the donor. The most common gift by the king was of a village. Prabhāvatīguptā, who claimed a special position in the dynasty, also granted land or a village. Regarding other elite women, it was only the daughter of the queen who made the grant of a temple, that too in memory of the queen mother, Prabhāvatīguptā. The gifts by the ministers were of plots of land, caves, etc. In the Kalacuri records the trend was quite different, as there were grants not only by the king and queen; a large number of grants were by the ministers and feudatories who gave a variety of items as gifts. There were gifts by other elite women, which included not only wives of the ministers and feudatories, but also a grant by a woman whose social status was not explicitly mentioned. The inscription only mentioned the name of her husband. Thus, women could make grants independently. This would also indicate that they had control over resources. Another very interesting feature was joint donation. There were donations jointly made by the king with the queen, prince or minister, or even merchants. Thus, the social network portrayed in these donations was unique. These donations mentioned various donors from different social backgrounds claiming a similar status, having access to a similar administrative apparatus.

Regarding the time and place of gift-giving, the inscriptions followed the Puranic instructions. For instance, the *Matsya Purāṇa* mentioned that grants could be made during eclipses, *saṅkrānti*, *śrāddha* and other occasions such as marriage, birth, etc., besides giving grants at sacred places such as *tīrthas*. The *Matsya Purāṇa*[148] mentioned that one should take a bath after the eclipse and give a donation of rubies and cows. One who would perform this ritual would attain bliss and never take birth in this world again. Even by reading or listening about this observance one would go to the realm of Indra, liberated from all sins and would be glorified. As a matter of fact, many inscriptions of the Kalacuri and the Candella dynasties mentioned grants made during eclipses. However, there was only one reference to grants during an eclipse in the Vākāṭaka inscriptions. The Kalacuri records mentioned grants during a solar or lunar eclipse in ten inscriptions. The Candellas mentioned eclipses in four records. Similarly, the Kalacuri inscriptions mentioned the performance of the *śrāddha* ceremony. One of the Candella grants mentions the death anniversary of the mother of the king. The Vākāṭaka inscriptions record donations after observing the *ekādaśī* fast by Prabhāvatīguptā. In the Kalacuri dynasty there was mention of a grant after taking a bath in a holy river. The Candellas, in one of the inscriptions, mention a grant being made after taking a bath at Vetravatī. Another frequently mentioned occasion was *saṅkrānti*. There were records of many grants on the occasion of the *uttarāyana-saṅkrānti*. One of the Candella records mentions *visuvat saṅkrānti*. There was also mention of a grant being made after the king was attacked by an alligator. Some of the Candella grants mention the brave deeds of the ministers during distress or against the Turks. In a different sense, the *satī* stones would also reflect distress. Overall, giving gifts after any important event was a trend, as mentioned in the Purāṇas.

The desired return from the act of giving gifts can be seen in terms of spiritual and worldly returns in the Dharmaśāstras. Thus, the expectation was not just of religious merit but included health, wealth, beauty, long life, etc. The texts mentioned prosperity, religious merit, and emancipation. The inscriptions generally referred to religious merit as the purpose of the grant. They also mentioned other desires such as prosperity, life, victory, power, etc. Elite women in most of the records do not mention such expectations.

The gift and its stated reasons changed over time and were gendered. Control or access to resources differed among elite men and women. What was given as a gift reflects what was considered significant in society. The inscriptions, representing the interest of the elites, mentioned land, villages, temples, wells, gardens, images, etc. They also challenge the notion about the property owned by women. The elite women had access to property and the right to alienate it as well. It was not just temples or gardens but also plots of land and villages, i.e. the grants were similar to those of the elite men. By the Candella period, we find a grant given by a dancer, which would reflect that the practice was common for elites (one can talk about grants by common men and women on the basis of the Buddhist and Jain inscriptions). The attempt of the elite was to legitimize their position and gain status from these donations. The joint donations of the Kalacuris and Candellas would suggest that the non-ruling elite claimed a higher status, but there were differences as well. The strategy of claiming status and identity through grants was practised by elite men as well as women. The elites identified themselves socially through donations. Their access to the administrative machinery was similar but a gendered pattern can be noticed in terms of access to resources.

*Both the spellings, Kalacuri and Kalachuri, are used by scholars. While I prefer the former spelling for orthographic consistency, I have also used the latter when citing the works of scholars who adopt this spelling. Similarly, both Candella and Chandella are in use. The principle of adhering to the specific practices of scholars who have been cited, and using other conventions of transliteration have been followed in other instances as well.

NOTES

1. Cynthia Talbot, 'Rudramā-devī, the Female King, Gender and Political Authority in Medieval India', in *Syllables of the Sky*, ed. David Shulman, Delhi: Oxford University Press, 1995, p. 392.
2. K.K. Shah, 'Legal Rights of Women to the Landed Wealth, A Case Study of Candella Queens', in *Women in Indian History*, ed. Kiran Pawar, New Delhi: Vision and Venture, 1996, p. 38.
3. Cited in P.V. Kane, *History of Dharmaśāstras*, vol. 2, pt. II, Poona: Bhandarkar Oriental Research Institute, 1974, p. 837.
4. Vijay Nath, 'Ritual Symbolism and Status-Conferring Role of Dāna', *Proceedings of the Indian History Congress*, 50th Session, Goa, 1989–90, p. 81.
5. Vijay Nath, 'Mahādāna: The Dynamics of Gift-Economy and the Feudal Milieu', in *The Feudal Order: State, Society and Ideology in Early Medieval India*, ed. D.N. Jha, Delhi: Manohar, 2000, p. 420.
6. Marcel Mauss, *The Gift: The Form and Reason for Exchange in Archaic Societies*, tr. W.D. Hallis, London: Routledge, (first published in 1950, translated in 1954), 1990.
7. Axel Michaels, tr. Philip Pierce, 'Gift and Return Gift, Greetings and Return Greetings from India. On a Consequential Footnote of Marcel Mauss', *Numen*, vol. XLIV, no. 3, 1997, p. 258.
8. Ibid., p. 260.
9. Romila Thapar, *Cultural Pasts: Essays in Early Indian History*, New Delhi: Oxford University Press, 2000, p. 96.
10. Vijay Nath, *Dāna: Gift System in Ancient India. A Socio-Economic Perspective*, Delhi: Munshiram Manoharlal, 1987, p. 9.
11. Cited in Nath, ibid., p. 18.
12. Ibid., p. 19.
13. Kane, *History of Dharmaśāstras*, vol. 2, pt. II, Poona: Bhandarkar Oriental Research Institute, 1974, p. 844.
14. Cited in Kane, ibid., p. 844.
15. Ibid., p. 845.
16. Nath, 'Ritual Symbolism', p. 21.
17. Kane, *History of Dharmaśāstras*, p. 847.
18. Michaels, 'Gift and Return Gift', pp. 249–51.
19. Kane, *History of Dharmaśāstras*, pp. 851–3.
20. Nath, 'Ritual Symbolism', p. 7.
21. Ellison Banks Findly, *Dāna: Giving and Getting in Pali Buddhism*, New Delhi: Motilal Banarsidass, 2003, p. 182.
22. Ibid., p. 199.
23. Cited in Nath, 'Ritual Symbolism', p. 26.
24. Kalpana Upreti, 'Institutional and Ideological Usage of Dāna in the *Divyāvadāna*', *Proceedings of the Indian History Congress*, 50th Session, Goa, 1989–90, p. 88.
25. Cited in Kane, *History of Dharmaśāstras*, p. 861.
26. James Heitzman, *Gifts of Power: Lordship in an Early Indian State*, Delhi: Oxford University Press, 1997, p. 181.

27. Cynthia Talbot, *Pre-colonial India in Practice: Society, Region and Identity in Medieval Andhra*, New York: Oxford University Press, 2001, p. 2.
28. B.D. Chattopadhyaya, *The Making of Early Medieval India*, 2nd edn., Delhi: Oxford University Press, 1998, p. 35.
29. Hermann Kulke, *State in India, 1000–1700 AD*, Delhi: Oxford University Press, 1995, p. 41.
30. Patna Museum Plates of Pravarasēna II, *Corpus Inscriptionum Indicarum* (henceforth *CII*), vol. V, p. 71.
31. Amoda Plates of Jājalladeva II: (Kalachuri) Year 91[9], *CII*, vol. IV, pt. 2, pp. 528–33.
32. Garrā Copperplate Inscription of Trailōkyavarman, VS 1261, *CII*, vol. VII, pt. 3, pp. 483–7.
33. Kālañjar Pillar Inscription of the Time of Madanavarman, VS 1186, *CII*, vol. VII, pt. 3, pp. 390–1.
34. Bhārat Kalā Bhavan Plate Inscription of Madanavarman, VS 1192, *CII*, vol. VII, pt. 3, pp. 399–405.
35. A.M. Shastri, *Vākāṭakas: Source and History* (henceforth *VSH*), New Delhi: Aryan Books International, 1997, p. 171.
36. F.E. Pargiter, *The Purāṇa Text of the Dynasties of the Kali Age*, Delhi: Deep Publications, 1913; repr. 1975, p. 73.
37. Shastri, *VSH*, p. 171.
38. A.M. Shastri, 'The Vākāṭakas: Original Home and Some Other Problems', in *The Age of the Vākāṭakas*, ed. A.M. Shastri, New Delhi: Harman Publishing House, 1992.
39. Hans T. Bakker, *The Vākāṭakas. An Essay in Hindu Iconology*, Groningen: Egbert Forsten, 1997.
40. V.V. Mirashi, *CII, Inscriptions of the Vākāṭakas*, vol. V, Ootacamund: Archaeological Survey of India, 1963.
41. Shastri, *VSH*, p. 5.
42. Waḍgaon Plates of Pravarasēna II, *CII*, vol. V, pp. 53–6.
43. D.C. Sircar, *Indian Epigraphical Glossary*, Delhi: Motilal Banarsidass, 1966, p. 220.
44. Yavatmal Plates of Pravarasena II (Year 26), K.M. Shrimali, *Agrarian Structures in Central India and Northern Deccan. A Study in Vākāṭaka Inscriptions*, henceforth *ASCI*, Delhi: Munshiram Manoharlal, 1987, pp. 63–5 and 95.
45. Pāṇḍhurṇā Plates of Pravarasēna II, *CII*, vol. V, pp. 63–8.
46. Kane, *History of Dharmaśāstras*, p. 861.
47. Pauni Plates of Pravarasena II Year 32, *ASCI*, pp. 69–71 and 98.
48. Poonā Plates of Prabhāvatīguptā, *CII*, vol. V, p. 7.
49. Riddhapur Plates of Prabhāvatīguptā, *CII*, vol. V, pp. 33–7.
50. Miregaon Charter of the Reign of Pravara Sena II, Year 20, in A.M. Shastri, *VSH*, pp. 91–3.
51. Masoda Plates of Pravarasena II, Year 29, *ASCI*, pp. 65–9 and 97–8.
52. According to Shrimali, this may mean that the land was given to a Vaiṣṇava religious establishment, *ASCI*, p. 112 (note 95).

53. Bakker reads the name of the donor as Atibhāvatī, daughter of Prabhāvatīguptā in Hans Bakker and Harunaga Issacson, 'Ramtek Inscriptions II: The Vākāṭaka Inscription in the Kevala-Narasimha Temple', *Bulletin of the School of Oriental and African Studies*, vol. LVI, no. 1, 1993, pp. 46–74.
54. Cynthia Talbot, 'Temples, Donors and Gifts: Patterns of Patronage in Thirteenth Century South India', *Journal of Asian Studies*, vol. L, no. 2, 1991, p. 333.
55. Chammak Copperplate Inscription of Pravarasēna II, *CII*, vol. V, pp. 22–7.
56. Indore Plates of Pravarasēna II, *CII*, vol. V, pp. 38–42.
57. Paṭṭan Plates of Pravarasēna II, *CII*, vol. V, pp. 57–62.
58. Hisse-Borālā Stone Slab Inscription of Deva Sena, Śaka 380, *VSH*, pp. 106–7.
59. Tirōḍī Plates of Pravarasēna II, *CII*, vol. V, p. 50.
60. Mirashi, *CII*, vol. V, *Inscriptions of the Vākāṭakas*, p. 49.
61. Waḍgaon Plates of Pravarasēna II, vol. V, pp. 53–6.
62. Pāṇḍhurṇā Plates of Pravarasēna II, *CII*, vol. V, pp. 63–8.
63. Patna/Balaghat Plates of Pravarasēna II, *CII*, vol. V, pp. 69–72.
64. Mandhal Plates of Pṛthivīṣeṇa II Year 2, *ASCI*, pp. 71–4 and 100.
65. Mandhal Plates of Pravarasēna II Year 16, *ASCI*, pp. 60–3, 89–91.
66. Hisse-Borālā Stone Slab Inscription of Deva Sena, Śaka 380, *VSH*, pp. 106–7.
67. Ajanta Cave Inscription of Varāhadeva, *CII*, vol. V, pp. 86–94.
68. Inscription of Ajanta Cave XVII, *CII*, vol. V, pp. 103–12.
69. Chattopadhyaya, *The Making of Early Medieval India*, p. 59.
70. Cited in J.N. Asopa, *The Origin of the Rajputs*, Delhi: Bharatiya Publishing House, 1976, pp. 173–4.
71. R.K. Sharma, *Kalachuris and their Times*, Delhi: Sundeep Prakashan, p. 3.
72. Mirashi, *CII*, vol. IV, pt. I, p. xlv.
73. Gurgi Stone Inscription of Kokalladeva II, *CII*, vol. IV, pt. 1, pp. 224–33.
74. Goharwa Plates of Karṇa, *CII*, vol. IV, pt. I, pp. 252–63.
75. Ratnapur Stone Inscription of Jājalladeva I, *CII*, vol. IV. pt. 2, pp. 409–17.
76. Pali Stone Inscription of Jājalladeva I, *CII*, vol. IV, pt. 2, pp. 417–19.
77. Bhera Ghat Stone Inscription of Narasiṃhadeva: (Kalachuri) Year 907, *CII*, vol. IV, pt. 1, pp. 312–21.
78. Bhera-Ghat Gaurī-Śaṅkara Temple Inscription of Vijayasiṃha, *CII*, vol. IV, pt. 1, pp. 363–4.
79. Sarnath Stone Inscription of Karṇa: (Kalachuri) Year 810, *CII*, vol. IV, pt. 1, pp. 275–8.
80. Kane, *History of Dharmaśāstras*, p. 883.
81. Rewa Stone Inscription of Karṇa: (Kalachuri) Year 812, *CII*, vol. IV, pt. 1, pp. 278–84.
82. Akaltara Stone Inscription of Ratnadeva II, *CII*, vol. IV, pt. 2, pp. 430–6.
83. Ratnapur Stone Inscription of Pṛthivīdeva II: Kalachuri Year 910, *CII*, vol. IV, pt. 2, pp. 483–90.
84. Sheorinarayana Stone Inscription of Jājalladeva II: Year 919, *CII*, vol. IV, pt. 2, pp. 519–27.
85. Karitalai Stone Inscription of Lakṣhmaṇarājā II, *CII*, vol. IV, pt. 1, pp. 186–95.

86. D.C. Sircar, *Indian Epigraphical Glossary*, New Delhi: Motilal Banarsidass, 1966, p. 155.
87. Bilhari Stone Inscription of Yuvarājadeva II, *CII*, vol. IV, pt. 1, pp. 204–24.
88. Banaras Plates of Karṇa (Kalachuri) Year 793, *CII*, vol. IV, pt. 1, pp. 236–50.
89. Goharwa Plates of Karṇa, *CII*, vol. IV, pt. I, pp. 252–63.
90. Khairha Plates of Yaśahkarṇa: (Kalachuri) Year 823, *CII*, vol. IV, pt. 1, pp. 289–99.
91. Kahila Plates of Sodhadeva: VS 1135, *CII*, vol. IV, pt. 2, pp. 382–97.
92. Bilaigarh Plates of Pṛthivīdeva II (Kalachuri) Year 896, *CII*, vol. IV, pt. 2, pp. 458–62.
93. Jabalpur Plates of Jayasiṃha: (Kalachuri) Year 918, *CII*, vol. IV, pt. 1, pp. 324–31.
94. Amoda Plates (2nd set) Pṛthivīdeva II: Year 905, *CII*, vol. IV, pt. II, pp. 491–5.
95. Amoda Plates of Jājalladeva II: (Kalachuri) Year 91[9], *CII*, vol. IV, pt. 2, pp. 528–33.
96. Simra Stone Inscription of Karṇa, *CII*, vol. IV, pt. I, pp. 288–9.
97. Koni Stone Inscription of Pṛthivīdeva II: (Kalachuri) Year 900, *CII*, vol. IV, pt. 2, pp. 463–73.
98. Jabalpur Stone Inscriptions of Jayasiṃha: (Kalachuri) Year 926, *CII*, vol. IV, pt. 1, pp. 331–9.
99. Rewa Plates of Jayasiṃha: (Kalachuri) Year 926, *CII*, vol. IV, pt. I, pp. 340–4.
100. Karitalai Stone Inscription of Lakṣmaṇarājā II, *CII*, vol. IV, pt. 1, pp. 186–95.
101. Saugor Stone Inscription of Śaṅkaragaṇa I, *CII*, vol. IV, pt. 1, pp. 174–6.
102. Banaras Plates of Karṇa: (Kalachuri) Year 793, *CII*, vol. IV, pt. I, pp. 236–50.
103. Bilhari Stone Inscription of Yuvarājadeva II, *CII*, vol. IV, pt. I, pp. 204–24.
104. Alha-ghat Stone Inscription of Narasiṃha: VS 1216, *CII*, vol. IV, pt.1, pp. 322–4.
105. Sheorinarayan Stone Inscription of Jājalladeva II: Chedi Year 919, *CII*, vol. IV, pt. 2, pp. 519–27.
106. Umariya Plates of Vijayasiṃhadeva: Year 944, *Epigraphia Indica* (hereafter *EI*), vol. XLI, ed. K.V. Ramesh, 1989, pp. 38–48.
107. H.V. Trivedi, *CII*, vol. 7, pt. 1, p. 86.
108. J.N. Asopa, *The Origin of the Rajputs*, Delhi: Bharatiya Publishing House, 1976, p. 215.
109. R.K. Dikshit, *The Candellas of Jejākabhukti*, New Delhi: Abhinav Publications, 1977, p. 3.
110. K.K. Shah, *Ancient Bundelkhand: Religious History in Socio-Economic Perspective*, Delhi: Gian Publishers, 1988, pp. 29–30.
111. Dikshit, *The Candellas of Jejākabhukti*, p. 3.
112. Ibid., p. 209.
113. Ajayagadh Satī Stone Inscription, VS 1346, R.K. Dikshit, *The Candellas of Jejākabhukti*, p. 210 .
114. Bamhnī Satī Stone Inscription, VS 1365, *CII*, vol. VII, pt. 3, pp. 525–7.
115. Ajayagaḍh Satī Stone Inscription of the Time of Hammīravarman, VS 1368, *CII*, vol. VII, pt. 3, pp. 527–8.

116. Khajurāhō Stone Inscription of Yaśōvarman, vs 1011, *CII*, vol. VII, pt. 3, pp. 337–46.
117. Khajurāhō Stone Inscription of Dhaṅgadēva of the Year 1059; Renewed by Jayavarmandēva in the Year 1173, *CII*, vol. VII, pt. 3, pp. 381–90.
118. Augāsī Copperplate Inscription of Madanavarman, vs 1190, *CII*, vol. VII, pt. 3, pp. 395–9.
119. Bhārat Kalā Bhavan Plate of Paramardidēva, vs 1247, *CII*, vol. VII, pt. 3, pp. 469–72.
120. Kālañjar Stone Inscription of Paramardidēva, vs 1258, *CII*, vol. VII, pt. 3, pp. 478–82.
121. Kālañjar Stone Inscription of Vīravarman, *CII*, vol. VII, pt. 3, pp. 507–10.
122. S.K. Sullerey, 'Kundeshwar Copper Plate of Chandella Queen Satyabhāmā, year 1060', in *Kṛṣṇa Smṛti: Studies in Indian Art and Archaeology*, ed. R.K. Sharma and R.C. Agrawal, New Delhi: Aryan Books International, 1995, pp. 105–7; *Indian Archaeology. A Review, 1971–72*, ed. M.N. Deshpande, New Delhi: Archaeological Survey of India, Government of India, 1975, p. 55.
123. Ajayagaḍh Rock Inscription of the Time of Vīravarman, vs 1317, *CII*, vol. VII, pt. 3, pp. 498–502.
124. Bhārat Kalā Bhavan Plate Inscription of Madanavarman, vs 1192, *CII*, vol. VII, pt. 3, pp. 399–405.
125. Khajurāhō Jaina Temple Inscription of the Time of Dhaṅgadeva, vs 1011, *CII*, vol. VII, pt. 3, pp. 347–9.
126. Fragmentary Jhansi Stone Inscription of Kanhapa, R.K. Dikshit, *The Candellas of Jejākabhukti*, p. 186.
127. Deogaḍh Rock Inscription of the Time of Kīrttivarman, vs 1154, *CII*, vol. VII, pt. 3, pp. 371–3.
128. Kālañjar Rock Inscription of the Time of Madanavarman, vs 1192, *CII*, vol. VII, pt. 3, pp. 405–6.
129. Horniman Museum Image Inscription of the Time of Madanavarman, vs 1208, *CII*, vol. VII, pt. 3, pp. 409–10.
130. Copperplate Grant of the Mahārāṇaka Kumārapāladēva. The vs 1297, *The Indian Antiquary*, vol. XVII, pp. 230–34; hereafter *IA*.
131. Kālañjar Pillar Inscription of the Time of Madanavarman, vs 1186, *CII*, vol. VII. pt. 3, pp. 390–1.
132. Khajurāhō Stone Inscription of Dhaṅgadēva of the Year 1059; Renewed by Jayavarmandēva in the Year 1173, *CII*, vol. VII, pt. 3, pp. 381–90.
133. Pachar Plate of Paramardideva, vs 1233, *EI*, vol. X, ed. Sten Konow and V. Venkayya, 1909–10; repr. 1959, pp. 44–9.
134. Kālañjar Rock Inscription of the Time of Madanavarman, vs 1192, *CII*, vol. VII, pt. 3, pp. 405–6.
135. Ajayagaḍh Stone Inscription of the Time of Madanavarman, vs 1208, *CII*, vol. VII, pt. 3, pp. 406–8.
136. Ajayagaḍh Stone Inscription of the Time of Paramardidēva, vs 1227, *CII*, vol. VII, pt. 3, pp. 436–8.
137. Sullerey, 'Kundeshwar Copper Plate of Chandella Queen Satyabhāmā, year 1060', pp. 105–7.

138. Three Chandella Copper-Plate Grants, *IA*, vol. XVI, 1886, pp. 202–7.
139. Ajayagarh Rock Inscription of Chandella Kirttivarman, *EI*, vol. XXX, ed. N. Lakshminarayan Rao and D.C. Sircar, pp. 87–90.
140. Garrā Copperplate Inscriptions of Trailōkyavarman, VS 1261, *CII*, vol. VII, pt. 3, pp. 483–7.
141. Dahi Copperplate Inscription of Vīravarman, VS 1337, R.K. Dikshit, *The Candellas of Jejākabhukti*, pp. 208–9.
142. Bhilsa Stone Inscription of Vācaspati, R.K. Dikshit, *The Candellas of Jejākabhukti*, p. 187.
143. Ajayagaḍh Stone Inscription of the Time of Paramardidēva, VS 1227, *CII*, vol. VII, pt. 3, pp. 436–8.
144. Ahār Statue Inscription of the Time of Paramardidēva, VS 1237, *CII*, vol. VII, pt. 3, pp. 455–8.
145. Ajayagaḍh Stone Inscription of the Time of Paramardin, VS 1243, *CII*, vol. VII, pt. 3, pp. 468–9.
146. Dhurētī Copperplate inscription of the time of Trailōkyamalla (Kalacuri), Year 963, *CII*, vol. VII, pt. 3, pp. 490–5.
147. Ajayagaḍh Stone Inscription of the Time of Vīravarman, VS 1325, *CII*, vol. VII, pt. 3, p. 503.
148. *Matsya Purāṇa*, 67.22-23, Pushpendra, *Matsya Mahāpurāṇa*, New Delhi: Mehrchand Lachhmandas, 1984.

REFERENCES

Archaeological Survey of India, *Corpus Inscriptionum Indicarum,* various issues, New Delhi: Archaeological Survey of India, Government of India.

———, *Epigraphia Indica,* various issues, New Delhi: Archaeological Survey of India, Government of India.

———, *Indian Archaeology. A Review*, *1971–72*, ed. M.N. Deshpande, New Delhi: Archaeological Survey of India, Government of India, 1975.

Asopa, J.N., *The Origin of the Rajputs*, Delhi: Bharatiya Publishing House, 1976.

Bakker, Hans T., *The Vākāṭakas: An Essay in Hindu Iconology*, Groningen: Egbert Forsten 1997.

Bakker, Hans and Harunaga Issacson, 'Ramtek Inscriptions II: The Vākāṭaka Inscription in the Kevala-Narasimha Temple', *Bulletin of the School of Oriental and African Studies*, vol. LVI, no. 1, 1993, pp. 46–74.

Chattopadhyaya, B.D., *The Making of Early Medieval India*, 2nd edn., Delhi: Oxford University Press, 1998.

Dikshit, R.K., *The Candellas of Jejākabhukti*, New Delhi: Abhinav Publications, 1977.

Findly, Ellison Banks, *Dāna: Giving and Getting in Pali Buddhism*, New Delhi: Motilal Banarsidass, 2003.

Heitzman, James, *Gifts of Power: Lordship in an Early Indian State*, Delhi: Oxford University Press, 1997.

Kane, P.V., *History of Dharmaśāstras*, vol. 2, pt. II, Poona: Bhandarkar Oriental Research Institute, 1974.

Kulke, Hermann, *State in India, 1000–1700 AD*, Delhi: Oxford University Press, 1995.

Mauss, Marcel, *The Gift: The Form and Reason for Exchange in Archaic Societies*, tr. W.D. Hallis, London: Routledge (first published in 1950, translated in 1954) 1990.

Michaels, Axel, 'Gift and Return Gift, Greetings and Return Greetings from India. On a Consequential Footnote of Marcel Mauss', tr. Philip Pierce, *Numen*, vol. XLIV, no. 3, 1997, pp. 242–69.

Mirashi, V.V., Inscriptions of the Kalachuri-Chedi Era, vol. IV, parts 1 and 2, Ootacamund: Archaeological Survey of India, 1955.

———, *Inscriptions of the Vākāṭakas, Corpus Inscriptionum Indicarum*, vol. V, Ootacamund: Archaeological Survey of India, 1963.

Nath, Vijay, *Dāna: Gift System in Ancient India: A Socio-Economic Perspective*, Delhi: Munshiram Manoharlal, 1987.

———, 'Ritual Symbolism and Status-Conferring Role of Dāna', *Proceedings of the Indian History Congress,* 50th Session, Goa, 1989–90.

———, 'Mahādāna: The Dynamics of Gift-Economy and the Feudal Milieu' in *The Feudal Order: State, Society and Ideology in Early Medieval India,* ed. D.N. Jha, Delhi: Manohar, 2000.

Pargiter, F.E., *The Purāṇa Text of the Dynasties of the Kali Age*, 1913; repr. Delhi: Deep Publications, Delhi, 1975.

Pushpendra, *Matsya Mahāpurāṇa*, New Delhi: Mehrchand Lachhmandas, 1984.

Shah, K.K., *Ancient Bundelkhand: Religious History in Socio-Economic Perspective*, Delhi: Gian Publishers, 1988.

———,'Legal Rights of Women to the Landed Wealth, A Case Study of Candella Queens', in *Women in Indian History*, ed. Kiran Pawar, New Delhi: Vision and Venture, 1996.

Sharma, R.K., *Kalacuris and their Times*, Delhi: Sundeep Prakashan, 1980.

Shastri, A.M., 'The Vākāṭakas: Original Home and Some Other Problems', in *The Age of the Vākāṭakas*, ed. A.M. Shastri, New Delhi: Harman Publishing House, 1992.

———, *Vākāṭakas: Source and History*, New Delhi: Aryan Books International, 1997.

Shrimali, K.M., *Agrarian Structures in Central India and Northern Deccan: A Study in Vākāṭaka Inscriptions*, Delhi: Munshiram Manoharlal, 1987.

Sircar, D.C., *Indian Epigraphical Glossary*, Delhi: Motilal Banarsidass, 1966.

Sullerey, S.K., 'Kundeshwar Copper Plate of Chandella Queen Satyabhāmā of the Year 1060', in *Kṛṣṇa Smṛti: Studies in Indian Art and Archaeology* (Prof. K.D. Bajpai Commemoration Volume), ed. R.K. Sharma and R.C. Agrawal, New Delhi: Aryan Books International, 1995.

Talbot, Cynthia, 'Temples, Donors and Gifts: Patterns of Patronage in Thirteenth Century South India', *Journal of Asian Studies*, vol. L, no. 2, 1991, pp. 308–40.

———, 'Rudrama-dēvī, the Female King, Gender and Political Authority in Medieval India', in *Syllables of the Sky*, ed. David Shulman, Delhi: Oxford University Press, 1995.

———, *Pre-colonial India in Practice: Society, Region and Identity in Medieval Andhra*, New York: Oxford University Press, 2001.

Thapar, Romila, *Cultural Pasts: Essays in Early Indian History*, New Delhi: Oxford University Press, 2000.

The Indian Antiquary: A Journal of Oriental Research, Delhi: Swati Publications (various issues).

Trivedi, H.V., 'Inscriptions of the Paramaras, Chandellas, Kachchapaghatas and Two Minor Dynasties', *Corpus Inscriptionum Indicarum*, vol. VII, pt. 3, New Delhi: Archaeological Survey of India, 1991.

Upreti, Kalpana, 'Institutional and Ideological Usage of Dāna in the *Divyāvadāna*', *Proceedings of the Indian History Congress*, 50th Session, Goa, 1989–90.

PART TWO

Norms and Narratives

3

Ensuring the Arrival of Sons: Birth *Saṃskāras* in the Gṛhyasūtras

Shwetanshu Bhushan

'IS IT A BOY OR A GIRL?'

Posed at the very first moment of life, this question embeds, expresses and enforces the common normative disposition towards the 'path of life'. It signals a discursive order in terms of which gender is established at the moment of birth and continues to exert its influence, definitive of nearly every human experience.

A certain degree of scepticism and uncertainty regarding life has perhaps always been a part of human societies. It is possible that some of these ideas found reflection in traditions regarding rites of passage, referred to as *saṃskāras* in ancient Sanskrit literature.

We all experience the key life events (turning points in our life) and, not surprisingly, in almost all cultures, the entry of a new member of society is celebrated with rites; this includes the transition from being single to married. From this perspective, the life of an individual in any society is a series of passages from one phase to another and for every one of these transitions there are rituals and ceremonies. The ostensible purpose of these rituals is to enable the individual to fortify him or her at the moments of transition that precede the passage into a new period of life or from one defined position to another.

The word *saṃskāra* is derived from the Sanskrit root *saṃskṛghan*. Though the term *saṃskāra* hardly ever occurs in Vedic literature, the root '*kṛ*' with '*sam*' and the passive participle '*saṃskṛta*' occur often enough.[1] *Saṃskāras* mean purificatory rites and ceremonies for sanctifying the body, mind and intellect of an individual so that he (and occasionally she) may become a full-fledged member of the community.[2] Literally meaning 'making a person perfect fit for a certain purpose',[3] the *saṃskāras* are meant to consecrate an individual and enable him to overcome the risks of a new stage of life, such as impregnation, birth, naming, initiation and investiture with the sacred thread, the return home of the youth ('Veda student') after the completion of his education, marriage, death.[4] So, covering all the important phases from conception until death and beyond, they make the individual gradually approach the state of the 'twice born', reach it and continue in it.[5]

At another level, *saṃskāras* were meant to elucidate social relations through their very performance. They constituted an expression of social relations through the language of rituals, which were meant to demonstrate the bonds between the larger society or community and the individual by indirectly focusing on values and reinforcing forms of classification. They attempted to accomplish their social purpose through/by different modes of communication of certain values. As is evident, rites of passage were not just about the changes in individual status but also about the dynamics of relations amongst members of society, as well as between past and present generations.

P.V. Kane, in his *History of Dharmaśāstras*, opines that in most of the digests the principal *saṃskāras* are said to be sixteen, viz., *garbhādhāna*, *puṃsavana*, *sīmantonnayana*, *viṣṇubali*, *jātakarma*, *nāmakaraṇa*, *niṣkramaṇa*, *annaprāśana*, *caula*, *upanayana*, *vedavrata* (four), *samāvartana*, and *vivāha*. He does not include the death rites in his list.

However, J. Holm and J. Bowker, in their work *Rites of Passage*,[6] present a somewhat different list of sixteen *saṃskāras*: *garbhādhāna*, *puṃsavana*, *sīmantonnayana*, *jātakarma*, *nāmakaraṇa*, *niṣkramaṇa*, *annaprāśana*, *cūḍākaraṇa*, *karṇavedha*, *vidyārambha*, *upanayana*, *vedārambha*, *keśānta*, *samāvartana*, *vivāha* and finally, *antyeṣṭi*.

While these lists and how they were standardized are indeed worthwhile subjects of investigation, our objective, at present, is to focus primarily on rituals associated with birth. In a sense, these are particularly important as they recognize the significance of creating, accepting, and defining new members of society. What we will demonstrate is how birth ceremonies represent the desire for a male child. In fact, this predilection for male progeny is evident in almost every *saṃskāra*.

What is noteworthy is that as far as the Gṛhyasūtras are concerned, women were most visible during pregnancy and childbirth, during which they were expected to undergo a series of rites. However, they were simultaneously present and absent in these rituals. In other words, while they were required to be physically present, they were viewed as being somewhat subordinate in terms of their status and roles, as instrumental in the procreative process. In this context, the insistence on ritual activities to produce 'good' offspring acquires significance.

A number of existing works on rituals, sacrifices, and literary traditions helped us in our analysis. One of the most significant scholars in our area of study is Arnold Van Gennep, whose crucial work *The Rites of Passage* is the English translation of his original French work *Les rites de Passage*.[7] Van Gennep belonged to a group of anthropologists, including the French scholars Emile Durkheim and Marcel Mauss, whose work on ritual and beliefs was of fundamental importance for the sociology and anthropology of religion. In the idea of *rites of passage* he believed he had discovered a key that would help unlock human behaviour, at least in the area of changing status in social life. He classified these rites into three categories: rites of separation, transition rites, and rites of incorporation. Rites of separation are prominent in funerals, and transition rites play an important part in pregnancy, betrothal and initiation, etc. Distinguishing the three phases and their subcategories, Van Gennep emphasized that all these ceremonies have their individual purposes. The author's views on transition are clear from his statement that man's life comes to be made up of a succession of stages with similar ends and beginnings: birth, social puberty, marriage, fatherhood, advancement to a higher class, occupational specialization and death; for every one of these events there are ceremonies whose essential purpose is to enable the individual to pass from one defined position to another which is equally well defined. He distinguishes between the secular and the religious worlds—between the profane and the sacred. In fact, this dichotomy of the sacred and the profane is the central concept for understanding Van Gennep's transitional stage in which an individual finds him/herself from time to time. He was insistent that ceremonies needed to be examined in their entirety and in the social setting in which they were found.

It is within this context that I examine the abundant material available in the four Gṛhyasūtras, namely, *Āśvalāyana*, *Āpastamba*, *Pāraskara*, and *Śāṅkhāyana*, focusing on the *saṃskāras* preceding the *upanayana*. This will highlight the strategies for ensuring the birth of sons through prenatal and natal rites as prescribed in the Gṛhyasūtras.

The references to the original texts have been, as far as possible, confined to the *Śāṅkhāyana*, *Āśvalāyana*, *Pāraskara*, and *Āpastamba Gṛhyasūtras* for the convenience of the general reader, to whom they are easily available in translated form, in vol. 29 of the *Sacred Books of the East*.[8]

Our understanding of this context has been greatly enhanced by the work of Jaya Tyagi on the Gṛhyasūtras.[9] Her book *Engendering the Early*

Household: *Brahmanical Precepts in the Early Gṛhyasūtras, Middle of the First millennium B.C.E.* focuses on the rites and rituals of the Gṛhyasūtras. She has identified how the Brahmanical thought on the *gṛha*, the household, evolved and how roles were crafted for men and women in the domestic realm. The compilation of the Gṛhyasūtras was not an isolated event and was part of a greater movement for consolidating Brahmanical ideological thought with practices and for legitimizing these with Vedic lore.

The Gṛhyasūtras deal with household rites, prescribe rituals in detail and lay down mantras and formulae to be recited at different stages of a particular *saṃskāra*. The Gṛhyasūtras were compiled over a period of time and the similarities in their style show that the earlier texts evolved a format that was subsequently followed. They rely heavily on the Vedas for legitimacy to perpetuate household rituals and sacrifices. By understanding the ideological and theological context of these texts, one can interpret the rituals and their symbolism and how they played a pivotal role in the social dynamics in creating and sustaining the gender and varṇa hierarchy.

Moving from the content of these texts to the question of authorship, it is one that has proved difficult to address. For instance, with regard to the authorship of the different sūtras, in almost all cases it is difficult to pinpoint it beyond doubt.[10] Further, there are individual peculiarities. The *Āpastamba Gṛhyasūtra* as compared with the *Āśvalāyana Gṛhyasūtra* is extremely brief and leaves out many rules that are given in other Gṛhya works. For example, in discussing the choice of a girl considered suitable for marriage, the *Āpastamba Gṛhyasūtra* mentions only a single rule.[11] Also, the *Āpastamba Gṛhyasūtra* is silent about the forms of marriage, about holidays, about the duties of *brahmacārins* and such other subjects, which are generally discussed in the other Gṛhyasūtras.

The dates of individual Gṛhyasūtras are difficult to determine and the only way to ascribe dates to the texts is by comparing them with each other, as one text can be relatively older than the other. P.V. Kane in his *History of Dharmaśāstras* (vol. I) dated the *Āśvalāyana Gṛhyasūtra* to 800–400 BC and the *Pāraskara Gṛhyasūtra* to 600–300 BC. The present work is based on this chronological framework. It is often said that the Gṛhyasūtras were composed a little later than the Śrautasūtras and a little earlier than the Dharmasūtras and therefore, the period of the composition of the Gṛhya and Dharma works no doubt largely overlapped.[12] Some authors wisely confine themselves to statements such as 'the general period of the sutras extends from the sixth and seventh century B.C. to about the second century B.C'.[13]

Stylistic criteria are also useful in establishing the relative chronological position of the texts. Generally, *sūtras* containing a greater proportion of prose are considered to be earlier than those which contain verse. Likewise it has been suggested that the *Āśvalāyana Gṛhyasūtra* must be earlier than the *Śāṅkhāyana Gṛhyasūtra*, which was followed by the *Pāraskara Gṛhyasūtra*.

Scholars such as Ram Gopal have compared the texts and point out that the *Pāraskara Gṛhyasūtra* contains more prescriptions than the *Śāṅkhāyana Gṛhyasūtra.* Ram Gopal has tried to classify the *sūtra* literature into three groups. According to this classification, the *Āśvalāyana Gṛhyasūtra* forms the earliest stratum of *sūtra* literature and the *Śāṅkhāyana Gṛhyasūtra*, *Pāraskara Gṛhyasūtra*, and *Āpastamba Gṛhyasūtra* constitute the second stratum.

Ram Gopal also feels that it is understandable that the emphasis on caste distinctions became more pronounced in later works.[14] Similarly, a comparison of the *Śāṅkhāyana Gṛhyasūtra* and *Pāraskara Gṛhyasūtra* would demonstrate that the short *sūtras* of the *Śāṅkhāyana Gṛhyasūtra* have been welded into larger ones in the *Pāraskara Gṛhyasūtra.* For instance, *sūtras* 8, 21–23, 26, 31, 33, 37 and 38 of the *Śāṅkhāyana Gṛhyasūtra*[15] have been incorporated in the *Pāraskara Gṛhyasūtra*[16] in a single *sūtra* by means of a long compound of six words. Therefore, the balance of probability is that the *Śāṅkhāyana Gṛhyasūtra* was composed slightly earlier than the *Pāraskara Gṛhyasūtra.*

The ideologies and the strategies behind the compilation of normative texts like the Gṛhyasūtras solely devoted to the household need to be analysed and emphasized. It is relevant to see how the *gṛha* came to be regarded as a sacred space for the conduct of rituals. By locating rituals in the household, the Gṛhyasūtras not only bring the household into focus, but also extend the scope of Vedic rituals to individual households. The need to trace the social significance of birth rituals led me to explore the content of these texts. Further, it is evident that there is an interplay among different constructs like varṇa, class and gender, and that there is an overemphasis on the varṇa system of the brāhmaṇas.

The rituals mentioned in the Gṛhyasūtras were commonly practised and conducted, and they reflect attempts to project various aspects of society—the way power was structured, who controlled and had access to resources, and the manner in which ideological constructs were disseminated—through rituals. Romila Thapar suggests that state formations are determined by many factors and one cannot but underline the significance of the rituals as they provide the rationale for ideological control, for the exercise of power, for the management of resources, and for social dynamics.[17]

As the householder counterposes the renouncer, the *gṛhastha* was expected to build his life around the rearing of a family, observing the social norms. The Gṛhyasūtras, through the household rites, attempted to create an 'ideal' construct of the household, which then allowed for the setting of norms for the social, material and behavioural activities of the household, and also for activities related to reproduction, socialization, building social linkages and the transmission of information and traditions within, and across generations.[18]

The *saṃskāras* preceding *upanayana*, as laid down in the Gṛhyasūtras, are of two categories: (1) the prenatal *saṃskāras*, which consist mainly of the *garbhādhāna* (conception of a child), *puṃsavana* (quickening of the male child) and *sīmantonnayana* (parting of the hair of women); and (2) The postnatal *saṃskāras* or the *saṃskāras* of childhood which include the *jātakarma* (birth ceremonies), *nāmakaraṇa* (naming ceremony), *niṣkramaṇa* (first outing of a child), *annaprāśana* (first feeding of a child), and *cūḍākaraṇa* or *caula* (tonsure or shaving of head). The last ritual occasionally formed a component of other rituals as well.

This chapter examines prenatal and postnatal ceremonies. It is divided into two sections. Section I includes the prenatal rituals where the 'would be' mother is relatively visible in the performance of the *saṃskāras*. Section II discusses postnatal ceremonies.

I

The rite through which a man placed his seed in a woman was called the *garbhādhāna*. The Gṛhyasūtras are unanimous on the point that the *garbhādhāna* was to be performed when the wife was physically prepared to conceive. The proper time for conception was thought to be from the fourth to sixteenth night after the monthly course of the wife.[19] Nights were prescribed for conception, while sexual intercourse during the day was prohibited.[20] What is noteworthy is that the rituals for producing a male child were expected to begin from the first conception. The mantra that was to be uttered was:

> May a male embryo enter thy womb, as an arrow the quiver; may a man be born here, a son after ten months. Give birth to a male child; may after him (another) male be born; In the male verily, in the man dwells the sperm; he shall pour it forth into the woman: thus has said Dhātar, thus Prajāpati has said. Prajāpati has created him, Savitar has shaped him. Imparting birth of females to other (women) may he put here a man. From the auspicious sperms which the men produce for us, produce thou a son; be a well breeding cow. Roar, be strong, put into her an embryo, achieve it; a male, thou male, put into her; to generation we call thee. Open thy womb; take in the man's sperm, may a male child be born, the most excellent of his kin.[21]

The mantras uttered in this *saṃskāra* are essentially prayers offered to help the bride conceive a good son. The deities mentioned in this context are Agni, Vāyu, Sūrya, Prajāpati, and Savitṛ. Agni or fire was the chief deity as all sacrifices meant to reach various deities were offered into the fire. Apte opines that prayers were used to avert misfortune in conjugal life and to ensure prosperity and the birth of hero sons.[22] Kane suggests that all *saṃskāras* other than the *garbhādhāna* could be performed by any agnate in the absence of the husband.[23] In other words, this indicates that male kinsmen of the husband were expected to play a crucial role in the ritual.

The *garbhādhāna* ceremony is not described as a separate *saṃskāra* in all the Gṛhyasūtras; perhaps originally it was considered as part of the marriage ritual. Further, there are variations in the way in which the rite is described. For instance, the *Śāṅkhāyana Gṛhyasūtra* mentions *garbhārakṣaṇa*, which means the ceremony for the protection of the embryo. According to the *Śāṅkhāyana Gṛhyasūtra*,[24] this ceremony was to be performed in the fourth month of pregnancy, after the performance of the *puṃsavana* in the third month. Thus, it seems that according to the tradition of Śāṅkhāyana, the *garbhārakṣaṇa* was slightly distinct from the *garbhādhāna*.

Further, the *Śāṅkhāyana Gṛhyasūtra*, *Pāraskara Gṛhyasūtra* and *Āpastamba Gṛhyasūtra*[25] mention another rite called the *caturthikarma* or *caturthihoma.* N.N. Bhattacharyya suggests that the *caturthikarma* is a variation of a tribal rite of ceremonial defloration, which was to be performed just after the first menstruation of women. He is of the view that in the Brahmanical texts, this is a part of the marriage rituals to be performed on the fourth day after marriage and may be equated with the rite of *garbhādhāna*. Its connection with the first menstruation is also suggested by its other name, *ṛtusaṅgamana.*[26] Since the increasing influence of patriarchy required the absolute chastity of women, the law books entrusted the function of ritual defloration to the husband. Bhattacharyya gives the examples of tribal people who observe a rite of seclusion when girls menstruate for the first time. He suggests that the lawmakers of the Brahmanical texts had to compromise with various local customs. Both the *Śāṅkhāyana Gṛhyasūtra* and *Pāraskara Gṛhyasūtra* that describe the rite of *caturthikarma* are placed in the second stratum of Ram Gopal's three strata. This would suggest that the incorporation of this rite within the textual tradition was a somewhat later development.

Unlike the other Gṛhyasūtras, the *Āśvalāyana Gṛhyasūtra*[27] refers to *anavalobhana* besides *garbhālambhana*. It distinguishes between the two, stating that *garbhālambhana* meant ceremonies for securing the conception of a child and *anavalobhana* meant rituals for preventing disturbances that could endanger the embryo. For a similar purpose, the *Śāṅkhāyana Gṛhyasūtra* proposes the ceremony of *garbhārakṣaṇa*[28] in the fourth month of pregnancy. It was a sacrifice consisting of six oblations. Kane[29] opines that the *garbhārakṣaṇa* of the *Śāṅkhāyana Gṛhyasūtra* and the *anavalobhana* of the *Āśvalāyana Gṛhyasūtra* are the same. We are in the dark regarding the character of these ceremonies because the *Āśvalāyana Gṛhyasūtra* does not describe these rituals. Nevertheless, one issue is clear: providing for as many as three ceremonies reveals the importance attributed to regulating conception and pregnancy. Perhaps variations in the names of the *saṃskāras* signify that the *sūtrakāras* were trying to accommodate various local practices and customs.

After the *garbhādhāna* comes the *puṃsavana*, the ceremony to secure the birth of a male child. This second *saṃskāra* in a row reveals that the desire for male progeny was so strong that an entire rite to this effect was introduced. The *Āśvalāyana Gṛhyasūtra* describes the rite in detail. It states:

> he should in the third month of her pregnancy, under the constellation of *Tishya* give to eat the wife, after she has fasted, in the curds of a cow which has a calf of the same colour (as the cow), two beans and one grain of barley for each handful of curds. On his asking, what dost thou drink? The wife should thrice reply, 'Generation of a male child! Generation of a male child!'

In addition, during the ritual, a few drops of the juice of the banyan stem were to be put into the right nostril of the pregnant woman to inhale, with a prayer for the birth of a son.[30]

It is apparent that this rite had several symbolic elements. Perhaps the *nyagrodha* or banyan stem juice had some medicinal qualities and properties of relieving trouble during pregnancy. Beans are symbolic of progeny and fertility. In Hindu society, barrenness is considered to be the worst evil, one that has to be counteracted by all possible means. Therefore, the remedy (which included the use of different forms of medicinal herbs or *oṣadhi* and fruits with their tonic properties) evokes and ensures the hope of offspring, especially birth of sons. The practitioners chose as cures for barrenness either plants belonging to the vitaliser (*jīvanīyagaṇa*) group or those belonging to the group of trees with milky sap (*kṣirivṛkṣa*). Most of these plants have to be mixed with cow's milk before they are swallowed.

The mention of curd or any milk product evokes the idea of fecundity. The idea relates to the sacred cow and its five products (milk, ghee, butter, urine, and dung). According to the Brahmanical perspective, these five products represent both the cosmic power of life and the clouds of the monsoon whose heavy rains provide fertility to the earth. This is why clouds are often compared to cows in Sanskrit poetry.

Helene Stork[31] suggests that barrenness was perceived as a curse and the effort was to overcome it in any way possible. She has given the following symbolic equation:

> Sterility (barrenness) = aridity (barren ground) = dryness.
> Fecundity (fruitfulness) = fertility = dampness.[32]

Hence the main aim was to pray to the deities for a great family of sons. In this context, Agni and Prajāpati were to be invoked in the rite as described in the Gṛhyasūtras.[33]

However, the *puṃsavana* was not designed to simply ward off barrenness; the desire for the male child was so strong that the main aim of the *puṃsavana* was to ask for sons, i.e. the generation of males.

According to the Gṛhyasūtras, the timing of the performance of the *puṃsavana* rite could vary. They maintain that it ought to be performed before the foetus began to move or throb in the womb. The *Pāraskara Gṛhyasūtra* states that it was to be performed when the moon was in conjunction with a male *nakṣatra.*[34] The Gṛhyasūtras (*Pāraskara Gṛhyasūtra*, *Āśvalāyana Gṛhyasūtra* and *Śāṅkhāyana Gṛhyasūtra*) prescribe that the rite was to be performed in the second or third month of pregnancy[35] (that is before the manifestation of the sex of the foetus), in the belief that it was capable of reversing the sex of the child in case it was a girl.[36] What needs to be highlighted is that the authors of the Gṛhyasūtras and Dharmasūtras may have been drawing on the tradition that the sex of the foetus was not completely fixed before the third month after conception. There is no mention of any other kinsfolk participating in the rite of *puṃsavana*. The absence of these groups suggests that the husband alone was expected to play the central role in the prenatal *saṃskāras* (as is also evident in the *sīmantonnayana*).

According to the Gṛhyasūtras, the third prenatal *saṃskāra* to be performed by the husband alone (with the wife as a necessary participant) was the *sīmantonnayana*. This word literally means parting of the hair (of a woman) in an upward direction. The *Āśvalāyana Gṛhyasūtra* describes it as follows:

> In the fourth month of pregnancy the *sīmantonnayana* (or parting of the hair, is performed). In the fortnight of the waxing moon, when the moon stands in conjunction with a Naksatra (that has a name) of masculine gender, then the husband establishes a fire, and having spread to the west of it a bull's hide with the neck to the east, with the hair outside, (he makes oblations) while (his wife) is sitting on that (hide) and takes hold of him, with the two verses 'May Dhātri give to his worshipper' with the two verses,
>
> 'I invoke Rākā, Negamesha, and Prajāpati, no other than thou'. He then parts her hair upwards (i.e. beginning from the front) three times with a bunch containing an even number of unripe fruits, and with a porcupine's quill that has three white spots and with three bunches of *kuśa* grass, with (the words), 'Bhur, Bhuvah, svar, om!' or four times. He then gives orders to two lute players, 'sing king Soma'. They sing, 'May Soma our king bless the human race'. They then name the river near which they dwell'.[37]

As we can see, among the prenatal *saṃskāras*, the *sīmantonnayana* is described at length in the Gṛhyasūtras. The ritual included prayers, as well as propitiation of the gods. The ambit of action of the sacrifice is especially noteworthy, for it was expected to produce a double effect, one on the object for which it was offered (here the unborn child) and upon which it was desired to act, the other on the moral person (here the husband who was expected to initiate the act) who desired and instigated that effect.[38]

Another interesting fact is that the *sūtrakāras* are divided in their opinion whether the *sīmantonnayana* was to be performed in every pregnancy or only in the first conception. The difference of opinion suggests that there may have been differences in the kinship pattern. For instance, if this *saṃskāra* was to be performed only in the first conception, it would imply that the eldest son was regarded as especially privileged. If performed in all conceptions, it would suggest a greater degree of equality amongst siblings. The *Āpastamba Gṛhyasūtra*[39] and *Pāraskara Gṛhyasūtra*[40] expressly state that this *saṃskāra* was to be performed only once, at the first conception.

The performance of the *sīmantonnayana* is described in different ways in each of the Gṛhyasūtras. On this point there is much difference of opinion in the texts, but there seems to have been a preference for performing it during the fourth month or later. For instance, the *Āśvalāyana Gṛhyasūtra* states that this *saṃskāra* was to be performed in the fourth month of pregnancy; the *Pāraskara Gṛhyasūtra* assigns it to the sixth or eighth month; and the *Śāṅkhāyana Gṛhyasūtra* states that it should be performed during the seventh month.[41] It is likely that these variations were associated with different regions and represent attempts to accommodate varied practices.

The variation in the timing of the parting of the woman's hair also suggests that there were no strict regulations. It is remarkable that the *Āśvalāyana Gṛhyasūtra* alone requires that the woman should be seated on a bull's hide, which shows that this was not regarded as impure as it would be at present within dominant strands of the Brahmanical tradition. The bull may have been regarded as the symbol of virility and masculinity and the bull's hide symbolizes fertility.[42] The *Pāraskara Gṛhyasūtra* suggests an alternative and recommends a soft chair or seat.[43] Clearly, if the latter was used, much of the symbolism associated with the alternative tradition would have been lost.

Almost all the Gṛhyasūtras agree that in parting the hair the husband was to use a bunch of unripe fruit (the *Pāraskara Gṛhyasūtra* and *Śāṅkhāyana Gṛhyasūtra* specify an *udumbara* fruit) and a porcupine quill with three bunches of *kuśa* grass.

Regarding the specific materials used (such as the porcupine quill, *udumbara* leaves, etc.) during the performance of the earlier mentioned *saṃskāra*, pregnant women were required to take utmost care to ensure their use, as it was believed that a pregnant woman was vulnerable to attack by evil spirits and therefore, some rites had to be performed to ward off these evil forces. In this regard, Kane says that the porcupine quill with three white spots resembles the three auspicious things associated with the gods, viz., the three meters, the three worlds, etc.[44] Perhaps it can also be suggested that the sharpness of the quill was expected to endow the child with intellect of similar qualities. In addition, the porcupine quill may have symbolized a bridge between the domestic and the wild, and could have signified an assertion of control over both domains.

Here too we see that masculinity in the tools was expected as the *Śāṅkhāyana Gṛhyasūtra*[45] emphasizes that 'the implements used and the Nakshatra should be of male gender'.

It is necessary to focus on the lute players or musicians and the mantras sung by them. There is evidence of a debate over whose praise was to be sung during the *sīmantonnayana*. The *Śāṅkhāyana Gṛhyasūtra* and *Pāraskara Gṛhyasūtra* state that the ballad sung must be in praise of the ruling king or anyone else who is valiant. The *Āśvalāyana Gṛhyasūtra*[46] prescribes a *gāthā* in honour of King Soma (the plant), perhaps because Soma was considered to be the symbol of fertility. In addition, Soma was revered as the king of the brāhmaṇas. Therefore, praising Soma instead of the human king may have been part of a process of brahmanizing the ritual.

As far as the priest and the brāhmaṇas were concerned, the *Āśvalāyana Gṛhyasūtra* and the *Śāṅkhāyana Gṛhyasūtra* expressly state that a bull is the fee for the officiating priest in this *saṃskāra.*[47] The *Āpastamba Gṛhyasūtra* and *Pāraskara Gṛhyasūtra* state that brāhmaṇas were to be fed in this rite.[48] It appears that although the participation of priests was marginal in these rites as laid down in the *sūtras*, their presence evidently provided legitimacy to the ritual. The content of the mantras nominally related to one single ritual act and their links with the ceremony are implicit or deducible from the terminology used.

The husband and wife were expected to seek the help of various deities to secure the birth of a child, ideally a son. The deity mainly invoked in the above *saṃskāra* is Rākā who is the presiding deity of the full moon. It seems that the sacrificer invoked Rākā so that the unborn child should be beautiful like the full moon. The full moon is also symbolic of completion. Indeed the *Āśvalāyana Gṛhyasūtra*[49] even says that the birth of a son brings purification to twelve descendants as well as twelve ancestors on both the husband's and wife's sides. Thus, here in the pre-birth *saṃskāras* we come across various references where the husband and wife approach the

Ṛgvedic and later Vedic deities with a definite purpose to produce what was considered to be the best possible progeny.

Thus, the pregnancy ceremonies included a great many rites, whose main purpose was to facilitate the delivery of a son and to protect mother and child against evil forces, which were regarded as both impersonal and personified. Obviously, the prenatal *saṃskāras* could not have been performed without the wife, yet she was assigned a subsidiary and inferior role during these ceremonies. It was the husband who was expected to offer the sacrifice and oblations and play a pivotal role in the ritual. Interestingly, the wife was to observe a fast during the whole ceremony though she was not allowed to perform the sacrifice independently. It can be highlighted that the dialogue hymns in the various rituals involve the construction of gender roles. The female acts in the service of her husband's ritual goals and she is not in the 'participatory' role.

The ceremonies of pregnancy and childbirth together generally constitute a whole. Often the first rites performed separate the pregnant woman from society, from her family group. They are followed by rites pertaining to pregnancy, marking a transitional period. Finally, come the rites of childbirth intended to reintegrate the woman into the group to which she previously belonged or to establish her new position in society as a mother, especially if she has given birth to a son.[50] What is evident is that in the Brahmanical version of these rituals the woman was regarded as at once central and subordinate.

II

Among the postnatal *saṃskāras*, the foremost was *jātakarma*, the ceremony performed when the child was born. P.V. Kane opines that this must have been a rite of hoary antiquity.[51] There is a great divergence in the Gṛhyasūtras on the different details that make up the *jātakarma*. Some texts such as the *Pāraskara Gṛhyasūtra*[52] lay down almost all the details, while other Gṛhyasūtras omit some of them. The order of the components of the ritual differs according to the Veda to which each text is attached. The *Āśvalāyana Gṛhyasūtra*[53] and *Śāṅkhāyana Gṛhyasūtra*[54] both belong to the *Ṛgveda* and it is noticed that both of these Gṛhyasūtras prescribe giving a secret name to the child on the day of birth and do not prescribe a separate *nāmakaraṇa* ceremony.

Moving to the chief rites of the *jātakarma*, they are: *medhājanana* or production of intelligence; *āyuṣya* where the father murmurs some mantras near the navel or the right ear of the child to ensure a long life; *aṃśabhimarṣaṇa*, which involves touching the child on the shoulder; *pañca brāhmaṇa sthāpana*, which involves five brāhmaṇas or the father himself breathing over the child, etc.[55]

In the *medhājanana* the father was to give the child honey and ghee with his finger and an instrument of gold.[56] The formula employed is as follows:

> Bhuh I put into thee;
> Bhuvah I put into thee;
> Svāhā I put into thee;
> Bhuh bhuvah svāhā everything I put into thee.[57]

The use of '*Bhuh Bhuvah Svāhā*' signifies the identification of birth rituals with the sacrifice, as these were the standardized formulae for offering to deities. The food the child was fed was also thought to be conducive to mental growth. Ghee was supposed to strengthen memory, talent and life; honey and gold, too, were thought to be conducive to mental progress and prosperity.

During the *āyuṣya* ceremony the father was to murmur:

> Agni is long lived; through the tree he is long lived. By that long life I make thee long lived; through the herbs etc. The Brāhman is long lived through the *brāhmaṇas* etc., the gods are long lived through ambrosia (*amrita*) etc. The *ṛṣis* are long lived; through observances etc., sacrifice is long lived; through sacrificial fire etc. the ocean is long lived; through the rivers etc. The fathers are long lived; through the *svadhā* oblations (or oblations made to the Manes) and Sacrifice is long lived; through sacrificial fee it is.[58]

In other words, the father was expected to mention the principal deities (Agni, Soma), important natural forces (tree, ocean), and significant social categories (*ṛṣis*) in the mantra that was to be uttered in the newborn child's ear. Thus, the purpose was perhaps to bring all types of forces to bear on what was regarded as a critical moment of transition, the entry of the child from the biological world into the social world, in a single ritual performance through a small mantra.

In the *pañca brāhmaṇa sthāpana* ritual, the father was expected to invite five brāhmaṇas and place them in five directions (north, south, east, west, and the fifth looking upwards). When the ceremonies were over, presents were to be offered to the brāhmaṇas and gifts and alms distributed. Connecting brāhmaṇas with the ritual was probably a means of lending added weight to it. Incidentally, the *Pāraskara Gṛhyasūtra*[59] states that the father could do the above rite himself if he could not find brāhmaṇas. This would suggest that the process of the Brahmanization of the ritual was by no means complete when the text was compiled.

Thus, we see that the Brahmanical *sūtrakāras* created an exalted position for the father even in the birth ceremonies, whereas the mother was an indispensable participant in the physical process of giving birth to the child.

Another *saṃskāra*, the *nāmakaraṇa* ceremony was meant simply for 'naming a child'. Here also the Brahmanical *sūtrakāras* emphasized the birth of the male child as auspicious and regarded the girl child as inferior.

Almost all the Gṛhyasūtras contain the rule that the name should begin with a sonant and contain a semi-vowel in the middle.[60] The *Pāraskara Gṛhyasūtra* states that the names of girls should end in '*ā*' with a *taddhita* (suffix) for a girl, while boys should have *kṛt* suffix and not a *taddhita.*[61] This open demarcation between the boy and girl child reveals the inferior position assigned to daughters. The *Āśvalāyana Gṛhyasūtra* attaches different kinds of virtues to names consisting of a different number of syllables.[62]

Apart from this, these Gṛhyasūtras state that the name for males should contain two or four syllables, i.e. an even number of syllables, while the girls' names should have an uneven number of syllables:[63] 'one who is desirous of fame, his name should consist of two syllables, one who desires holy lustre, his name should contain four syllables'. It is to be noted that for boys an even number of syllables was prescribed because the Brahmanical authors wanted their sons to be meritorious and valiant. It is also obvious that such qualities were not desired for daughters. This demarcation between the ways of naming the boy and girl child reveals the gendered perspective of the *sūtrakāras.*

With reference to the varṇa order, the *Pāraskara Gṛhyasūtra* states that men belonging to different varṇas should have different titles: 'The name of a brāhmaṇa should end in śarman (for instance Viṣṇuśarman), that of a Kṣatriya in varman (viz., Lakṣmivarman), that of a vaiśya in Gupta (for e.g. Candragupta)'.[64] There is no reference to the śūdras in this context, so it is evident that there was no place for them in this scheme of things. That the idea of the varṇa order was reinforced through variations in the names assigned to men is clear from the earlier example.

The *niṣkramaṇa*, which means taking the child out of the house in the open, was generally considered a minor rite. The procedure of this *saṃskāra* involved the father taking the child out and making him look at the sun.[65] The radiant sun in this *saṃskāra* was probably symbolic of energy and vigour and, therefore, perhaps the father wanted that the infant child should start his first exposure to the world with seeing the sun so that he would be endowed with strength and life like the sun. The *Āśvalāyana Gṛhyasūtra* and *Śāṅkhāyana Gṛhyasūtra* do not mention this *saṃskāra.* The *Pāraskara Gṛhyasūtra* mentions that after the *nāmakaraṇa saṃskāra*, 'In the fourth month is the going out. He makes (the child) look at the sun, pronouncing (the verse), "That eye".'[66]

After the first outing of the child, the next major ritual was the *annaprāśana saṃskāra*, which is described at length in the *Pāraskara Gṛhyasūtra*[67] and *Śāṅkhāyana Gṛhyasūtra.*[68] All of them prescribe the sixth month from birth as the time for this *saṃskāra.* The ritual feeding with rice as the first solid food is usually performed when the infant's first tooth appears. This is believed to sanctify the process of weaning. The father was expected to prepare the food for the child and make him eat it to the accompaniment of the recitation of mantras and the offering of oblations. In the case of a girl child, the rite was to be performed without the mantra and ritual.[69] An important thing to note here is that normally cooking food would have been women's work, but in the ritual it was ideally taken over by men. The man was expected to sacrifice with the food that was cooked. Besides, after having eaten, he was to feed his son. This was to be followed by the ritual feeding of the brāhmaṇas. Thus, women were obviously marginalized in the ritual. Only one text, the *Śāṅkhāyana Gṛhyasūtra* states: 'Let the mother eat the remnant.'[70]

The *cūḍākarma* is known by various names such as *cūḍākaraṇa* or *caula* (first tonsure), that is the first cutting of the hair on the child's head. This *saṃskāra,* mentioned in every Gṛhyasūtra,[71] involved keeping the lock or tuft of hair on the head while the remaining part was shaved. The principal act in this ceremony was the cutting of the hair of the child. We get '*cauḍa*' from '*cūḍa*', meaning 'a rite the purpose of which is keeping a lock of hair' and 'ḍa' and 'la' often interchange places. Therefore, we get '*cauḍa*' or '*caula*' also as the name of the ceremony.[72]

The *Śāṅkhāyana Gṛhyasūtra* assigns different years to the three varṇas for the performance of the *cūḍākaraṇa*: 'After one year or in the third year for the brāhmaṇa, the fifth year for the kṣatriya and in the seventh for a vaiśya.'[73] All the other Gṛhyasūtras describe this *saṃskāra* in detail.

The *kuśa* grass is the most important ingredient in this ceremony, with the father being expected to point and touch the head and hair of the boy with the *kuśa* bunches while uttering: 'Herb! Protect him!'[74] The other subsidiary matters included the performance of *homa*; feeding of brāhmaṇas, receiving their benedictions and giving of *dakṣiṇā*, etc.[75]

According to the *Pāraskara Gṛhyasūtra*,[76] the *caula* could be performed in the first or third year; the *Āśvalāyana Gṛhyasūtra*[77] says it could be performed in the third year or in the year in which it was the custom of the family to perform it. The *Pāraskara Gṛhyasūtra* also refers to family usage. The *Āpastamba Gṛhyasūtra*[78] states it should be performed when the moon is in conjunction with the *punarvasu nakṣatra*. Therefore, there is divergence among the *sūtrakāras* regarding the proper time for the performance of the *cūḍakarma*. However, what is common in the description of this rite is the cutting of the hair of the child.

Among all the Gṛhyasūtras, the most exhaustive treatment of this ceremony has been provided in the *Āśvalāyana Gṛhyasūtra*. The description is as follows.

> To the north of the fire are placed four vessels, each of which is separately filled with rice, barley, beans, and sesamum seeds. The mother, with the boy on her

lap, is to be seated to the west of the fire and two vessels, one filled with the dung of the bull and other with *śami* leaves, are to be placed. To the right of the mother, the father sits holding twenty-one bunches of *kuśa* grass or the brāhmaṇa should hold them. To the west of the boy, the father pours warm water (with the words), 'With warm water, O Vāyu, come hither!' After the *homa* is performed, the principal matter (of cutting the hair) is to begin. With the words 'Axe do not harm him' he presses a copper razor (on the kuśa blades). The hair is cut with the mantra: 'With that razor with which Savitṛ, the wise, cut (the hair) of king Soma and of Varuṇa, cut now his (the boy's hair), oh brāhmaṇas, so that he may be endowed with long life and (reach) old age'.[79]

Each time the hair was cut, the father was supposed to give the cut hair with their ends turned towards the east together with the *śami* leaves to the mother, who had to put it down on the bull's dung. Once again, the principal role was assigned to the father while the mother of the child was expected to play a subordinate role.

The hair was to be cut a second time, with another mantra: 'With what Dhātri shaven (the head) of Brihaspati, Agni and Indra, for the sake of long life, with that I shave thy (head) for the sake of long life, of glory, and of welfare.'

For the third round the mantra was: 'He may after night, see the sun again and again with that I shave thy head for the sake of long life, fame and happiness.'

All the mantras were to be repeated in the fourth round. The hair was to be cut three times on the left side in an identical manner. The edge of the razor was to be wiped off with the mantra: 'When thou shavest as a shaver the hair (of the boy) with the razor that wounds and is well shaped purify his head but do not deprive him of life.'

Then the father was to order the barber: 'Without causing him any wound arrange his hair well.' There was also provision for variations in practice. This is evident from the statement: 'Let him have the hair of the boy arranged according to the custom of the family.'[80]

It is stated that the rite for the girl child was to be performed without mantras. The *Śāṅkhāyana Gṛhyasūtra* says: 'Silently the rites (are performed) for the girl.'[81] The *Āśvalāyana Gṛhyasūtra*[82] also contains the same provision. The continuous exclusion of the girl child from the performance of the rituals of *saṃskāra* would have served to reinforce the gender hierarchy that was of basic importance to the development of a patrilineal kinship structure.

The Gṛhyasūtras and Dharmasūtras are entirely silent on what was done for the child's education between the third year when *caula* was usually to be performed and the eighth year (from conception) when the *upanayana* was expected to take place (in the case of brāhmaṇas).

Shaving the head (*cūḍākaraṇa*) and piercing of the ear (*karṇavedha*)[83] are both Brahmanical rites that are prescribed in the literature pertaining to domestic rituals (Gṛhyasūtras). The priest pierces the ears of the child 'in a spot made by the gods' (*daivakarte chidre*), where the skin is very soft and illuminated by the sun's rays. Traditionally, the first words the child should hear after the ear piercing ritual are the sacred words of Vedic mantras. It is generally believed that once the child's hair has been offered as a sacrifice to god, the ear piercing ceremony will enable that child to understand divine words. Piercing a baby's ears is also commonly believed to be a useful method of protecting it from disease.

As is the case with all such rites, their objective appears to have been to sanctify and refine the body and mind of the individual from conception onwards, as it was believed that life started from the moment of conception and not simply from the moment of birth.[84] Prenatal and childhood rites were intended to protect the son, and the birth of the daughter was considered an unwelcome event. Everywhere the son was valued more than the daughter. Therefore, one can say that all the rituals were performed to protect the child, especially the son, and the *sūtrakāras* were not attentive to the wife or the mother. Only in one instance was the wife asked to wear gold ornaments,[85] if she so desired, otherwise at no other place was the opinion of the wife in particular or women in general taken into consideration.

As is obvious, the ceremonies of pregnancy and childbirth together, generally constitute a whole. These could have been used to underline and strengthen the position of the mother/wife. What is significant is that while these possibilities were inherent in the *saṃskāras* we have discussed, they were not always realized through the ritual. As we have seen, there the focus was far more on producing a son and integrating him within the patrilineage.

Overall, it has been aptly pointed out that the imagery of miscarriage in the later Vedic texts shows an increased anxiety over the parental loss of lineage, and in doing so wrests the embryo further and further away from the body of the mother. Through a series of ritual linkages the womb was no longer viewed as a part of the woman's body, and, therefore, as a kind of detached item it was subjected to control through the technology available at the time—that of the Vedic mantra.[86] The woman who hopes to become a mother goes through a series of rituals, first to promote fertility, and second to protect the child, especially the son once he is born.

To conclude, the ritual texts exhibit variations in the provisions for specific rites. However, at the same time, we can see that there was an overwhelming concern with ensuring the birth of male offspring. Special provisions were also made to recognize and socialize the boy child, while there was a marked indifference towards the girl child. Also, while the mother was regarded as significant, there was a certain ambivalence towards her; most major ritual roles were either assigned to the father, or to priests. In this context, this cluster of rites of passage associated with the prenatal and postnatal situations, if actually performed would have introduced ideas of gender difference within everyday life. Young children would have been socialized into the notion that boys and girls were different, and that the former were more valued than the latter. Older men and women, the parents of children, would also be expected to conform to hierarchical roles. Given that these practices were sanctified through rituals, using mantras, and occasionally in the presence of priests, they would have acquired added weight.

Rites of passage can have more than one significance, but in the case of these Brahmanical rituals, the preoccupation with constructing a gender-stratified world seems to have been particularly dominant.

NOTES

1. P.V. Kane, *History of Dharmaśāstras*, vol. II, pt. I, Poona: Bhandarkar Oriental Research Institute, 1930–64, p. 190.
2. R.B. Pandey, *Hindu Saṃskāras*, New Delhi: Motilal Banarsidass, 1969, p. 17.
3. Kane, *History of Dharmaśāstras*, vol. II, pt. I.
4. Jan Gonda, *The Ritual Sūtras, History of Indian Literature*, vol. II, pt. I, Weisbaden: Otto Harrassowitz, 1997, p. 469.
5. Ibid., p. 557.
6. J. Holm and J. Bowker, eds., *Rites of Passage*, London: Pinter Publishers, 1994, pp. 72–3.
7. Arnold Van Gennep, *The Rites of Passage*, 1st edn., 1908; London: Routledge and Kegan Paul, 1960.
8. H. Oldenberg, tr., *The Gṛhyasūtras*, pts. I–II, *The Sacred Books of the East*, ed. F. Max Muller, vol. 29, 1886, New Delhi: Motilal Banarsidass, repr. 1964.
9. Jaya Tyagi, *Engendering the Early Household: Brahmanical Precepts in the Early Gṛhyasūtras, Middle of the First Millennium B.C.E.*, New Delhi: Orient Longman, 2008.
10. Kane, *History of Dharmaśāstras*, vol. I, pt. II, p. 689.
11. *Āpastamba Gṛhyasūtra* (hereafter *ApGS*) I.3.19. The Gṛhyasūtras, pt. II, *The Sacred Books of the East*, ed. F. Max Muller, vol. 29, tr. H. Oldenberg, 1886; New Delhi: Motilal Banarsidass, repr. 1964.
12. Gonda, *The Ritual Sūtras*, pp. 478–9.
13. Ram Gopal, *India of the Vedic Kalpasutras*, 2nd edn., New Delhi: Motilal Banarsidass, 1983, p. 89.
14. Ibid., pp. 71–3.

15. *Śāṅkhāyana Gṛhyasūtra* (hereafter *SGS*) IV.7. The Gṛhyasūtras, pt. I, *The Sacred Books of the East*, ed. F. Max Muller, tr. H. Oldenberg, vol. 29, 1886; New Delhi: Motilal Banarsidass, repr. 1964.
16. *Pāraskara Gṛhyasūtra* (hereafter *PGS*) II.11.6. The Gṛhyasūtras, pt. I, *The Sacred Books of the East*, ed. F. Max Muller, tr. H. Oldenberg, vol. 29, 1886; New Delhi: Motilal Banarsidass, repr. 1964.
17. Romila Thapar, *Recent Perspectives of Early Indian History*, Bombay: Popular Prakashan, 1995.
18. Tyagi, *Engendering the Early Household*, p. 31.
19. *PGS* I.11.1.
20. *ApGS* II.1.16–17.
21. *SGS* I.19.6.
22. V.M. Apte, *Social and Religious Life in the Gṛhyasūtras*, Ahmedabad: Ramnik Pitambar Das, 1939, p. 12.
23. Kane, *History of Dharmaśāstras*, vol. II, pt. I, p. 206.
24. *SGS* I.21.1–3.
25. *SGS* I.18–19; *PGS* I.11; *ApGS* VIII.10–11.
26. N.N. Bhattacharyya, *Ancient Indian Rituals and Their Social Contents*, New Delhi: Manohar Book Series, 1996, pp. 177–9.
27. *Āśvalāyana Gṛhyasūtra* (hereafter *AsvGS*) I.13.1. The Gṛhyasūtras, pt. I, *The Sacred Books of the East*, ed. F. Max Muller, tr. H. Oldenberg, vol. 29, 1886; New Delhi: Motilal Banarsidass, repr. 1964.
28. *SGS* I.21.1–3.
29. Kane, *History of Dharmaśāstras*, vol. II, part I, p. 220.
30. *AsvGS* I.13.2–7.
31. Helene Stork, 'Mothering in Tamil Nadu: Some Magico Religious beliefs', in *Roles & Rituals for Hindu Women*, ed. J. Leslie, Delhi: Motilal Banarsidass, 1999, p. 92.
32. Ibid.
33. *AsvGS* I.13.2–7; *PGS* I.14.1–5; *SGS* I.20.1–5.
34. *PGS* I.14.3.1.
35. *AsvGS* I.13.2; *PGS* I.14.3.1; *SGS* I.20.1.
36. Stork, 'Mothering in Tamil Nadu', p. 92.
37. *AsvGS* I.14.1–9.
38. Henri Hubert and Marcel Mauss, *Sacrifice: Its Nature and Function*, tr. W.D. Hallis, Chicago: University of Chicago Press, 1964, p. 10.
39. *ApGS* VI.14.1.
40. *PGS* I.15.1.
41. *SGS* I.22.1.
42. In the *vivāha* rites, too, the bride is seated on the bull's hide to make her fertile.
43. *PGS* I.15.4.
44. Kane, *History of Dharmaśāstras*, vol. II, pt. II, p. 222.
45. *SGS* I.22.6.
46. *AsvGS* I.14.9.
47. *AsvGS* I.14.9; *SGS* I.22.18.

48. *ApGS* VI.14; *PGS* I.15.
49. *AsvGS* I.6.1.
50. Van Gennep, *The Rites of Passage*, p. 41.
51. Kane, *History of Dharmaśāstras*, vol. II, pt. II, p. 228.
52. *PGS* I.16.1–25.
53. *AsvGS* I.16.4.
54. *SGS* I.24.5.
55. *PGS* 1.16.11–16.
56. *PGS* I.16.4.
57. Ibid.
58. *PGS* I.16.6.
59. *PGS* I.16.16.
60. *AsvGS* I.15.4; *PGS* I.17.2; *SGS* I.24.4; *ApGS* I.15.9.
61. *Kṛt* has an active role while *taddhita* has a passive role.
62. *AsvGS* I.15.5.
63. *PGS* I.17.3; *AsvGS* I.15.7; *ApGS* VI.15.11.
64. *PGS* I.17.4.
65. *PGS* I.17.5–6.
66. *PGS* I.17.6.
67. *PGS* I.19.1–13.
68. *SGS* I.27.1–11.
69. *AsvGS* I.16.6.
70. *SGS* I.27.11.
71. *AsvGS* I.17.1–19; *ApGS* VI.16.3–11; *PGS* II.1–25; *SGS* I.28.1–24.
72. Kane, *History of Dharmaśāstras*, vol. II, pt. II, p. 260.
73. *SGS* I.28.
74. *AsvGS* I.17.8; *SGS* I.28.12.
75. *AsvGS* I.17.1–18; *ApGS* VI.16.3–11.
76. *PGS* II.1.4.
77. *AsvGS* I.17.
78. *ApGS* VI.16.3.
79. *AsvGS* I.17.9–10.
80. *AsvGS* I.17.11–18.
81. *SGS* I.28.22.
82. *AsvGS* I.17.19.
83. Holm and Bowker, *Rites of Passage*, pp. 72–3.
84. Stork, 'Mothering in Tamil Nadu', p. 97.
85. *SGS* I.22.17.
86. L. Patton, *Jewels of Authority*, New Delhi: Oxford University Press, 2002, pp. 61–3.

REFERENCES

Apte, V.M., *Social and Religious Life in the Gṛhyasūtras*, Ahmedabad: Ramnik Pitambar Das, 1939.

Bhattacharyya, N.N., *Ancient Indian Rituals and Their Social Contents*, New Delhi: Manohar Book Series, 1996.

Gonda, Jan, *The Ritual Sūtras*, *History of Indian Literature*, vol. II, pt. I, Weisbaden: Otto Harrassowitz, 1997.

Gopal, Ram, *India of the Vedic Kalpasutras*, 2nd edn, New Delhi: Motilal Banarsidass, 1983.

Holm, J. with J. Bowker, eds., *Rites of Passage*, London: Pinter Publishers, 1994.

Hubert, Henri and Marcel Mauss, *Sacrifice: Its Nature and Function*, tr. W.D. Hallis, Chicago: University of Chicago Press, 1964.

Kane, P.V., *History of Dharmaśāstras*, vol. II, pt. I, Poona: Bhandarkar Oriental Research Institute, 1930–64.

Oldenberg, H., tr., *The Gṛhyasūtras*, pts. I & II, *The Sacred Books of the East*, ed. F. Max Muller, vol. 29, 1886; repr., New Delhi: Motilal Banarsidass, 1964.

Pandey, R.B., *Hindu Saṃskāras*, New Delhi: Motilal Banarsidass Publishers, 1969.

Patton, L., *Jewels of Authority*, New Delhi: Oxford University Press, 2002.

Stork, Helene, 'Mothering in Tamil Nadu: Some Magico Religious beliefs', in *Roles & Rituals for Hindu Women*, ed. J. Leslie, Delhi: Motilal Banarsidass, 1999.

Thapar, Romila, ed., *Recent Perspectives of Early Indian History*, Bombay: Popular Prakashan, 1995.

Tyagi, Jaya, *Engendering the Early Household: Brahmanical Precepts in the Early Gṛhyasūtras, Middle of the First Millennium B.C.E.*, New Delhi: Orient Longman, 2008.

Van Gennep, Arnold, *The Rites of Passage*, 1st edn, 1908, London: Routledge and Kegan Paul, 1960.

4

Re-viewing Elite Sexuality: Erotic Love, Adultery, and Chastity in the *Kathāsaritsāgara*

Tara Sheemar

The Narrative and the Characters

IN THIS CHAPTER, I PROPOSE to highlight the construction of masculine and feminine sexualities as ideal types and deviant types in the voluminous work of narrative literature, the *Kathāsaritsāgara*. I assume that these narratives would have served as guides to behaviour, as much as they might reflect it. These will be viewed within the larger concerns of gender, caste, and class hegemonies. The chapter is divided into sections with separate themes relating to premarital sexuality, specifically the *gāndharva* 'marriage', marital sexuality focusing on adultery and chastity, and the sexuality of religious practitioners and semi-divine beings. In essence, through these masculinities and femininities, we have the depiction and creation of identities of individuals situated at the innumerable intersecting levels of gender, caste, and class.

The *Kathāsaritsāgara* (henceforth *KSS*) is a Sanskrit text composed between 1063 and 1081 CE by Somadeva, a brāhmaṇa poet at the court of King Ananta of Kashmir, for the 'amusement' of Queen Sūryamatī. Devika Rangachari has discussed the controversial portrayal of the queen by Kalhaṇa when she talks of the queens in Kashmir as powers behind the throne.[1] Somadeva has claimed that the work is derived from a much larger collection, which he purports to remain 'true' to, titled *Bṛhatkathā*, which was composed by Guṇāḍhya in the Paiśācī dialect much earlier in the sixth century CE. It has been considered as the first and the greatest Indian 'novel'[2] as well as a conceptual category signifying the *Volksgeist*, the Great Repository of Folk Narratives.[3] There is no mistake about the popularity of the narratives of the *KSS* since many of them also form the themes of other literary works of the early medieval period, such as the plays of King Harṣa. One can assume that the stories may have been popular in Kashmir and in the early medieval literary and public space, which is also apparent from the fact that another Kashmiri writer from the same period, Kṣemendra, also wrote a text based on the same work. In addition, the text is composed in the epical *śloka* (*anuṣṭubh* metre), which would make it more broadly comprehensible than the sophisticated metres of the usual *kāvya* literature.

However, in the act of composing its Sanskrit Kashmirian *kāvya* version, Somadeva places it in the Sanskrit 'literary culture' of the subcontinent, the cosmopolitan, elite and political nature of which has been expounded by Sheldon Pollock. Pollock considers literature as 'an act in the field of power'; power being specifically tied with the state/*rājya*.[4] Daud Ali places literature within the wider context of material life, interpersonal protocols, and ethical practices of the court in the early medieval period, treating texts as modes through which individuals were 'educated' and 'interpolated' into the structure of courtly life in a highly reflexive manner.[5]

While literature could be turned into the 'voice' of power structures and hierarchies, it was certainly not limited by intentions of authors and patrons, especially not narratives like those of the *KSS*, which, as stated earlier, had popular antecedents. Ostensibly, the accessibility of the text itself, but not the stories, seems to have been largely limited to the royalty and the urban elite of Kashmir, a significant section of society; one can assume Somadeva himself to be an urban man of learning. Through the *KSS* we can see how elite sexuality (and that of others) was meant to be constructed, since the text to an extent echoes their concerns including that of monarchies. It reflects the concerns that underline the normative Brahmanical literature to some extent, through application of its world view in its narratives and characterization. In addition, its placement in the courtly context makes it part of the systems of power that seek to regulate the 'practice of sexuality'.[6]

While narratives and oral literature may be subtler means of spreading ideology that encompasses power relations (that would include gender, caste, and class hierarchies), a text like the *KSS* can reveal the intricacies of the functioning of the system since it contains 'popular' elements. It is obvious that the boundaries between the high/courtly/elite and low/common/popular culture were thin and porous with osmotic effect. The 'popular' antecedents (and future) of the stories have to be emphasized. Its significance can be grasped from the statement of A.K. Ramanujan:[7] 'Folklore pervades childhoods, families, and communities as the symbolic language of the non-literate parts of the people and culture.' Thus, the *KSS* stands at the juncture of various mutually interconnected locations: the literary, oral, court/elite society, the past (associated with Guṇāḍhya) and the present (of Somadeva). From this point of view, it can reveal to us how individuals reacted to the norms and traditions regarding sexuality. We will see that it presents a picture of complexity in the sphere of sexual relations, fluidity in the interplay between norms, tradition, and behaviour.

Who are these elites that we speak of? How are they represented in the text? How do class and caste intersect in defining the elite identity of an individual? Crucial for us to understand the manner in which the text depicts social categories is the fusion that Sherry Ortner has envisioned between class and race/ethnicity in American cultural thought, thinking of fusion in the Lévi-Straussian sense of a particular relationship between categories, so that none can be found in pure form and each is hidden within the other.[8] Class is seen as a culturally and historically constructed identity to be examined within a discursive field of related terms of social identity and difference like gender. Thus, when we begin our discussion on elites as a social category we have to necessarily include caste, class, and gender.

The elite of society can be understood as a broad group with control over economic resources; the aristocracy can be considered as a smaller segment within it, having political power as well. The proximity of the elite to the court and royalty is significantly represented in the text. From this it can be safely assumed that the category 'common' can be used as the inverse of the elite, the even broader non-elites—those who were largely involved directly in production (including what is today defined as the service sector) but had little control over substantial economic resources. Individuals from varied backgrounds occur in the text, but the elite courtly bias cannot be ignored since individuals from these backgrounds form the main protagonists in the narratives. Romila Thapar has significantly shown that while in the early historical period the elite was composed of three upper varṇas ritually, there was a difference between ritual and actual status in terms of politico-economic power, while there was wide ranging social mobility across regions and castes.[9]

The elite category protagonists that appear in the text include, to a large measure, kings and queens, princes and princesses, i.e. characters belonging to the royal lineage. In addition to royal protagonists, the significant presence of brāhmaṇas and merchant men and women can be seen, and they are mostly located in urban backgrounds. However, there are other social groups that figure in the narrative as part of the wider social context. These include various urban and rural occupational groups like ministers, companions, maids, barbers; the 'outcastes' or *cāṇḍālas*; the foresters, interchangeably referred to as *śavaras/bhillas*, *kirātas*, and *mātaṅgas*; religious personages like ascetics, hermits, and wandering mendicants. There are also non-human beings with 'evil' characteristics including *piśācas*, *rākṣasas*, *vetālas*, and witches (*ḍākinī/śākinī*). And there are divine and semi-divine beings who are instrumental in the narrative, including *apsarās*, *gāndharvas*, *asuras*, *yakṣas*, *gaṇas* and, above all, *vidyādharas*. The *vidyādharas* are the most prominent and appear to be a projection of the fantasies of the ruling classes. This is apparent from the connecting narrative, whose hero, prince Naravāhanadatta, is depicted as gaining the kingdom of the *vidyādharas*.

What we see in the urban space is a highly stratified society, where to a great extent, occupation constituted the identity of the individual; caste or varṇa being subsumed within the occupational identity except in the case of brāhmaṇas who are called *dvija* or *vipra*, and sometimes *brāhmaṇa*. Their brāhmaṇa identity and ancestry is highlighted, whatever occupation they may be depicted as performing. This assertion of identity is apparent from the naming pattern followed in the text; brāhmaṇa individuals are almost always named along with their father's name.[10] In fact, the term *kula* is used mostly for individuals belonging to the brāhmaṇa varṇa.[11] This emphasis on the status of the brāhmaṇas seems to be a general trend in the *kāvya*. Kaul has pointed out that *kāvyas* 'display intense socio-economic diversity by a lack of formal attention to the caste status of characters; the brāhmaṇa caste is an exception'.[12]

In contrast to the brāhmaṇas, the term vaiśya is rarely used to designate merchants (*vaṇik*). Merchants are identified not so much in terms of *kula*, but in terms of wealth. They are certainly elite and very closely linked to the monarchy. For instance, the father of Unmādinī is called a wealthy merchant (*mahādhanavaṇik*),[13] while Dharmagupta is called great merchant (*mahāvaṇik*).[14] Kings, queens, princes, and princesses occasionally identified with the kṣatriya varṇa. King Udayana of Vatsa is referred to as of the Pāṇḍava lineage, the whole earth being his by heredity descent (*kulakrama*).[15] However, equally noteworthy, elite identity is often revealed through physical and mental attributes. For instance, when the legendary queen Vāsavadattā was staying in disguise as a brāhmaṇa woman, she was thought to be of 'noble' birth on account of her shape, softness, grace, and fragrance.[16]

The background of state functionaries is never mentioned unless they are of brāhmaṇa origin. Others who are designated in terms of their occupation include the potter, garland maker, guard, maid, etc. Amongst the non-elite groups are the 'outcastes' whose identity is derived from the 'pollution' inherent in their status instead of the presence or absence of economic resources. One of the terms used for outcastes is *vṛṣalī*; when a princess is reluctant to marry, her father tells her that if a daughter reaches puberty unmarried she is an outcaste and her husband is the husband of an outcaste (*vṛṣalīpati*).[17] In a story, the queen expressed her bewilderment when her son who belonged to the royal family (*rājavaṃśa*) fell in love with a *cāṇḍāla* girl, also described as *antyajām* (outcaste).[18] A brāhmaṇa is said to have been reborn in the fisher caste (*kula*) due to the pollution of his desires.[19] Thus, the terms *kula* and *jāti* are used for social categories, and notions of 'high' and 'low' or 'good' and 'bad' are used to classify them.[20] These resonate with the suggestions made by Uma Chakravarti for a much earlier period (fifth century BCE to first century CE), when a two-tier system of stratification is indicated with a basic opposition between high and low in the context of the *jāti*, *kula*, *kamma* (work), and *sippa* (craft).[21]

Class also intersects with caste in many instances. For example, the state functionaries are often brāhmaṇas (the high ministers) or kṣatriyas (*rājaputras* as warrior servants). Entry to these categories seems to have been available to the political elite of the forest. Entry to the royal house in a few cases is also depicted as being open through marital alliances, to individuals (and families) of varied backgrounds, high and low. But in cases of succession, individual claimants with mothers of 'higher' lineage are given definite preference, as seen in the story of Bhīmabhaṭa and Samarabhaṭa.[22] This demonstrates the openness of channels of power, and access to it of women (and men) from disparate backgrounds. But it shows how, in the construction of masculinities, birth becomes the basis for innate qualities of heroism and righteousness, and access to courtship, friendship and the loyalty of 'followers'. The prince of the 'wrong' birth is stripped of these traits, and in fact needs the protection of his father to survive politically, which of course was attributed to the king's love for his dancer wife. The elder prince could uproot the younger only after the death of the father-king.

Thus, members of three higher varṇas, as depicted in the text, are in essence, also members of the elite sections of society, or vice versa. They are depicted as being connected with each other through ties of marriage generally following the *anuloma* (hypergamy) mode. While caste/class identities were maintained through gender relations, the text does not display an obsession with maintaining caste purity by avoiding *varṇasaṃkara*. In fact, we will see how such norms are subverted, suggesting that class was as significant as caste.

Contexts and Concepts

The context of the text is Kashmir in the early medieval period, with its well developed monarchy, administration, religious establishments; religious traditions ranging from orthodox Brahmanism to unorthodox Tantrism and 'heterodox' Buddhism; trade and commerce; close political, economic and personal ties with neighbouring kingdoms; and a very sophisticated Sanskrit literary tradition. The production of a large number of religious, political, philosophical, theoretical narratives and poetical works was undertaken in Kashmir under royal patronage, as well as independently. Devika Rangachari[23] refers to Bilhaṇa's praise of Sūryamatī and of the women of Kashmir and his statement that in every house in Kashmir Sanskrit and Prakrit words were spoken even by women and others. Kumkum Roy[24] has made a pertinent observation regarding the varṇa order being contested, if not irrelevant in the context of early medieval Kashmir. Rangachari[25] has brought out the role of women in the political sphere in Kashmir using the available evidence for women's agency and power in the sources of the period. Women appear as rulers, advisers, court participants, donors, builders, and in a range of other roles.

The sociopolitical context of Kashmir, as evident in the *Rājataraṅgiṇī*, represents fluid sexual relations, with ministers presenting their wives to the king, and with queens consolidating their power by entering into relations with ministers: '. . . sexual relations were probably part of a spectrum of political strategies used by men and women belonging to a range of social categories in their attempt to both retain and gain power'.[26] That these strategies and resolutions were complex is evident from the story of Queen Sūryamatī, for whom the *KSS* was composed.[27] According to Kalhaṇa, Haladhara, the son of a vaiśya watchman at a temple, rose higher in her service and became the prime minister. When Sūryamatī committed sati on the death of her husband, she took an oath to establish the purity of her character and put an end to the rumours that had grown due to Haladhara's position as her confidante. This just highlights for us the fact that textual representations were not divorced from 'actual' events.

Issues related to sexuality have become central to understanding the operation of gender relations in societies. Michel Foucault brought it into focus by the extremely significant premise that sexuality must not be thought of as a natural given and that power tries to hold in check; it is produced.[28] Foucault's assumption that the deployment of sexuality took place first among the ruling classes as part of the strategy of preserving hegemony in the eighteenth-century West is very instructive for us,[29] though our period and context is entirely different. In the early Indian context, Uma Chakravarti[30] has pointed out how the subordination of women occurred due to the needs of Brahmanical patriarchy and the necessity of maintaining control over their sexuality. In another context Gerda Lerner[31] showed how encouraging homogamy—the marriage between partners of equal social status—through laws assured that property stayed within the class of propertied people.

Morality, a term closely associated with sexuality, includes a set of values and rules of action prescribed for individuals as well as the behaviour of individuals in interrelation to these.[32] The doctrines may provide space for compromises and loopholes to deal with variations or transgressions through which individuals may conduct themselves. This accommodation and elasticity is reflected in the *KSS*. One way of dealing with acts of transgression is the philosophy of karma and rebirth and the belief in fatalism. All actions and events form part of a chain of causation—almost inescapable and predetermined. Wendy Doniger[33] has stated that '. . . characters in tight spots often blame fate or *karma*, while the narrator in a tight spot hastily conjures up a previous incarnation to explain an otherwise awkward twist of the plot or inconsistency of character'. Another explanatory device used in the *KSS* is related to *kāma* or desire/love. Amongst other gods and goddesses, Kāmadeva, the god of love is frequently mentioned in the text. At various junctures in the narratives the actions of individuals are said to be driven by *kāma* and are, therefore, excusable even if they do not conform with the norms.

More generally, hegemony has been used in different contexts to understand the phenomena of Brahmanism and gender hierarchy. Kunal Chakrabarti[34] has used the concept of cultural hegemony, understanding it as the organization of consent, as the theoretical premise for his understanding of the phenomenon of Brahmanism in Bengal, which happened through the codification of the Purāṇas. Ortner[35] attempted to understand how gender hegemony relates the 'whole social process' to specific distributions of power and influence organized by specific dominant meanings and values.

Through the *KSS* we can see how elite sexuality (and that of others) was meant to be constructed since the text mainly echoes their concerns. Since the elite formed part of the monarchical apparatus, their concerns were those of the monarchy itself. This has to be viewed with reference to the system of deployment of alliance (marriage, kinship, inheritance, licit/illicit alliances, maintaining law, statuses). We can also state that sexuality was also deployed, to a large extent, for the creation of masculinities and femininities.

We understand that the sexuality of both men and women was subordinated, or was attempted to be subordinated, to suit patriarchies, for reproduction and maintaining statuses. But along with that there is the awareness that resistance, overt or covert, conscious or unconscious, of varying degrees, would have been present. Sexuality is a key variable in gender studies, while gendering history operates with the premise that in all possible aspects of analysis the relative male-female dimensions must be included. The understanding is that these are relational categories and any discussion of one would be incomplete without reference to the other. This in a way takes us a big step ahead of 'women's history'.

In this chapter, I essentially interrogate the heterosexual premarital interactions, the marital relationship and extramarital relations represented in the narratives of the *KSS* with a focus on the themes of love, adultery, and chastity. I also examine the manner in which identities, both masculine and feminine, are constructed in certain cases. These will reveal the interface between normative injunctions, social attitudes, and individual behaviour. Sexuality, as I have stated above, becomes a crucial theme in the study of gender since it became the interior of the difference between the two basic gender identities of male and female.

Urban Lovers and the *Gāndharva* Union

Unrequited, unfulfilled love is not the concern of the *KSS*. Its grand conceptualization of love standardizes the male and female actors in their physical attributes and emotional responses (in keeping with general *kāvya* style) and ultimately fulfils it in their sexual union, which is marriage by mutual choice or the *gāndharva* marriage.

In recognizing this form of marriage (even though it is not highly approved and certainly discouraged) the lawmakers appropriated the sexuality of individuals to fit into the pattern of patriarchal marriage and social reproduction based on Brahmanical varṇa, class, and gender norms. The *KSS* reflects a channelization of elite premarital sexuality to fit into certain patterns and within certain parameters. I endeavour to demonstrate this in this section. For that we have to understand how love is structured in the text—who loves whom, how do they love, who helps them—these are the issues that I will mainly enquire into. This is the logic behind my focus on three themes as being significant in the depiction of premarital sexuality: the caste and class status of the protagonists, the intermediaries involved, and its consequences.

Love is a very elite phenomenon in the text; usually it is between high status individuals in terms of caste and class, or at least one of them has a high status. The literature produced in the early medieval period was dominated by erotic themes forming the *śṛṅgāra rasa*, as pointed out by Shalini Shah,[36] and love within it was an elite 'androcentric phenomenon'.[37] In the *prema* tradition in classical Sanskrit tradition, according to Shah, including all data from narrative literature such as *KSS*, *Śukasaptaśatī* and

Bṛhatkathāślokasaṃgraha, we find evidence of the celebration of female erotica that subverts the hegemonic masculine tradition, including tales of adultery and women centric tales.

According to Daud Ali, the generic and abstract character of the *nāyaka* and *nāyikā* in courtly poetry made these personae eminently open and 'habitable' categories which members at court were implicitly encouraged to 'enter'.[38] It also made them susceptible to investment with wider concerns of self and society. We may suggest that elite members of the audience could identify with the characters and would be, to a certain extent, influenced by the widely popular narratives of the *KSS*.

Attributes of Lovers: Youth and Beauty

As far as age is concerned, the tales recount encounters between young men and women who have acquired a certain maturity including consciousness about sexuality. There is no direct reference to the exact age of the characters, except in one or two cases that refer to the age of men. Sūryaprabha is said to be sixteen years old when he was made crown prince and *asura* Maya began to instruct him in the magic sciences.[39] It was after completing his education that he embarked upon his journey of sexual conquests by carrying off one princess after another. Īśvaravarman, the son of a merchant, was sixteen years old when he fell into the trap of a courtesan and he had already completed his education by then.[40] In these and other instances, the young men's transition to a stage of erotic bonding coincides with the completion of their education.

There are quite a few instances of kings being the centrepiece of romances, and their beauty as well as martial qualities are highlighted. The king also figures as the *nāyaka*, the hero in love, expressing 'true' (and stylized) romantic love. The language used in each instance of kingly or princely sexuality, such as the numerous liaisons of Naravāhanadatta, is that of overpowering romantic love.

The women are also young and obviously beautiful and they desire the same in their partners. In premarital romances one does not find the kind of misogynous language that one finds in the cases of adultery. There are no references to the insatiable desire of women or their innate sexual nature and, thus, it seems that premarital romance and bonding is more 'acceptable', 'understandable', and even desirable. What we do have is stylized lengthy descriptions of women, in many cases emphasizing their physical attributes. Consider the description of one of the *vidyādharī* wives of Naravāhanadatta: '. . . that fair one, with eyes rolling like bees, with her lips red like shoots, beautiful with breasts firm as clusters, having her body yellow with the dust of flowers, removing fatigue by her loveliness . . .'.[41]

Physically attractive men were also valorized. The danger of a princess getting married to an old king and accompanying anxiety on that ground can be seen in the conversation between Somaprabhā and Princess Kaliṅgasenā[42] when the princess is told that the king whom her parents favoured as her future husband was old and she would be pitied if she married him. She told her that 'of all the desirable requisites in a suitor, youth (*vayo*), good looks (*rūpa*), noble birth (*kula*), good disposition (*śīla*) and wealth (*vitta*), youth is of the greatest importance, high birth and so on are of subordinate importance'.[43] She convinced her friend to choose Udayana, the king of Vatsa, praising his beauty (*rūpa*), attractiveness (*lāvaṇya*), and lineage (*kula*). The two most desirable qualities in men besides youth seem to be beauty and valour. Descriptions such as the following one are quite common: 'Vajramukuṭa, the hero, dashed the god of love's pride in his beauty and his enemies' confidence in their valor.'[44]

There are very few instances where we find the expression of parental worry about the marriage of a daughter once she had attained the 'right' age. A king of the *vidyādharas* voiced his concern to his queen about their daughter Ratnaprabhā, who in his opinion was 'fit' to be given away in marriage.[45] He stated that a daughter was misery even though she was an ornament of her family, and, despite the fact that Ratnaprabhā was modest, learned, young, and beautiful she caused him stress as she had not yet gained a husband.

It has been pointed out that with the gradual triumph of patriarchy, in post-Vedic literature a tendency developed to lower the age of marriage of girls since patriarchy demanded total eradication of women's independent existence.[46] However, contrary to *śāstric* expectations, the *KSS* has woven tales of love between young men and women who are obviously of a mature age. Still, there is expression of some anxiety about the marriage of daughters. This probably reflects general fears regarding the maintenance of female chastity and control over women's sexuality.

Initiative, Kinship, and the Role of Intermediaries

The text represents various means through which young men and women harbouring romantic feelings for each other established contact in a society that normatively restricted premarital interaction between the sexes. Various strategies were employed in communication and intermediaries were involved as aides in bringing lovers together. Another aspect that emerges is regarding the role of the family, especially parents, as being supportive and/or antagonistic regarding the lovers' choice of each other.

The story of prince Vajramukuṭa and Padmāvatī can be taken as typifying premarital sexual relations in its various aspects, as represented in the text:[47]

While hunting in a forest along with his friend and minister Buddhiśarīra, Prince Vajramukuṭa saw a maiden of heavenly appearance bathing in a lake with her attendants and was captivated by her, and she was also attracted to him. As he was looking at her and wondering who she was, she made a sign to tell him details about herself.[48] After the exchange they both left for their respective residences, full of love sickness. Later, Buddhiśarīra interpreted the meaning of the signs for the prince and informed him that her name was Padmāvatī. She was the daughter of an ivory carver who was the favourite courtier of King Karṇotpala in the country of Kaliṅga, and she had given him the message that her heart was his. The prince set out with his friend to Kaliṅga on the pretext of hunting. There they lodged themselves at the house of an old woman near the ivory carver's place. The old woman knew the ivory carver well as she had been his nurse and had also attended to Padmāvatī. The old woman was quite greedy, and in return for various gifts she went to Padmāvatī thrice with Vajramukuṭa's message.[49] The third time Padmāvatī conveyed to the prince the secret passage he was to take when he would come to see her by sending the old woman back by the very same way. Thus, that very evening, the prince crossed the wall between the old woman's and the ivory carver's house and was pulled up a window by a rope with the help of Padmāvatī's female servants. They married by the *gāndharva* rite and he remained with her in concealment for some days. He had to leave when she found out that Buddhiśarīra had interpreted the signs. She was angry and full of jealousy, thinking him to be a rival to the exclusive devotion of the prince to her. Henceforth the story is full of intrigue and plotting. Padmāvatī tried to murder Buddhiśarīra but he anticipated her actions and convinced the prince to persuade her to leave her relations instead. He then invented a scheme to carry her off and got her branded as a witch and banished from the city to the forest. Finally, the prince took her to his own kingdom, while her parents died of grief thinking their daughter to be dead.

The narrative of Devadatta and Śrī is similar to the above in the use of signs as a means of communication in cases when secrecy was required.[50] In both the stories the girl was angered when she found out that it was someone other than her lover who had interpreted the meaning of the signs. Penzer[51] has pointed out that the method of communicating through signs, represented by objects, was widespread throughout the East and has also been noticed in different parts of Africa and America. The depiction of communicating through signs made by objects was probably because of the seclusion of elite women. Another aspect of the sign language is that it seems available only to men and women from high status. In both stories the crucial intervention of the companion of the male heroes can be seen. And, there is the transgression of parental authority and norms along with the secretive *gāndharva* marriage.

As far as initiative is concerned, it is taken by women in quite a few tales, and no value judgement is attached to it, nor is it gender specific. On comparison, in fact, the tales in which the initiative in establishing premarital relations is taken by women seem to outnumber those in which men do so. At the same time, the initiative taken by women was viewed with some ambivalence. When Princess Kaliṅgasenā took the bold step of abandoning her palace to approach Udayana, the King of Vatsa, the consequences were not in keeping with her desire.[52] The male initiative on the other hand is more in the nature of 'seizing' the woman from her relations and, thus, obtaining a wife. In the two tales of Puṣpadanta and Vajramukuṭa a plan is hatched by the young men along with their 'aides' to obtain their love interests by whatever means possible. The female lovers are kept in the dark about these plots throughout and the initiative is taken away from them in the second half of the stories.

Coming to the role of the kinship network we find that many of the tales imply a transgression of parental authority, especially that of the father over the daughter as a protector with the right to marry her to a suitable bridegroom at the appropriate time. The devices employed may differ, but the protagonists always succeed and Beck's[53] point about Indic tales involving a subversion of authority in their depiction of hierarchical relationships seems significant in this context. The tales of Puṣpadanta and Vajramukuṭa also bring into focus the question of the authority of the king. The function of kingship as the upholder of dharma has been elaborated within normative literature. However, in these tales the king is instrumental in circumventing the authority of the father, even though the protagonists use deception to achieve their ends. In Puṣpadanta's story, the king's authority comes into conflict with paternal responsibility, though both are embodied in the same person. The king as Princess Śrī's father is forced to give away his daughter for fear of being cursed due to his failure to perform his duty as a king in protecting another man's wife. Overall, victory belongs to the lovers, but specifically to the male lover: it is the man's adventure which results in his gaining the woman he desires, who also, of course, desires him.

The person of the father emerges as significant in various tales and the role of the mother is more or less sidelined in comparison. Sometimes brothers are mentioned but they are figures of no consequence; sisters are not mentioned, nor are any other kinsfolk. There is an incident which represents a dispute regarding the claims of the father and mother over the right to give away their daughter in marriage, the consequences of which lead to the king's court for settlement. The commander-in-chief of the new king of the *vidyādharas*, Naravāhanadatta, arrested the *vidyādhara* Ityaka while he was spotted attempting to carry off a woman who was crying out for her husband.[54] He based his claim upon the woman on the grounds that she had been promised to him by her mother, but her father had bestowed her upon another man. The assessors decided that while the father was alive the mother had no authority to give away the daughter.

Fathers are also depicted in a supportive role. In the story of Vararuci and Upakośā the wider kinship network, including the girl's father, make possible the union of the two lovers.[55] This story occurs in the first book and is linked to the narrative about the origin of the *KSS*. The entire story encompasses an ideal premarital love situation depicting strong mutual attraction, and an ideal marriage with a chaste wife. The manner in which the marriage is arranged is interesting. Upakośā's friend informed her mother about the love of her daughter for Vararuci; her mother informed her father, who turned out to be the brother of Vararuci's teacher and who approved of the match.

The only case in which the mother plays a central role as a mediator and agent is in the story of the young fisher boy (*kaivartakumāra*) named Suprahāra,[56] who fell in love with a princess and, thinking of the impossibility of their union, fell into depression. His mother Rakṣitikā promised to fulfil his desire and went to the princess regularly with a gift of a fish, eventually gaining the goodwill of the princess in the process. The princess made her a promise and Rakṣitikā informed her of Suprahāra's obsession, begging her to meet him. The princess, torn between obligation and embarrassment, finally agreed and asked her to bring her son to the palace secretly in the night. Here we notice that, due to the difference in caste and class status, the fisher boy is represented as being unable to approach the princess; no gestures are involved. The representation of the mother ties in with an understanding of gendered roles being different for different classes/castes.

There are rare stories which envisage an obstructive role for the fathers in premarital interaction. Śṛṅgabhuja was a prince who fell in love with Rūpaśikhā, the daughter of the *rākṣasa* Agniśikhā, living in a great city in a distant forest.[57] The girl introduced him to her father, threatening to commit suicide if they were not allowed to marry. Thus, in a sense, she knew beforehand that she would face opposition in her choice of husband. Agniśikhā agreed with immense reluctance only due to his daughter's insistence. In his view the match was undesirable since men were the food of *rākṣasas*. In order to prevent the marriage he put Śṛṅgabhuja through a series of trials after placing the condition that he must never disobey him if he wanted to become his son-in-law. But his daughter anticipated all his tricks and guided her lover through the arduous tasks placed before him.

Her father was rendered helpless, never suspecting her, and had to agree to the marriage eventually. Similarly, King Caṇḍamahāsena killed an *asura* with the help of the *asura's* daughter Aṅgāravatī and then married her.[58] It has been pointed out that the *rākṣasas* were anti-Vedic tribes and have been represented in the *Rāmāyaṇa* as the antithesis of dharmic humanity.[59] In a sense this is exemplified by Agniśikhā, who is opposed to his daughter marrying a 'human'.

Turning to friends, they are invariably represented as playing a supportive role as intermediaries in premarital interaction. The only situation where friendship between women is discussed at length is that of Somaprabhā and Kaliṅgasenā.[60] Somaprabhā, the daughter of *asura* Maya, and thus, possessing magical powers, informed the princess that her prospective suitor King Prasenajit was old, and therefore, to be shunned even though her parents had chosen him. Moreover, she also influenced her to choose the king of Vatsa. When the princess voiced her helplessness in the matter as she was under the authority of her parents, Somaprabhā convinced her to leave her parental house. After showing her king Prasenajit she took her to Kauśāmbī to meet the handsome Udayana, the king of Vatsa, advising her to wait for the opportune time to approach him.

Similarly, there are various instances of confidantes (*sakhīs*) helping out their friends by acting as messengers. Upakośā's confidante goes with her love message to Vararuci, and then upon his insistence informs her mother about their wish to be married.[61] A rich kṣatriya's daughter, Madirāvatī, sent her foster sister (*dhātreyī*), who was also her friend and her maid servant's daughter, to a brāhmaṇa youth she loved with a garland, a message and other gifts. The youth sent back his message through the same friend reciprocating her feelings.[62] In another tale, Princess Mṛgāṅkavatī sent her dear friend (*priyasakhī*) named Bhāvanikā to Śrīdatta on the pretence of returning his ring, with the message that he should become her husband or she would die.[63] Later, Bhāvanikā was also the accomplice in her elopement from the palace.

Male friends also assist each other in their romantic pursuits. In the tale of two brāhmaṇa friends one of them encouraged his friend not to give up his lady-love and made a plan for carrying her off.[64] Also, as mentioned earlier, Śrīdatta was helped by his friend Bahuśālin to make a plan to carry off Princess Mṛgāṅkavatī and elope to Mathurā. Likewise, Buddhiśarīra, the son of the minister of Prince Vajramukuṭa's father, and his companion, proved invaluable to him in pursuing Padmāvatī.

A significant difference can be discerned in the depiction of companions of men and women. As far as women are concerned, except in the case of Somaprabhā, the social status of the friend or companion seems obscure and in many instances they are also referred to as handmaids (*ceṭī*), obviously of common status. On the other hand, the friends of men seem to be of higher status; that is they at least belong to the elite section of society, even though the hero may belong to the royal lineage. Also, friends and confidantes of whatever background seem to be available only to men and women of high status. There might be some exceptions as in the case of Kanakamañjarī, discussed below, who was a handmaid herself and who also had a friend of the same status named Aśokakarī who helped her in her deception.

The next important category of intermediaries may be classified as low status groups and include mainly serving maids, ascetic women, old and poor women, bards, and painters. Some of them appear at points in the narrative that propel the story further, some act as catalysts; some perform the function of messengers. These handmaids seem to have played an important role as messengers in a situation where women of the upper classes seem to be forbidden direct and open premarital contact with members of the opposite sex. Also their 'friendship' with their mistresses appears to have been socially accepted.

An interesting example is of the confidante (*sakhīrahasyagyām*, also called maid/*ceṭī*) Kanakamañjarī, in the story of Prince Kamalākāra and Haṃsāvalī.[65] She was sent by the princess in secret to check if the prince she was to be married to was the one whose picture she had seen and fallen in love with or someone else. The maid went to meet the prince in the disguise of an ascetic, was fascinated with him and decided to obtain him for herself. By tricking the trusting and simple Haṃsāvalī, Kanakamañjarī got married to the prince with the help of her own intimate friend Aśokakarī. In the end she was discovered as an imposter because she lacked the gift of curing fever with the touch of the hand, which the princess possessed.

There appear, in certain situations, characters of varying status who act as catalysts. They trigger off the romantic instincts in the principal character/s and start off a chain of events in the process. In the tale of Kamalākāra and Haṃsāvalī, mentioned above, it was the bard named Manorathasiddhi who performed this function. In another story, King Kanakavarṣa was described to Madanasundarī by the painter named Roladeva.[66] These characters are described as travelling widely (especially the mendicants) and going off to the courts of various kings. The bards and painters seem to be a category of men who even had access to the women's apartments. A mature female ascetic named Kātyāyanī, who is said to have returned from a distant foreign country, fuelled passion in the heart of Prince Sundarasena by showing him the picture of Mandāravatī that the ascetic had painted herself.[67] However, while various low-status individuals are instrumental in interactions between lovers, courtship essentially is pre-marital and is not made available to them.

Resolving Lovers' Status-Problematique

We have seen how love is made available to individuals of elite status in the *KSS*, and actualized through the support network consisting of a wide variety of persons belonging to varied statuses and through the use of some strategies including sign language, cross-dressing, secret meetings, etc. The problematique of love in the urban space is represented when the statuses of individuals are widely different in terms of class and caste. This is especially so when it involves groups that are not supposed to intermingle. For example, we have seen the case of the maid Kanakamañjarī who attempted to replace her mistress but met with only temporary success. Maids were expected to play vital roles, but were also placed within certain social boundaries.

The love story of Prince Avantivarman and Suratamañjarī, and the tales inserted within as explanatory devices, are exceptional in illuminating boundaries, hierarchies, and the intersection of tradition, flexibility and power.[68] The story is as follows:

Prince Avantivarman, son of King Pālaka of Ujjayinī, fell in love with a *cāṇḍāla* girl. The girl, named Suratamañjarī, was endowed with considerable sexual charm. The prince saw her when the news of her taming a mad elephant (which had run loose in the city and could not be controlled by anyone) with the touch of her hand had spread. The situation was problematic, as the friends of the prince pointed out, that her touch would pollute the prince. The king, on the other hand, believed that since his son was so inclined, the girl had to be some 'heavenly being' or a 'celestial nymph' who had fallen among the *mātaṅgas* for some reason. Also that she must have been the beloved (*priyatamā*) of the prince in a former birth due to which he had fallen in love with her at first sight. In between are interspersed three other stories, discussed below, relating to *pratiloma* unions to illustrate these points. When Utpalahasta, the girl's father, was entreated by the king's messengers to give his daughter in marriage to the prince he placed a curious condition on the alliance. He could do so only if 18,000 brāhmaṇas of the city of Ujjayinī were made to eat in his house. The king without any hesitation ordered all the brāhmaṇas in the city to comply with the demand, which landed them in a grave dilemma: to obey the king's command would mean touching the food of a *cāṇḍāla*; to disobey would mean receiving his punishment. The situation was saved when after the performance of austerities (*tapas*) at a shrine, Śiva appeared to them in a dream and told them that Utpalahasta and his daughter (and the whole family/*kuṭumba*) were *vidyādharas* cursed by Śiva and the curse would end when the earlier condition would be fulfilled. Nonetheless, the brāhmaṇas made the king construct a structure outside the quarters of the *cāṇḍāla* and get the food cooked by 'pure' cooks and Utpalahasta served them dressed in white clothes almost as if he himself was 'purified'. Thus, took place the marriage of Avantivarman and Suratamañjarī.

The mad elephant has been used as a symbol of uncontrollable male sexuality and forms the backdrop for the first meeting of lovers in some tales in the *KSS*. However, in the other stories it is the man who rescues the girl from the dangerous elephant. This is the only tale in which the girl tames an elephant with her touch and goes on to amuse herself by playing with the beast and thus becomes a source of wonder for all those watching, and the object of the prince's desire. The touch itself is symbolic of sexuality and fertility and emphasizes, here, the extraordinary sexual power of the girl. Her name, Suratamañjarī, further drives home the point of her overpowering sexuality since *surata* is literally sexual union or intercourse and *manjarī* means a cluster of blossoms. The nature of the condition is interesting because it comes from a man of 'low' caste as well as class status. The feeding of brāhmaṇas has been considered as an important source of legitimacy. Utpalahasta, by placing his demand before the king's messengers, appears to be asserting himself and at the same time attempting to raise his social status.[69]

We do have instances in the text of inter-caste and inter-class *anuloma* unions—when a prince falls in love and obtains as his wife the daughter of a rich ivory carver (*dantaghātaka*); a brāhmaṇa named Śrīdatta marries a *śavara* chieftain's daughter;[70] a brāhmaṇa named Haṭhaśarman marries a kṣatriya woman named Aśokamālā.[71] Mention may be made of Kadalīgarbhā who is the daughter of the sage Maṅkanaka and who gets married to a king named Dṛḍhavarman.[72] Assuming that she belongs to the brāhmaṇa caste, this is a *pratiloma* union.

Avantivarman's fascination for the girl is justified through the logic of the narrative through reference to other *pratiloma* unions and past life. The stories that are interpolated involve a fisher boy and a young *cāṇḍāla* who marry princesses, and this makes these *pratiloma* unions that also transcend the extremities of class. The manner in which the situations are resolved is very interesting; brāhmaṇa lineage is established for both the young men. Thus, while the force of erotic love and the bindings of past life are considered so strong that norms are twisted and the young men from 'low' origins gain entry into the royal house, this can be done only if their former identity is supplanted. In one of the stories, the abandoned child theme is used, a theme which in many cases explains obscure or 'low' origins of prominent personalities in narratives. Further, it is only death and attempted ritual suicide that resolves the situation.

In one of the stories, Kuraṅgī, the daughter of King Prasenajit of Supratiṣṭhita, was saved by a young *cāṇḍāla* from a 'mad' elephant, thus displaying great bravery.[73] They both fell in love with each other, and the young man, tortured by her thoughts, considered the idea of their union impossible due to the vast gulf between them. So he decided to burn himself with the prayer that she would be his wife in a future birth and made a pyre in the cremation ground. However, the fire god appeared before him and told him that he was the god's son , born secretly to the daughter of a brāhmaṇa in whose home fire he had dwelled. He had been enticed by the girl's beauty and had made her his 'wife'by promising her immunity from disgrace. When the boy was born, she had thrown him out on the street due to shame and he had been brought up by some *cāṇḍālas* on goat's milk. Thus he was not impure. The fire god appeared in a dream of the king urging him to unite the two, which he did.

The other story is that of a young good-looking fisherman named Suprahāra who fell in love with Princess Māyāvatī of Rājagṛha when he saw her playing in a garden in spring.[74] The role of his mother, Rakṣitikā, has been discussed earlier. When the mother dropped him off at the palace, the young man, exhausted due to the fire of separation (*virahāgni*), fell asleep due to the touch of the princess which was 'cool as sandalwood'. The princess avoided being 'disgraced' by him and slept in another room. He woke up, and not finding her there, his 'breath left his body'. The princess, blaming herself, decided to burn herself on his funeral pyre. Her father, King Malayasiṃha, was told by a heavenly wife that the princess and the fisherman had been a brāhmaṇa couple in a previous birth. The man had been born in the fisher caste (*kula*) as he had desired fish while performing penance, while his wife had remained firm in her resolve and had been reborn as a princess. Then the princess restored the youth to life by giving half her life, and they were married by the king.

These narratives assume significance in a text which largely focuses on specifically three caste and class categories as part of the urban elite in depicting premarital sexuality—the ruling kṣatriyas (kings, princes, princesses), the rich merchants, and the learned brāhmaṇas. Also the marital unions are almost always either *anuloma* (hypergamous) or *savarṇa* (homogamous) unions. The same applies for premarital relationships, since they invariably end up in marriage, especially for women (though not always for men if we consider adultery, which will be discussed later). The point being made is that that if such *pratiloma* (hypogamous) unions could have been possible then why not the *anuloma* union of the prince.

What is clear from these instances is that they do not follow the usual pattern of narratives involving love between individuals of elite status. One may suggest that the text projects wealthy and powerful individuals and groups as capable of twisting the norms to suit their own purposes. Thus, the *KSS* reflects flexibility in the approach to caste as well as gender.

The stories overall encourage the idea of love among individuals who belong to the same status. The fact that only some specific types of unions are problematized can perhaps be linked with the history of Kashmir. The *Rājataraṅgiṇī* has described in some detail (and considerable abhorrence) the marriage of two 'untouchable' *ḍomba* sisters with King Cakravarman and the elevation of one of them to the status of chief queen.[75] This turned out to be the main reason for the king's eventual assassination by the *ḍāmaras*, who had been instigated by his other wives.

In fact, the communities termed as the *cāṇḍālas* in texts appear to have had some political (and social) presence in Kashmir. Jayāpīḍa was followed in the fight to regain his throne from the usurper Jajja by a large number of villagers and men from the forests who were unable to bear Jajja's rule. It was a village *cāṇḍāla* named Śrīdeva who went to the battle with his villagers and is said to have killed Jajja by using a catapult with a sling stone after having resolved to do so.[76] The attempts of the *KSS* in these few depictions to somehow 'explain' the presence of the 'outcastes' can be seen in this context.

Overall, the representation of caste hierarchies in the *KSS* in the context of sexual relations is both simplistic and complex at the same time. In its representation of premarital relations the text glosses over, rather it does not envisage any possibility of complexity other than the one discussed earlier. The tales are laden with adventure, heroism and success, and a preoccupation with the caste hierarchy is hardly ever expressed. There is, for example, no problematization of a *pratiloma* situation in which a brāhmaṇa woman could desire a man of the merchant group. There is no dread of the mixture of castes or classes. It echoes the interests (or what should be the interests), concerns, fantasies of the elite and the values they uphold or are supposed to uphold. When there are transgressions, these are made to fit into the general paradigms of Brahmanical ideology.

Gāndharva 'Marriage': Transforming the Sexual Choice

The outcome of premarital relations in more cases than one is represented as leading towards the *gāndharva* union in the *KSS*, i.e. intercourse by mutual choice. Penzer, in his note on the *gāndharva* marriage, is of the opinion that it occurs most frequently in the text because the heroes usually belong to the warrior category and this form of marriage was particularly recommended for them.[77] But in the stories this is not limited to the kṣatriya varṇa. There are also some examples where the young lovers do not take recourse to the *gāndharva* union and get married through the 'proper channels', i.e. the marriage ceremony in which the bride is given away by the father in the presence of kinsmen, etc., as in the story of Vararuci and Upakośā.

The *gāndharva* marriage, as the outcome of the sexual desire of two individuals in love, involves some complexities. The attitude towards this form of marriage is ambivalent even in the *KSS* (as we shall see ahead). Penzer[78] has pointed out that the only witnesses of this form of marriage are the Gandharvas, the spirits of the air, and the participants realized that there was a certain irregularity in the action (thus the secrecy) even though they also knew that they were 'within the law'.

The protagonist in one story, Putraka, married a princess secretly by the *gāndharva* rite and they continued their sexual relations till the 'intrigue' was discovered by the guards.[79] Putraka is due to be punished by the king but escapes. Puṣpadanta, whose story has been discussed earlier, gained entry into the *antaḥpura* dressed as a woman in order to gain the princess Śrī, who had previously gotten in touch with him. There he married her secretly and she became pregnant. In the end he obtained her as his wife and their son was appointed as the successor of the kingdom, as the king had no son. Śrīdatta, a brāhmaṇa, was approached by Sundarī, the daughter of a *śavara* chieftain who had captured him, with the promise of freedom if he married her.[80] He made her his wife by the *gāndharva* ceremony and she became pregnant. He had to leave after that upon the insistence of his mother-in-law due to a threat from the chief. Later in the story he takes Sundarī as one of his wives when he becomes king. Thus, there are numerous instances where the *gāndharva* union is accepted in the end.

However, in the story of the brāhmaṇa Manaḥsvāmin and Princess Śaśiprabhā, another point of view is expressed. Manaḥsvāmin remained in the form of a woman in the *antaḥpura* with the princess and they married by the *gāndharva* ceremony.[81] But after this he was separated from her, and she was given by the king to Śaśin, who was the friend of the teacher of Manaḥsvāmin. This resulted in a dispute over the princess between the two men. Upon being asked to judge, the king replied that the princess belonged to Śaśin as she was his lawful wife, openly given to him by her father in a lawful way. On the other hand, the brāhmaṇa had married her in an underhand way, like a thief, by the *gāndharva* rite and had no lawful claim over her.

However, the issue of a girl's virginity before marriage is entirely ignored. It is in fact expressed nowhere in the text, showing that the sexuality of married women was much more problematic than that of unmarried girls. The issue in this case is more about paternal authority, since unmarried girls fell under the authority of the father in patriarchies, and its transgression by the male lover. Ultimately such unions are brought under the ambit of Brahmanical social reproductive norms by incorporating them into the structure of marriage. Male sexuality is problematic only when it involves the 'outcastes' or people at the margins; otherwise, married or not, they are free to take whatever chances that come their way. However female sexuality is allowed expression at least to the extent of choice and freedom to love.

Thus, we may state that premarital sexual relations are represented as being embedded in a complex social context in the *KSS*. A wide variety of characters from diverse backgrounds play an intricate role in these stories. The parameters of the behaviour of these characters are outlined clearly in the narrative, just as is done for the protagonists. The protagonists, regardless of their gender, figure as agents shaping their own destiny with the support of various strategies and intermediaries.

The standardization in the characterization of the heroic male and his beautiful willing beloved creates a perceptive pattern, an idealized situation. Shonaleeka Kaul has seen the significance of standardization in Sanskrit literature in their creation of archetypes, repeated occurring patterns or motifs, as social imagery and symbolism.[82] The archetype of lovers in the *KSS* creates masculinity and femininity that is as conforming as it is contesting. The variations crop up when the focus shifts to 'low' status individuals as protagonists, or when they belong to the groups (for example the *rākṣasas*) that are not entirely a part of Brahmanical society. The process of their legitimization is itself very significant.

Deviant Femininity: Contest and Control in Marital Sexuality

Common Monogamy and Courtly Polygyny

We may now shift our focus to the depiction of marital relations, polygyny and its implications, and adultery. The text does not focus much on 'routine' marital situations since these would inspire neither excitement nor anxiety. Marriage as such is not sensualized or eroticized in the text, yet a little concern can be seen in the establishment of conjugal relations. The consent of women is considered crucial in both fixing their marriage and after marriage.

Neither the sanctity of marriage, nor sexual relations within it is taken for granted in the tale of Aśokamālā, the daughter of a kṣatriya named Balasena.[83] When she was a virgin (*kanyā*) she was demanded from her father by a rich brāhmaṇa Haṭhaśarman who was captivated by her beauty. However, she was unwilling to marry him as she found him physically unappealing and told her father that she would not remain in his house if she was given to him. Despite her protest she was married and as stated she left her husband for another man.

The tale of the old merchant and his young wife is about how a favourable situation leads to the development of sexual/conjugal relations between the husband and wife when there was considerable age difference.[84] An old merchant married a young girl, who was also the daughter of a merchant, with the help of his wealth. But she was always averse to him due to his age. One night a thief entered the house while the husband and wife were in bed. The wife embraced her husband out of fear when she saw the thief. Thus, the merchant saw it as good fortune and spared the thief.

In the story of Somaprabhā, the daughter of a rich merchant of Pāṭalīputra, the husband had to make considerable efforts to establish his conjugal rights over his wife.[85] She had asked her father not to give her in marriage to anyone, but a young merchant named Guhacandra fell in love with her. His father forced the father of the girl to give his daughter in marriage to his son by bribing the king and surrounding their house with the help of the head of police. Somaprabhā agreed on the condition that her father would make an arrangement with her father-in-law that Guhacandra must never treat her as a wife (i.e. establish sexual relations with her). The father of Guhacandra agreed, assuming that everything would fall into place after the marriage took place, and in the evening after the ceremony asked his son to take his wife to bed as no man abstained from his wife. Upon hearing that, Somaprabhā looked angrily at her father-in-law and he died on the spot. Guhacandra concluded that his wife was evil and avoided her company, even though she lived in the house. He made a vow and feasted brāhmaṇas every day, while his wife, observing strict silence, gave a fee to them after they had eaten. In the end, he obtained her as a loving wife with the help of a charm given to him by a brāhmaṇa to appease the god of fire who showed him that she was a heavenly nymph and did not desire the society of a mortal. Guhacandra dressed himself up, after writing the charm, and went to converse with a courtesan in the presence of his wife. Out of jealousy, she stopped him from visiting the courtesan and asked him to be with her as she was his wife.

In this context, the case of Kanakarekhā, daughter of a king ruling over Vardhamāna city, can be cited.[86] When Kanakarekhā 'grew up', her father was worried about finding a suitable match for her and expressed this to her mother. But the queen told him that his daughter did not wish to be married. The daughter had told her mother that it was not inevitable that she should be separated from her parents, and that if she were to marry she would die. There was a certain reason behind this, which she did not disclose. However, she agreed to get married when her father gave her a speech about the unrighteousness of keeping a daughter unmarried and the sin incurred if she reached puberty.

All the situations discussed earlier have been represented in the context of monogamous marital situations. However, the concept of mutual fidelity is largely absent in the marital bond, since it allowed men to have more than one wife and access to women outside marriage. On the other hand, the wife could maintain legitimate sexual relations only with her husband. The portrayal of polygyny as an urban courtly phenomenon is prominent in the text.

A polygynous situation is clearly linked with the social status of a person. In the story of Guṇaśarman we find a passage in which the brāhmaṇa Agnidatta considers his daughter fortunate when, after inspecting her moles, Guṇaśarman states that she would have many rival wives (*sapatnaya*).[87] The reason given by Agnidatta is that wives generally have many rivals when the husband is wealthy, as a poor man would find it difficult to support even one wife.

Thus, polygyny is associated with the wealthy, especially kings, and not with any varṇa in particular. All the tales in which the protagonists belong to rich merchant families depict a monogamous marital bond. The tales that deal with occupational categories such as those of a barber, carpenter, or kṣatriya in the service of the state also portray monogamous marriages. The brāhmaṇa households of teachers are also monogamous. On the other hand is the instance of a brāhmaṇa youth named Śrīdatta who, by the end of the story, gains the sovereignty over a kingdom and also gains many wives in the process.[88] We may note here that sexual prowess was a significant aspect of the depiction of kingship, and the 'love' of kings extended to innumerable women.

The most outstanding example in the text is that of Naravāhanadatta, the hero of the main narrative, who is stated to be an incarnation of Kāma and is destined to be the emperor of the *vidyādharas*.[89] Before he attains that position, he marries, one by one, a number of maidens who are the daughters of *vidyādhara* kings or chiefs, many of whom approached him of their own accord and are also destined to become his wives.

Kingship is inseparable from the chief queen, a figure of great prominence in the text. Śrīdatta's chief wife is Mṛgāṅkavatī (and his magical sword is named Mṛgāṅka); Vāsavadattā, the chief queen of the king of Vatsa, is given great instrumentality in obtaining for her husband Padmāvatī, the daughter of the rival king standing in the way of his conquest of the earth; Madanamañcukā is inseparable from Naravāhanadatta.

The tales also reflect what effect the polygamous situation had on the marital life of women. Mahallikā, who was to be married to Sūryaprabha, expresses her discontent over what it was like to be in love with a 'man of many favorites', as she herself called Sūryaprabha, after she had a jealous encounter with one of his other wives.[90] She decided to persuade her father to give, along with herself, also her twelve friends in marriage to Sūryaprabha. Upon their protestation she stated that she was anyway not going to be the only wife of Sūryaprabha and that it would do her no harm if her friends were amongst these women. At least she would have some company of friends among other women with whom she could establish little intercourse, as they were her enemies (*virudha*). Sūryaprabha is said to have divided his body by magic science and thus, lived at the same time with all his ladies, but with his 'real' body he lived with his 'best' beloved (*priyatamā*), Mahallikā, the daughter of the *asura* king Prahlāda.

In the end he placed Kāmacūḍāmaṇī, the daughter of Sumeru, a prince of the *vidyādharas* and his main ally, above all his other wives and respected her the most on the orders of Goddess Durgā.[91] After they were married he told Kāmacūḍāmaṇī that the other women lived outside of him, but she alone lived in his heart. The morning after their first night together as husband and wife, he went and paid compliments to his head wives who were all together. They, '. . . were rejecting him, as being in love with a new wife, with playful, sarcastic, sweet, affectionate and bashful turns of speech . . .'.[92] Incidents such as these appear to be setting the standards of behaviour for women in the courtly context of polygyny.

When Kadalīgarbhā, the daughter of a sage, married King Dṛḍhavarman, she was faced with a situation where his principal wife tried to get rid of her. The chief queen first tried to bribe a minister to make her rival depart, and upon his refusal took the help of a wandering mendicant.[93] In the end, the plot was discovered and Kadalīgarbhā was reunited with the king, but she had to face a period of adversity when the king abandoned her. This story itself was narrated by Somaprabhā to her friend, Princess Kaliṅgasenā, about the false accusations of co-wives, so that she remained aware of her possible fate when she married a king.

Thus, the tale reflects intense competition and rivalry among co-wives, which ultimately has to be linked to their desire to gain the maximum possible influence over their husband through maximum sexual access. Queen Vāsavadattā had a difficult time coping with the situation soon after her marriage, as she was probably used to the excessive and exclusive love of Udayana during the period of prolonged courtship when he was prisoner in her father's court and her music teacher. With time she came to find out about his sexual 'intrigues' with other women (including an attendant of the harem). One time she witnessed the king secretly 'marrying' Mañjulikā, a princess whom the minister Gopālaka had captured by force and presented to the queen, by the *gāndharva* ceremony in a summerhouse. In retaliation in her fury she had Vasantaka, another minister and close companion of the king, captured.[94] The king later mocked her at her misplaced anger; but she had had obviously no choice for she could not have put the king himself behind bars, or done anything else to either control him or to alter her situation.

In such situations of jealousy and conflict the king is depicted with his 'hands full'. Udayana, the king of Vatsa, had to conciliate Vāsavadattā by clinging to her feet (when he addressed her by the name of another lover by mistake) and it is stated that '. . . bathed in her tears he was anointed a fortunate king'.[95] He continually made use of the 'soft and sweet' tales of the ingenious Vasantaka to conciliate his wife 'while he sat at her feet'.

Thus, we see that the polygamous situation is represented in the text as an almost exclusive feature of kingship. It is a situation which may or may not be reflected as resulting in rivalry and jealousy amongst co-wives. There is, for example, the case of Vāsavadattā and Padmāvatī, who became friends even before the marriage of the latter takes place to the king of Vatsa.[96] Friendships between co-wives when the king had multiple wives and concubines are, in this manner, depicted as a source of strength and power. The case of Mahallikā, who preferred to get married with twelve of her 'friends', has been discussed earlier. But never is the situation such that there is a reflection of conflict between the king and any of his wives. The kings happily reign with their chief queens by their side, women who are resigned to the idea of sharing their husband sexually with other women; their main concern becomes power over the king-husband, or influence, which may be attained through their lineage, kinship, resources, and sexuality.

Conflict arises in a situation in which they see their position under threat, as it happened with the queen when the new bride Kadalīgarbhā enters the scene as the beloved of the king. In conclusion, the correlation between kingship and polygyny and the depiction of chief queens in the *KSS* is an extension of the earth as feminine, which has been pointed out by Kumkum Roy.[97] She points out that in the *Rājataraṅgiṇī* 'the ideal masculine *rājā*, who protects, controls and enjoys the feminine earth', is utilized to characterize royalty. Thus, the king's sexuality belongs to an entirely different realm.

Uninhibited Sexuality: The Adulterous Female Archetype

This section deals with the depiction of extramarital relations in the text, an aspect which has been given considerable space in the narrative of the *KSS*. Since in a patriarchy men are granted relatively more sexual freedom than married women, adultery becomes a transgression by the wife, and an adulterer is a man who violates the authority of the husband by having sexual relations with the wife of another (*paradāra*). The *KSS*, in the attention that it draws towards adultery, is echoing the normative concerns with the fidelity of the wife. But in doing so the narrative has also brought into focus certain other aspects. We may discuss the portrayal of adultery with two themes as reference points—the question of initiative, and the eventual outcome of the relationship. Within these, differences according to the status and gender of the protagonists will also be highlighted.

The greatest possible 'collective flaws' of men and women, as envisaged in the text, can be seen in the stories related by a hen-mynah and a parrot in the judgement hall of King Vikramakesarin of Pāṭālīputra to settle a dispute between them over the question of the comparative wickedness of the sexes.[98] The mynah narrated the story about the greed and violence of males in which a 'worthless' merchant's son, addicted to gambling and other vices, had wasted his wealth, killed his virtuous wife while she was asleep, and ran away with her ornaments. Thus, the worst possible 'offence' a man could commit seems to be against a virtuous wife by misbehaving, neglecting or abandoning her, and using violence. In the case of women, the problem of sexuality emerges. In the story told by the parrot, a woman named Vasudattā, though married to a young, wealthy and handsome merchant, carried on a secret affair with a lover, and later tried to get her handsome husband executed on false charges in order to hide her own guilt. This is one of the *vetāla* tales where the *vetāla* questions King Tṛvikramasena about who was more wicked. The king concluded that women were the worst, since men could be wicked once in a while, but females were, as a rule, always so everywhere.

This puts into perspective the lopsided depiction of the sexuality of women in the text, since in most of the stories the initiative for establishing sexual relations is represented as being taken by married women. The archetype of the adulterous female constructs deviant femininity, posited against the powerful conforming femininity of the chaste wife. There are quite a few passages describing the unrestrained wicked behaviour of women. Thus, when Queen Rājadattā[99] approaches a merchant's son in her state of intoxication it is stated that a woman maddened by the god of love is incapable of discriminating: '. . . when there are these five fires, feminine nature, intoxication, privacy, obtaining of a man, and absence of restraint what chance for the subtle of character?'[100]

While the polyamorous behaviour of kings is extolled, as seen above, that of queens is made a prominent problematique in the text. While the *antaḥpura* was a secluded space, there were men like ministers, functionaries and courtiers who had legitimate access to it. While the kings gathered wives in numbers, their emotional and sexual fulfilment remained a cause for concern, as is seen in the depiction of polygyny. The proximity of other males in the king's household is resolved in the stories through the construction of the 'servile' masculinity—the male devoted in the service of his master, restrained and brave. Daud Ali has highlighted this in the courtly context, the context of bhakti ideology and medieval polity.[101] The issue was not just the sexuality of women of the king's household, it was also the threat posed to the political position of the king in the situation of close connections of queens with men of the court. This has been highlighted earlier in this chapter in the context of Kashmir and the events related in the *Rājataraṅgiṇī*.

As an example illustrating the above is the story of Aśokavatī and Guṇaśarman.[102] Aśokavatī, the beloved consort of King Mahāsena of Ujjayinī, became enamoured with the king's brāhmaṇa friend Guṇaśarman upon witnessing his skills in dance, music, use of weapons, etc. In order to get closer to him, Aśokavatī artfully asked her husband to make him teach her to play the *vīṇā*. Guṇaśarman, suspecting mischief, avoided the task but eventually had to start teaching her. Aśokavatī tried immense coquetry to seduce him; he asked her to desist as she was his master's wife. She referred to his beauty and skill being wasted, tried to bribe him, threatened to die and kill him also, but he is portrayed as steadfast in his righteousness. In addition, he saved the king's life several times in the story and at the same time kept resisting the advances of the queen. Finally, she took her revenge (through the king by telling him that Guṇaśarman had tried to use force on her) by getting him branded as a traitor, but he escaped before he could be punished. He later became a king himself.

Indeed it might be that all the social hierarchies seem somehow hinged on the sexuality of women; certainly caste and class hierarchies, and political hierarchies. In the next story, the student-teacher hierarchy of brāhmaṇa households is threatened, the education system based on the male-brahmanical monopoly over learning, the logic of 'violation of the preceptors bed' being a *mahāpāpa*, great sin, in the *śāstras*.

The story is of a handsome brāhmaṇa student, Sundaraka, whose beauty was matched by his excellent character, and Kālarātrī, the wife of his teacher who taught many pupils from different lands, made sexual advances towards him.[103] It is another issue that Kālarātrī was also a witch (*ḍākinī/śākinī*); consequently, the depiction of her sexuality does not follow normative patterns.[104] Kālarātrī made advances to Sundaraka one day when her husband was away, but he, though tempted, resisted with his whole soul the crime; 'however women may misbehave, the mind of the good is not to be shaken'.[105] In anger, Kālarātrī marked and tore her own body with bites and scratches and remained weeping with dress and locks in disarray till her husband came back. The angered teacher and his pupils attacked Sundaraka and flung him on the road. Sundaraka sought shelter in a neighbouring cow-house and took his meals in the almshouse of the brāhmaṇas. Kālarātrī approached him once more in the market one day, but he refused her on the grounds that she was the wife of his teacher, and addressed her as mother. She again lied to her husband and he got Sundaraka's food stopped at the almshouse.

While the sexuality of such women did not work on the men whose virtue is highlighted, it worked on the very husbands they intended to deceive. The women turned against the men the very sexuality they had rejected, and accused them of committing a crime they had refused to commit. The kings were close to brāhmaṇa household communities,[106] while the brāhmaṇa households themselves were hinged on the teacher-student relationship. The sexuality of women was a threat in each situation—kings had many wives and the learned brāhmaṇas were linked with knowledge. Female desire was brought within the ambit of deviant femininity and one might say 'excused' on that basis; male sexuality had to be curbed in this situation by outlining the ideals of masculinity that restrained itself. In light of the powerful rhetoric of masculine and feminine sexualities it would definitely influence and place even powerful women within the paradigm of being innately 'low' while men represented innate virtuosity.

In the story of Unmādinī, the king's righteousness is put to test in a potentially adulterous situation.[107] Unmādinī was the extremely beautiful daughter of a wealthy merchant, who was refused in marriage by King Devasena of Śrāvastī. Instead, she was married to his commander-in-chief. All through she held a proud resentment in her heart against the king. One day, in an act of revenge, she exhibited herself to the king from the terrace of her palace and the distracted king fell ill upon discovering that it was the same lady he had rejected. The commander-in-chief offered his wife to the king, but the king refused the offer as being unrighteous. The king consequently died, 'consumed by love's burning'.

There are variations in the eventual end of these situations—Guṇaśarman lost his position at the king's court and swore revenge only to become a king later; Sundaraka succeeded in exposing Kālarātrī and also became a king; King Devasena died and left the impression that no harm would have come to anyone (except dharma) if he had accepted Unmādinī, since even the citizens of the city had implored him to take the woman.

There are a few tales in which the men take the initiative in establishing an adulterous affair. These are tales that test the duty of the wives and in these the virtuous wives emerge triumphant, as in the stories of Upakośā and Devasmitā discussed ahead in the section on chastity. Thus, in the text adultery or the possibility of adultery is used also as a background against which the virtuousness of young men and women is put to the test.

The next story illustrates some aspects which have been related to adultery in the text—the situation which propels a wife to engage in extramarital sex, the possible reflection of adultery as strife in a marital relation, victimization of the husband, the treachery of the wife, and a correction of the 'wrongs'. The story is as follows.[108]

Devadatta was the son of a merchant of Pāṭāliputra, married to the daughter of a rich merchant of Puṇḍravardhana. He squandered away all his wealth in gambling after his father's death, and so his father-in-law took away his daughter as she was distressed by poverty. When Devadatta went to his father-in-law to borrow money to set up his own business, he discovered that his wife was having an affair with another young merchant. His wife told her lover about four jars of gold buried in her husband's house, which she had not revealed to her husband despite his poverty as she disliked him because of his addiction to gambling. Devadatta overheard the conversation between his wife and her lover and outwitted their plan to acquire his property. But the dispute over the wealth was finally settled in the king's court, where the king punished the adulterous (*paradārikam*) merchant by confiscating his property, while Devadatta cut off the nose of his wicked wife and married another. In all this, Devadatta's addiction to gambling and the consequent misery of his wife, which was the root of the problem, was forgotten.

Thus, we see that the punishment of the merchant is inflicted by the king. It should be noted that the main reason appears to be the attempted theft of another's property and the moral of the story focuses upon theft rather than on adultery by asserting that any treasure should be obtained only through virtuous methods. The wife, on the other hand, is punished by her husband. The cutting of the nose could actually mean that her behaviour was revealed in public and therefore led to loss of respect, represented by the literal mutilation and loss of face. As such disfigurement is depicted as the standard punishment of adulterous women in the text. The adulterous wife was superseded by Devadatta's new wife, but it is not clear if she was abandoned. In the tale told by the parrot, the adulterous wife Vasudattā's nose is bitten off by her dead paramour's corpse as it was animated by a *vetāla*.[109] She accused her husband of the act, adding that she had done nothing wrong, and the king ordered his execution. But the husband was saved by a thief who had witnessed the truth.

Adultery is, in addition, combined with other offences like theft of property and attempt to murder. There seems to be no standard pattern relating to the punishment of adulterous men in the text. In the tale of Devadatta, the merchant's property is confiscated by the king, but that seems to be a penalty for the attempted theft, compounded by adultery no doubt. There is a story in which the maimed lover of a Bodhisattva's wife was not punished and was banished along with the woman.[110] Vasudattā's lover had already been hanged by the city guards on suspicion of being a thief, and thus had met his punishment at the hands of fate. In the tale of the virtuous wife Śaktimatī, it is mentioned that in the city of Takṣaśilā whenever a man was found in the night with another man's wife, he was placed with her in the inner chamber of a *yakṣa's* temple.[111] In the morning they were taken to the king's court to be punished. The punishment is not specified, but what is apparent is that their behaviour was made public. King Yogānanda orders the execution of Vararuci on the suspicion that he had seduced his queen; this could point to the sterner treatment of adultery involving the king's wife.[112]

Adultery may not always meet with punishment. For example, we may take up the instance of the barber and his wife.[113] The king, who is indicated to be immoral, saw the wife of his barber and was attracted by her youth and beauty. This is also a rare tale of an adulterous king in the *KSS*; kings are mainly depicted as the executioners of justice in cases of adultery (and as lovers of queens, and unmarried women soon to be made their queens). Deciding that the barber was in no position to do anything about the matter, the king approached his wife when the barber was away from home. The next day the wife told the barber about the incident with a lot of pride. The king continued his liaison with the woman, while the barber was powerless to prevent it. The barber finally put an end to the affair by making the king believe that his wife was a witch who extracted a man's entrails by sucking them out through her mouth (the notion that overly sexual women 'damage' male bodies?).

Thus, the barber resolved the situation through the use of cunning. It is an interesting case as the wife was extremely proud of the fact that the king had chosen her as his lover. The tale reflects the variation in the attitude towards adultery in relation to the caste and class status of the actors and also voices the opinion of the female. Adultery per se is not the right action, since the king is branded as immoral. But the barber is content with the rehabilitation of his wife and no question of any kind of punishment is brought up since it is the king, who, instead of upholding the law, used his coercive power to transgress dharma.

There are also some narratives dealing with adultery that actually reflect the outmanoeuvring of the system by women through the means available to them. In one story, a young, handsome, brave, generous and high-minded kṣatriya who was in the king's employ (*rājopasevinaḥ*) had a wife who was wicked enough to enter into an 'intrigue' with another man. Her husband came to know and was determined to punish her. However, her confidante informed her and she escaped before she could be punished, but fell into a well in the forest.[114] She was rescued by a man described as a reincarnation of a portion of a Bodhisattva, and went on to become the maid (*dāsī*) to the principal queen (*mahādevī*) of a king named Gotravardhana. But the Bodhisattva lost his power due to contact with the 'sinful' woman (*kulaṭā*). Besides revealing aspects of adultery, this is one of the rare stories where we find mention of the kind of background the maids could have had.

It is noteworthy that numerous tales of adultery occur in the section on fools' stories, many of which are also situated in villages. Thus, to be a fool is to be emasculated, through adultery by his wife (or his own other acts), creating the model of a man-who-is-not-a-man (and who is also a 'rustic'). Some of them are very unlikely situations as the ones discussed ahead, though they reverse gender hierarchies in showing female cunning and male stupidity. In these instances we may see the fluidity of gender identities at various levels and gender seems to become 'performative', the tantalizing suggestion of Judith Butler.[115] This is most apparent in the story of Vajrasāra, where gender is reversed and sex is power, and marital conflict is expressed in violence.

Vajrasāra, a servant of the king of Vatsa, came to know that his wife had formed sexual connections with another man while he had left her in the house of her father in Mālava.[116] He decided to bring her home and led his wife into a dense wood beyond earshot of anyone. There he interrogated her and asked for the truth, threatening to punish her. But she refused to answer and told him to do as he liked. So Vajrasāra tied her up and beat her with creepers. While stripping off her clothes he felt his passion renewed and asked her for forgiveness. She consented on the condition that he let her tie him up in the same manner and beat him. He agreed, being 'blinded with passion', but she cut off his ears and nose with his own sword and ran away disguising herself as a man with his clothes and sword, thus, symbolically emasculating him. He was discovered and saved by a kind physician. He searched unsuccessfully for his wife and related the entire incident in the court of the king of Vatsa. All the people there mocked him saying that his wife had justly taken his man's dress and suitably punished him, since he had lost all his manly spirit and faculty of just resentment and so had become a woman. But in spite of the ridicule he remained in court.

In the story of the foolish carpenter and his adulterous wife, the wife escapes being caught with her lover, and also punishment in the process.[117] The carpenter was hiding under the bed with his pupil to verify the information given to him by his neighbours that his wife was in love with another man. But she discovered his presence and artfully told her paramour (*upapatim*) that she loved her husband more than him and would surrender her life for her husband. She also said that unfaithfulness was natural to women; the carpenter was pleased to hear these words. He told his pupil that though his wife had a lover, she was devoted to him and carried them both, the wife and the lover, as they sat on the bed, on his head.

There are rare cases in which the adulterous lovers actually end up as married couples: the brāhmaṇa Manaḥsvāmin developed sexual relations with the wife of a minister's son while he was staying in their house disguised as a woman.[118] The minister's son was away for six months and his wife regretted his absence as he went away immediately after their marriage. When he was to return, she ran away from the house with Manaḥsvāmin, already having developed relations with him. It is apparent in the tale that sexual relations had not yet been established between the husband and wife, and, therefore, her status as a wife was not yet complete. In another story a young and brave brāhmaṇa saved a new bride from an elephant while her groom (a merchant) and attendants had deserted her.[119] She expressed her grief to the youth at being married to such a coward and told him that he had become her husband from the time he had saved her life. So the youth followed the procession, while she avoided any sexual intercourse with her husband. Later, both of them escaped and the youth was even rewarded by Naravāhanadatta for his bravery. Again, in this story, though the girl was lawfully married to another, she was a new bride and had not had sexual relations with her husband. In addition, the heroism of the youth is contrasted with the cowardice of the merchant and he is represented as being more worthy of being her husband.

The outcome of the transgression of adultery seems open-ended, as reflected in the text. Taken in the context of marriage it clearly reflects a situation of conflict between the spouses in many cases. Besides the overall projection of Brahmanical norms and comments on the wickedness and evil nature of women, etc., we also find representation of the dissent of women. The norms related to gender hierarchy are represented as being contested and questioned by women and besides outright transgression they are depicted as finding ways and means of asserting their own will and, thus, subverting the system.

It has been pointed out that in Brahmanical patriarchy the chief concern was with the sexual behaviour of upper-caste and upper-class women due to the need to maintain patrilineal succession and caste purity.[120] Thus, the *KSS* in a way reflects the obsession with the sexuality of elite status women. Significantly, it is in the tales dealing with merchants, brāhmaṇas, and the royalty that adultery results in the punishment of the offenders, whereas in the instances of the barber, carpenter, and the king's servant there is a marked difference in the attitude of the narrator.

Overall, while adultery is considered a 'sinful' act, women are represented as subverting the system and the constraints on their sexual behaviour. They are willing to establish relations with any man who catches their eye or is available, including thieves, sick men, and maimed men. The adulterous men largely meet an adverse fate in the tales, since their behaviour in the context of sexual relations is nowhere linked to their inner propensity to wickedness, deceit, fickleness and lack of restraint, as in the case of women. These women represent the 'deviant' femininity archetype and a 'negative' female identity, while the male identity is associated with valour, self-control and enhanced sexual capability typical of kings and heroes. The issues of masculinity are different; it is not profligate sexuality, but rather the loss of manhood, especially in the inability to control the wife, that becomes a serious issue, seen in the depiction of the 'rustic fool'.

Idealized Femininity: The Chastity Motif

The representation of the chaste woman in the *KSS* forms the idealized femininity, which presents a direct contrast to the deviant model. In this context we can bring up the point made by Uma Chakravarti about the ideology of *strīdharma/pativratādharma* (duty of women/duty of devoted wife) that was created by Brahmanical patriarchy, which was to be internalized by women.[121] The chaste wife appears rarely in the narratives in contrast to unchaste females, the instances of adultery being far more numerous. However, when put together with the denigration of unchaste women, the valorization of the chaste woman and the powers conferred on her form a very influential model of femininity, all the more formidable when contrasted with the adulterous archetype.

The story of King Ratnādhipati is narrated by Ratnaprabhā, one of the wives of Naravāhanadatta, to illustrate her viewpoint that the strict seclusion of women was a mere social custom or folly produced by jealousy, as women of good family (*kulastriyah*) were guarded by their own virtue and even God could not guard unchaste women.[122] She was basically making the point in objection to the female warder (*dvāhsthyāh*) of her apartment, and asked the warden not to close the door to prevent the entrance of her husband's friends as they were as dear to her as her own body.

In the story narrated by her, King Ratnādhipati received a white elephant that could fly through the air as a reward from God Viṣṇu and he used him to conquer the earth and gain 80,000 wives. One day the elephant was severely wounded and a heavenly voice told the king that if a chaste woman (*sādhvī*) was to touch the elephant then he would be healed. So the king asked his carefully guarded wife (*nijām-surakṣitām*) Amṛtalatā to touch the elephant, but he did not rise. After that all of his wives and the women of his capital touched the elephant in succession, he still remained as he was, proving that there was not a single chaste woman in the city. At that time a merchant named Harṣagupta had arrived from Tāmraliptī and in his train was a servant (*karmakarī*) named Śīlavatī who was devoted to her husband (*pativratā*). She touched the elephant while stating that if she had not even thought of any man other than her husband then the elephant should rise up. The elephant rose up and the people praised Śīlavatī saying that chaste women were few and far between, comparing them to Śiva in their ability to create, preserve, and destroy the world. The king rewarded her (and her master) and she is stated to have reaped the fruit of her vow of chastity (*prāpta-sādhvīvrata-phala*).

Thus, it appears that a clear dichotomy is drawn between 'good' women who are chaste and quite rare and 'bad' women who are unchaste and who are numerically preponderant. In the tale while all the princesses of high lineage prove to be unchaste even though they are guarded, a low status *karmakarī* is chaste, who is in fact part of the retinue of a merchant travelling from Tāmraliptī and not kept in seclusion. The narrative, by placing the chaste devoted wife on a pedestal, rewarding her and comparing her power to that of Śiva, appears to be giving the women in the audience a not so subtle message (since it is also told by a woman). As stated earlier, the purpose was to make women internalize the ideology, which would solve the problem of the control of the sexuality of women in Brahmanical society. It almost appears as if chastity was for women a *tapasyā* that did not fail to reward them with some fruits sooner or later.

Some of the tales point towards an obsession with wifely virtue and chastity. One of the central figures of the narrative, Vāsavadattā, has to prove her chastity as her husband had doubts about her conduct during the time she spent away from him.[123] Ironically, Vāsavadattā had been in the kingdom of Magadha as part of the plot to obtain Padmāvatī as a wife for her husband. Everyone was willing to prove Vāsavadattā's 'innocence' while she was away when the whole plot was revealed to the Vatsa king. Yaugandharāyaṇa, his prime minister, stated that the entire undertaking was for the sake of the king so that he could become a universal emperor. But still the king seemed to be in doubt, so Vāsavadattā resolved to enter the fire to remove all suspicion from his mind. But Yaugandharāyaṇa, who had masterminded the plot, came to her rescue and facing the east addressed the 'guardians of the world' and implored them to speak if he had been a benefactor to the king and if the queen had been free from 'stain'. After that a heavenly voice was heard which proclaimed Vāsavadattā to be blameless and a goddess in a former birth.

We see that the parallels with the *Rāmāyaṇa* are obvious. Vāsavadattā endured her separation from her husband by seeing a painting of Sītā on the walls of the palace and she also resolved to go through the ordeal of fire. But the situation is averted by what Penzer calls the 'Act of Truth' motif in folklore which was taken recourse to by the minister.[124] According to Penzer, the Act of Truth could be a useful motif in the hand of the storyteller when the hero/heroine was in a tight corner. Here it proved the innocence of Vāsavadattā.

The question of wifely chastity is brought into focus in another context also, that is when their behaviour is put to test in the face of adversity. This situation can be found in the story of Upakośā[125] and Devasmitā.[126] We will focus on the latter. Devasmitā tricked four young merchants who had planned to seduce her out of curiosity upon hearing of the vow of chastity she and her husband had taken together when he had to leave on business.[127] To procure an interview, they sent a woman ascetic named Yogakaraṇḍikā to her house. She tried to influence Devasmitā by relating the story of her former birth in which she was the wife of a brāhmaṇa who travelled frequently. She had lived with other men and had, therefore, not cheated her senses of their lawful enjoyments. But Devasmitā perceived the treachery in the story and was able to outwit the four merchants. She marked them on the forehead with the mark of a dog's foot and cut off the ears and noses of the female ascetic and her disciple.

After doing this Devasmitā was scared that the young merchants might try to harm her husband, so after consulting her mother-in-law she, along with her maids, went disguised as a merchant on a ship to the country of Kaṭāha where he was. There she petitioned the king, asking him to assemble all his subjects. She then claimed that four of her escaped slaves were in hiding and pointed out the four young merchants, showing the marks on their foreheads as proof of identity when the other merchants objected to her claim, announcing that they were the sons of distinguished merchants. The king made them pay a huge sum to the chaste wife to redeem themselves from slavery, in addition to a fine to his treasury. Devasmitā returned happily with her husband. The moral of the story, as told by the narrator Vasantaka to Vāsavadattā, was that women of good family worship their husbands, are chaste, and never think of other men.

The chaste virtuous wives of these tales not only protect their own virtue but also prevent calamity: Devasmitā saved her husband from danger. In such situations, women characters are endowed with immense ingenuity and their achievement is recognized. However, nowhere in the tales is the chastity of men brought into focus: any conception of an unchaste man is non-existent in the narrative. Only in the story of Devasmitā do we find the concept of mutual fidelity. She was too jealous to approve of her husband's journey to a distant country, fearing that he would be attracted to another woman. So both the husband and wife performed a vow after which Śiva appeared to them in a dream and gave them two red lotuses, stating that if either of them was unfaithful during separation the lotus in the hand of the other one would fade, but not otherwise. It was this very red lotus that had attracted the curiosity of the four merchants.

To conclude, it can be stated that the *KSS* represents a situation in which all the problems in a marital relationship are linked with the question of the sexuality of women. But, just as in the case of premarital relationships, it is the extramarital relations which point towards a flexibility in the text's handling of deviations from the norms. The norms are upheld no doubt, but transgressions are accommodated. As in the earlier instances, variations are apparent and dependent on the status of the protagonists. What is also obvious is that the marital bond is represented as being fragile and fraught with tension. Chastity, while normative, seems to have been rare enough in practice to be valorized through stories of exemplary women.

Conclusion

We have seen the manner in which sexuality in its different aspects—related to premarital love and sex, marital relationships, and extramarital relationships—is depicted in the *KSS*. These reveal the interface between norms, traditions, and behaviour in matters relating to sexuality. Premarital love is brought within the ambit of patriarchal marriage and reproduction with the legitimization of the *gāndharva* marriage. Premarital courtship in certain stylized aspects (like sign language) is available only to elite men and women. But various urban common status groups are placed strategically as intermediaries in these. In premarital interactions in the text, women are depicted as subverting norms through various means and exercising their choice. The sexuality of women in these instances is not problematic; it is a bodily asset. The text worked out solutions to rationalize the behaviour of individuals to fit broadly into Brahmanical societal norms.

Within marriage there is the depiction of considerable dissent by women, in not accepting the marriage partners chosen for them and resisting conjugal relations. In representing the archetype of the adulterous woman we have the reflection of 'deviant' femininity. When viewed together with the idealized femininity of the chaste woman, we see how women were simplistically divided into 'good' and 'bad' types as the conforming and non-conforming. These may be seen as models of what to be and what not to be (but is). For men, notions relating to sexuality follow different patterns; their chastity is not an issue, and the king as the embodiment of perfect masculinity is also linked with a kind of copious sexuality. Masculinity is associated with restraint in sexuality, in contrast to femininity which gives in to sexual desires as an innate quality of women.

Uma Chakravarti significantly pointed out the plurality of meanings in the *Jātakas* while discussing the issues related to the production of the text (by Buddhist monks) and its recomposition by the readers/audience:[128] 'Thus, despite the fact that the relationship of the popular to high culture remains a grey area within the *Jātakas*, there is a strong possibility that the narratives contained in them could be decoded and used differently from the way the *bhikkhus* had intended.' The tales of the *KSS* could be interpreted in a variety of ways by the audience.

It raises very pertinent issues regarding how women can be perceived as participants in patriarchies, and their inseparability from issues relating to caste and class. Upper-caste and upper-class women were party to the various benefits that were conferred on them as being part of these categories, but were expected to restrain themselves sexually. However, due to their innate nature, they did not. The innate 'wicked' and sexual nature ascribed to women has to be seen as more than the mere rationale for their subordination or seclusion. It, in fact, depicts female behaviour patterns which resisted norms, and is also used as a justification for their non-conforming behaviour itself. It shows that gender norms functioned in extremely complex ways. This is not to say that caste or varṇa categories are insignificant in the text; they just do not follow the neat hierarchical pattern that is often assumed to be the norm; nor do gender relations.

NOTES

1. Devika Rangachari, *Invisible Women, Visible Histories: Gender, Society, and Polity in North India (Seventh to Twelfth century A.D.)*, New Delhi: Manohar, 2009, pp. 136–9.
2. A.K. Warder, *Indian Kāvya Literature*, vol. II, Delhi: Motilal Banarsidass, 1974, pp. 114–16.
3. Sheldon Pollock, *The Language of Gods in the World of Men: Sanskrit Culture and Power in Premodern India*, Delhi: Permanent Black, 2006, p. 92.
4. Ibid., p. 5.
5. Daud Ali, *Courtly Culture and Political Life in Early Medieval India*, New Delhi: Cambridge University Press, 2006, p. 18.
6. Michel Foucault, *The History of Sexuality Vol. I: The Will to Knowledge*, 1978; repr., New Delhi: Penguin Books, p. 14.
7. A.K. Ramanujan, Introduction to *Folktales From India*, ed. A.K. Ramanujan, New Delhi: Penguin, 1991.

8. Sherry Ortner, 'Identities: The Hidden Life of Class', *Journal of Anthropological Research*, vol. 54, no. 1, Spring 1998, pp. 1–17.
9. Romila Thapar, *Ancient Indian Social History*, 2nd edn., Delhi: Orient Blackswan, 2010, pp. 113–15.
10. For example, Agnidatta, the father of Somadatta and Vaiśvānaradatta, divided his royal grant/*agrahāra* between them; *Kathāsaritsāgaraḥ*, ed. Durga Prasad, Bombay: Motilal Banarsidass; 1889. All citations are from this version of the text, hereafter *KSS*. III. 6. 8.
11. The brāhmaṇa woman named Piṅgalikā who applies to the king's court for protection is said to be of 'good' caste or family/lineage (*brāhmaṇīkulajā, brāhmaṇī kulavatyeṣā*) See *KSS* IV. 1. 42, 103.
12. Shonaleeka Kaul, *Imagining the Urban: Sanskrit and the City in Early India*, Ranikhet: Permanent Black, 2010, p. 103.
13. *KSS* III. 1. 64.
14. *KSS* III. 3. 64.
15. *KSS* III. 1. 6.
16. *Ākṛtyā saukumāryena śayanāsansausṭhavaih. Śarīrasaurabhenāpi nīlautpalasugandhinā. Tām uttamām vinisvatya mahāhairātmanah sameh. Padmāvatī yathākāmupacārerūpācarat.* See *KSS*, III. 2. 28–9.
17. *KSS* V. 1. 40.
18. *KSS* XVI. 2. 86.
19. *KSS* XVI. 2. 141.
20. See *KSS* I. 4. 33 (Upakośā tells a prince's minister that she was from a respectable family/*satkula utpanna*).
21. Uma Chakravarti, *Everyday Lives, Everyday Histories: Beyond the Kings and Brahmanas of 'Ancient' India*, New Delhi: Tulika Books, 2006, pp. 59–62.
22. See the Story of Bhīmabhaṭa and Samarabhaṭa, which depicts the strife between stepbrothers on the issue of succession. A definite bias is shown towards the claims of the elder on the grounds that he was born from a mother equal in birth to the king, a kṣatriya, while the younger's claims are negated mainly on the grounds that his mother was a dancer. The former was the older brother and son of the high born queen and surpassed the younger in all the accomplishments. The latter is called *mūrkha nartakī putra*, 'foolish son of a dancing girl' (*KSS* XII. 7. 35–309).
23. Rangachari, *Invisible Women, Visible Histories*, pp. 136–9.
24. Kumkum Roy, *The Power of Gender and the Gender of Power*, New Delhi: Oxford University Press, 2010, p. 155.
25. Rangachari, *Invisible Women, Visible Histories*, p. 17.
26. Kumkum Roy, *The Power of Gender*, p. 58.
27. *Rājataraṅgiṇī*, VII. 207–8, pp. 477–8. All references to the text are from Stein, M.A., tr., *Kalhana's Rājataraṅgiṇī: A Chronicle of the Kings of Kashmir*, vols. I–II, 1900, 1st edn.; Delhi: Motilal Banarsidass, repr. 1989.
28. Foucault, *The History of Sexuality*, vol. I, pp. 57, 69, 92.
29. Ibid., pp. 106, 122, 127.
30. Chakravarti, *Everyday Lives, Everyday Histories*, p. 138.

31. Gerda Lerner, *The Creation of Patriarchy*, New York: Oxford University Press, 1986, p. 108.
32. Michel Foucault, *The History of Sexuality Vol. II: The Use of Pleasure*, 1985; repr., New Delhi: Penguin Books, 1998, p. 25.
33. Wendy Doniger, ed., *Karma and Rebirth in Classical Indian Tradition*, New Delhi: Motilal Banarsidass, 1983, p. 13.
34. Kunal Chakrabarti, *Religious Process: Purāṇas and the Making of a Regional Tradition*, New Delhi: Oxford University Press, 2001, p. 11.
35. Sherry B. Ortner, 'Gender Hegemonies', *Cultural Critique*, no. 14 (The Construction of Gender and Modes of Social Division II), Winter 1989–90, pp. 37–9.
36. Shalini Shah, *Love, Eroticism and Female Sexuality in Classical Sanskrit Literature (Seventh–Thirteenth Centuries)*, Delhi: Manohar, 2009, pp. 29, 109, 163–6, 184.
37. She considers the construction of the *nāyaka* in the erotic tradition as the embodiment of 'hegemonic masculinity'—one who attempts to dominate, subordinate and feminize the rest, and objectifies the female. In contrast is the 'love tradition', *prema*, essentially a feminine tradition which deals with reciprocity and emotions in sexual relations (which may or may not be physical).
38. Ali, *Courtly Culture and Political Life*, p. 234.
39. *KSS* VIII. 1. 1-41.
40. *KSS* X. 1. 50-175.
41. *KSS* VII. 1. 10-12; tr. Tawney, vol. III, 1924, p. 156. All translations cited, unless otherwise indicated, are from N.M. Penzer, ed., *The Ocean of Story, Being C.H. Tawney's Translation of Somadeva's Kathā Sarit Sāgara*, vols. 1–10, 1924; repr., Delhi: B.R. Publishing, 2001; hereafter referred to as Tawney.
42. *KSS* VI. 4. 21–30.
43. Tawney, vol. III, 1924, p. 66.
44. *KSS* XII. 8. 62; Tawney, vol. VI, 1924, p. 168.
45. *KSS* VII. 1. 123–6.
46. N.N. Bhattacharyya, *History of Indian Erotic Literature*, Delhi: Munshiram Manoharlal, 1975, pp. 43–4.
47. *KSS* XII. 8. 61–194.
48. She took a lotus from her own garland and put it in her ear and remained for a long time twisting it into the form of an ornament called *dantapatra* (tooth leaf). Then she took another lotus and placed it on her head and laid her hand significantly on her heart.
49. During two of these meetings Padmāvatī showed hostility towards her and left her coloured (camphor and red dye) finger imprints on the old woman, which were coded messages and were again interpreted by the prince's friend. In this entire communication the old woman was unaware of what was going on.
50. Devadatta (*KSS* I. 7. 57–103) was the son of a brāhmaṇa residing in a royal grant named Bahusuvarṇaka. He went to Pratiṣṭhāna to acquire learning, after which the daughter of the king, Princess Śrī, saw him from a window

and he saw her and they fell in love. She immediately communicated with him through the window by using signs to indicate the day and the place of their rendezvous. He could not understand them and his teacher Vedakumbha, seeing his pitiable condition, told him their meaning. The princess had told him to go to the temple rich in flowers called Puṣpadanta and wait there for her. They met in the inner shrine of the temple as the princess entered it alone. When he told her that his teacher had interpreted her signs she was furious at his stupidity and left out of fear that her secret would be discovered. However, a *gaṇa* named Pañcaśikha was instructed by God Śiva to help him as the god had been appeased by Devadatta earlier. The *gaṇa* disguised him as a woman and himself as a brāhmaṇa and went to King Suśarman, the father of the princess. He requested him to keep his daughter-in-law, the disguised Devadatta, safe as he had to go in search of his son who was abroad. The king placed the 'woman' in his daughter's apartments. One day he revealed himself to the princess when she was full of regretful longing in the night and married her by the *gāndharva* rite. When she became pregnant the *gaṇa* carried off Devadatta and then went in the disguise of the brāhmaṇa to ask for his daughter-in-law. The king, fearing the curse of the brāhmaṇa, offered his daughter in marriage to his son. Thus, Devadatta is said to have flourished in the power and splendour of his father-in-law and his son was made the successor of the kingdom, since the king had no son.

51. Penzer, *The Ocean of Story*, vol. 1, 1924, p. 81.
52. Ibid., 6.5. 1–90; 6. 7. 164–180; Kaliṅgasenā desired to marry Udayana but instead was deceptively married through the *gāndharva* 'ceremony' by Madanavega, a *vidyādhara*.
53. Brenda E.F. Beck, 'Social Dyads in Indic Folk Tales', in *Another Harmony*, ed. S.H. Blackburn and A.K. Ramanujan, Delhi: Oxford University Press, 1986, p. 82.
54. *KSS* XVI. 2. 1–40.
55. *KSS* I. 4. 1–30.
56. *KSS* XVI. 2. 89–108.
57. *KSS* VII. 5. 1–247.
58. *KSS* II. 3. 39–75.
59. N.N. Bhattacharyya, *Indian Erotic Literature*, p. 42; R.P. Goldman and Sally J. Sutherland, Introduction to *The Rāmāyana of Vālmīki: An Epic of Ancient India*, vol. V, tr. Robert P. Goldman and Sally J. Sutherland, pp. 3–98, Princeton, New Jersey: Princeton University Press, 1996, p. 65.
60. *KSS* VI. 2. 100–112, 3. 1-68, 4. 15–35.
61. *KSS* I. 4. 1–18.
62. *KSS* XIII. 1. 40–50.
63. *KSS* II. 2. 101–104.
64. *KSS* XIII. 1. 120–149.
65. *KSS* XII. 4. 71–226.
66. *KSS* IX. 5. 36–38.
67. *KSS* XII. 34. 53–56.

68. *KSS* XVI 2. 73–88, 109–110, 170–214.
69. *KSS* XII. 8. 49–196.
70. *KSS* II. 2. 135–140.
71. *KSS* IX. 2. 30–65.
72. *KSS* VI. 6. 98–120.
73. *KSS* XVI. 2. 111–146.
74. *KSS* XVI. 2. 89–108.
75. Stein, *Kalhana's Rājataraṅgiṇī*, vol. I, V. 351–413.
76. Ibid., IV. 475–78, 516. Further, in the *Rājataraṅgiṇī,* the theory of karma is used to explain the origins of Suyya, the engineer of the Kashmir waterworks under king Avantivarman (CE 855/6-883), which led to great increase in productivity and got him the epithet of *annapati*/lord of food. Suyya's origins are said to have been unknown (it is said that he was not born from a woman's womb) and he was brought up by a *cāṇḍāla* woman (named Suyyā) who found him while sweeping a dust heap (Ibid., V. 72–78).
77. Penzer, *The Ocean of Story*, vol. I, p. 87.
78. Ibid.
79. *KSS* I. 3. 30–79.
80. *KSS* II. 2. 115–40.
81. *KSS* XII. 22. 1–115.
82. Kaul, *Imagining the Urban*, pp. 130–60. The male archetype is the *nāgaraka*, the man-about-town, including the king and princes, brāhmaṇas, professionals and their sons, and merchants and their sons. Among the female archetypes she includes the free-sexual-cultured courtesan (*gaṇikā*), and her supposedly sequestered opposite, the family woman (*kulastrī*), whose secluded space of the inner apartments is routinely subverted through acts of adultery. She also speaks of a third type, the *abhisārikā*, the beloved slipping out onto the streets after dark for a secret tryst with her lover; the *kulastrī* by day was the *abhisārikā* by night.
83. *KSS* IX. 2. 30–65.
84. *KSS* X. 6. 83–88.
85. *KSS* III. 3. 63–132.
86. *KSS* V. 1. 6–30.
87. *KSS* VIII. 6. 203–209.
88. *KSS* II. 2. 10–210.
89. *KSS* IV. 3. 72–80.
90. *KSS* VIII. 2. 232–310.
91. *KSS* VIII. 7. 124–162.
92. Tawney, vol. IV, p. 118.
93. *KSS* VI. 6. 98–125.
94. *KSS* II. 6. 60–90.
95. Tawney, vol. II, 187–8.
96. *KSS* III. 2. 20–34.
97. Roy, *The Power of Gender*, p. 146.
98. *KSS* XII. 10. 1–95.
99. *KSS* VII. 2. 84–88.

100. Tawney, vol. III, p. 175.
101. Ali, *Courtly Culture and Political Life.*
102. *KSS* VIII. 6. 1–151.
103. *KSS* III. 6. 104–182.
104. Kālarātrī is also the name of one of the fierce forms of Durgā, worshipped during the *navarātras*, the nine-day festival dedicated to the goddess.
105. Tawney, vol. II, p. 105.
106. Ali, *Courtly Culture and Political Life*, pp. 49–50, 56.
107. *KSS* XII. 24. 1–62. It is a *vetāla* story, where the *vetāla* asks Tṛvikramasena whose loyalty was superior—that of the king or the general? The reply was that it was the king's, since there was nothing astonishing in the fact that the commander-in-chief acted for the benefit of his master since servants are bound to preserve their master's life, even by sacrificing their own. However, kings are arrogant, uncontrollable like elephants, and when they want enjoyment, they snap and forget the scriptures. But this king did not. Contrast this with the *Rājataraṅgiṇī*, where the king accepted the wife of a prominent merchant and she became his chief queen and the mother of the successor.
108. *KSS* III. 5. 15–63.
109. *KSS* X. 12. 1–95.
110. *KSS* X. 9. 1–40.
111. *KSS* II. 5. 163–178.
112. *KSS* I. 5. 32–55.
113. *KSS* VI. 6. 146–171.
114. *KSS* X. 9. 94–100.
115. Judith Butler, *Gender Trouble: Feminism and the Subversion of Identity*, New York: Routledge, 1999, p. xv.
116. *KSS* X. 2. 79–106.
117. *KSS* X. 6. 104–116.
118. *KSS* XII. 22. 1–115.
119. *KSS* VI. 1. 207.
120. Chakravarti, *Everyday Lives, Everyday Histories*, p. 138.
121. Ibid.
122. *KSS* VII. 2. 1–50.
123. *KSS* III. 2. 106–120.
124. Penzer, *The Ocean of Story*, vol. II, pp. 31–3.
125. *KSS* I. 4. 1–86.
126. *KSS* II. 5. 45–196.
127. Ibid., 2. 5. 45–196.
128. Chakravarti, *Everyday Lives, Everyday Histories*, pp. 203–4.

REFERENCES

Ali, Daud, *Courtly Culture and Political Life in Early Medieval India*, New Delhi: Cambridge University Press, 2006.

Beck, Brenda E.F., 'Social Dyads in Indic Folk Tales', in *Another Harmony*, ed. S.H. Blackburn and A.K. Ramanujan, Delhi: Oxford University Press, 1986.

Bhattacharyya, N.N., *History of Indian Erotic Literature*, Delhi: Munshiram Manoharlal, 1975.

Butler, Judith, *Gender Trouble: Feminism and the Subversion of Identity*, New York: Routledge, 1999.

Chakrabarti, Kunal, *Religious Process: Purāṇas and the Making of a Regional Tradition*, New Delhi: Oxford University Press, 2001.

Chakravarti, Uma, *Everyday Lives, Everyday Histories: Beyond the Kings and Brahmanas of 'Ancient' India*, New Delhi: Tulika Books, 2006.

Doniger, Wendy, ed., *Karma and Rebirth in Classical Indian Tradition*, New Delhi: Motilal Banarsidass, 1983.

Durga Prasad, ed., *Kathāsaritsāgaraḥ*, Bombay: Motilal Banarsidass, 1889.

Foucault, Michel, *The History of Sexuality Vol. II: The Use of Pleasure*, 1985; repr., New Delhi: Penguin Books, 1998.

———, *The History of Sexuality Vol. I: The Will to Knowledge*, 1978; repr., New Delhi: Penguin Books, 1998.

Goldman, R.P. and Sally J. Sutherland, 'Introduction' to *The Rāmāyana of Vālmīki: An Epic of Ancient India*, vol. V, tr. Robert P. Goldman and Sally J. Sutherland, pp. 3–98, Princeton, New Jersey: Princeton University Press, 1996.

Kaul, Shonaleeka, *Imagining the Urban: Sanskrit and the City in Early India*, Ranikhet: Permanent Black, 2010.

Lerner, Gerda, *The Creation of Patriarchy*, New York: Oxford University Press, 1986.

Ortner, Sherry B., 'Gender Hegemonies', *Cultural Critique*, no. 14 (The Construction of Gender and Modes of Social Division II), Winter 1989–90, pp. 35–80.

———, 'Identities: The Hidden Life of Class', *Journal of Anthropological Research*, vol. 54, no. 1, Spring 1998, pp. 1–17.

Penzer, N.M., ed., *The Ocean of Story, Being C.H. Tawney's Translation of Somadeva's Kathā Sarit Sāgara*, vols. 1–10, 1924; repr., Delhi: B.R. Publishing, 2001.

Pollock, Sheldon, *The Language of Gods in the World of Men: Sanskrit Culture and Power in Premodern India*, Delhi: Permanent Black, 2006.

Ramanujan, A.K., 'Introduction', *Folktales From India*, ed. A.K. Ramanujan, New Delhi: Penguin, 1991.

Rangachari, Devika, *Invisible Women, Visible Histories: Gender, Society, and Polity in North India (Seventh to Twelfth century A.D.)*, New Delhi: Manohar, 2009, pp. 136–9.

Roy, Kumkum, *The Power of Gender and the Gender of Power*, New Delhi: Oxford University Press, 2010.

Shah, Shalini, *Love, Eroticism and Female Sexuality in Classical Sanskrit Literature (Seventh – Thirteenth Centuries)*, Delhi: Manohar, 2009.

Stein, M.A., tr., *Kalhana's Rājataraṅgiṇī: A Chronicle of the Kings of Kashmir*, vols. I–II, 1900, 1st edn.; repr., Delhi: Motilal Banarsidass, 1989.

Thapar, Romila, *Ancient Indian Social History*, 2nd edn., Delhi: Orient Blackswan, 2010.

Warder, A.K., *Indian Kāvya Literature*, vol. II, Delhi: Motilal Banarsidass, 1974.

Notes on Authors

SNIGDHA SINGH is Associate Professor of History at Miranda House, University of Delhi. Her Ph.D., from the Centre for Historical Studies, Jawaharlal Nehru University, New Delhi, is titled 'Gender Relations and Regional Contexts: A Study of Early Historical Votive Inscriptions, *c.* 2nd century BCE to 2nd century CE'. Her research interests include gender relations, especially as represented in inscriptions and visual sources, with a special focus on the early historic period.

SHATARUPA BHATTACHARYA is Assistant Professor of History at Lady Shri Ram College, University of Delhi. She holds a Ph.D. in History from the Centre for Historical Studies, Jawaharlal Nehru University, New Delhi. Her research focuses on exploring society through the lens of gender, using epigraphs as well as texts. Her papers have been published in reputed journals like the *International Journal of the Social Sciences and Humanities* and the *Indian Historical Review*.

SHWETANSHU BHUSHAN is teaches history at Lady Shri Ram College, University of Delhi. Her area of interest includes early Indian social history with a focus on gender and varna. Her research also deals with *samskaras* (rites of passage) as represented in normative texts such as the Grihya Sutras, Dharma Sutras, and epic literature. Her doctoral thesis, from the Centre for Historical Studies, Jawaharlal Nehru University, New Delhi, is titled '*Samskaras* in the Sutras and the *Ramayana*: A Comparative Study'.

TARA SHEEMAR is Assistant Professor of History at Janki Devi Memorial College, University of Delhi. Her doctoral thesis, from the Centre for Historical Studies, Jawaharlal Nehru University, New Delhi, is titled 'A Study of Gender Relations in the *Kathāsaritsāgara*'. Her research includes examining the intersections of caste, gender, and political institutions. She has contributed papers to the Indian History Congress and received an award from the organization for her presentation on 'Merchants, Wealth and Monarchy'. Her forthcoming book, based on her thesis, is titled *Plunging the Ocean*: *Courts, Castes and Courtesans in the Kathasaritsagara.*

KUMKUM ROY is Professor at the Centre for Historical Studies, Jawaharlal Nehru University, New Delhi. Her publications include *The Power of Gender and the Gender of Power: Explorations in Early Indian History* (2010); *A Historical Dictionary of Ancient India* (2009); and *The Emergence of Monarchy in North India: Eighth to Fourth Centuries B.C.* (1994). She has edited and contributed to anthologies on issues of gender and social history. Her research interests encompass gender, histories of political institutions and social relations, and the representation of marginalized groups. She is also interested in issues of pedagogy.

Index

adultery 14,124, 131–2, 144, 148–9, 151–6, 164–81
Agrawala, V.S. 53n106
Ali, Daud 125, 132, 140, 160n5
Allchin, F.R. 49n2
Altekar, A.S. 2–3, 15n2
annaprāśana 104, 108, 116
apsarās 45, 47, 127
Apte, V.M. 109, 121n22
Asopa, J.N. 83, 95n70, 96n108
autonomy for women 8, 23

Bakker, Hans T. 71, 94n39
Barua, B.M. 24, 50n31
Beck, Brenda E.F. 135, 163n53
Bhandarkar, D.R. 76
Bharhut 10–11, 21, 23–31, 33–44, 48–9
Bhattacharyya, N.N. 109, 121n26, 162n46, 163n59
bhikkhu(s) 25–30, 39, 41–5, 160
bhikkhunī(s) 22, 24–5, 27–31, 37–9, 41–5, 160
Bowker, J. 104
brāhmaṇa(s) 6, 34, 63, 67–8, 71–3, 77, 83, 85, 107, 113–15, 117–18, 126–8, 139–40, 145, 151, 155
Brahmanical 4, 7, 9, 11, 13–14, 27, 41, 75, 82, 85, 106, 109–10, 114–16, 118, 120, 125, 131–1, 142, 144, 155–7, 159
Brekke, T. 50n11
Buddha 24, 26, 29, 43–4, 48
Buddhism 2, 22, 34, 67, 78, 129
Butler, Judith 150, 165n115

Candella(s) 10, 13, 65, 68–9, 82–6, 88–92
Chakrabarti, Kunal 130, 162n32
Chakravarti, Uma 2–3, 15n1, 16n12, 128, 134, 156, 160
Chastity 109, 124, 131, 133, 151, 157–9
Chattopadhyaya, B.D. 68, 78
childbirth 104, 114, 119
coping-stones 23, 25, 37, 39–40, 44
cūḍākarma 108, 117
Cunningham, A. 26–8, 33, 36

dāna 11, 22–3, 25, 27, 40–1, 43, 64–70, 84–6, 89
Dehejia, V. 38, 51n39
Dikshit, R.D. 83, 96n109
Doniger, Wendy 130, 162n33

early historic 10–11, 21, 126
elite women 8, 37, 43, 64, 70–1, 74–5, 78–9, 82, 86–9, 91–2, 134

Findly, E.B. 15, 27, 50n9
Foucault, Michel 129

gāndharva 14, 124, 127, 131, 134–5, 142–3, 147, 160n50
  attributes of lovers 132
  initiative, kinship, and role of intermediaries 133
  transforming sexual choice 142
garbhādhāna 104, 108–10
Ghosh, A. 50n16
gift-giving 11–13, 22–3, 65–6, 76, 80, 91
gift-making 22–3, 64
Goldman, R.P. 163n59
Gombrich, R.F. 50n18
Gonda, Jan 120n4, 120n12
Gṛhyasūtra(s) 6, 13, 104–5, 106–119
Gutschow, K. 50n12

Heitzman, James 68, 93n26
Hinduism 3
Holm, J. 104

Jainism 2, 22
jātakarma 104, 108, 114
jāti 7, 81, 128
Joshi, Shubhada 3–5, 15n5

Kalacuri(s) 10, 13, 76, 78, 83, 86–8, 90, 92
Kane, P.V. 49n6, 104, 106, 109, 113–14
Kathāsāritsagara 10–11, 14, 124
  brāhmaṇa identity and ancestry 127
  contexts and concepts 129–31
  elite of society 122–3
  marital sexuality 124, 144
  members of three higher varṇas, depiction of 128
  narrative and characters 120–4
    representation of the chaste woman 156–159
  urban lovers and the *gāndharva* union 131–44
Kaul, Shonaleeka 6, 16n15,144, 161n12
kāvya 6–9, 125, 127, 131
kingship 14, 135–6, 146, 148
kinship 8, 14, 25, 33–5, 41–2, 44, 112, 118, 130, 133, 135–6, 148
Konow, Sten 43, 53n127
Kulke, Hermann 94n29

Laymen and laywomen 39, 41
Lerner, Gerda 130
Luders, H. 26–8, 30, 33, 50n41, 51n35, 52n70

Mahathera, A.P.B. 50n28
matronage 15, 23, 25, 40, 50n13
Mauss, M. 49n5, 65, 93n6, 105, 121n38
merchant(s) 35–6, 48, 76, 79, 91, 197, 141, 155, 158–9, 164n81
Michaels, Axel 65–6, 93n7
Mirashi, V.V. 71, 74, 76, 94n40, 95n60, 95n72
Mishra, Kamalakar 4, 15n7
Misra, R.N. 49, 53n141
Mitra, D. 36, 53n104
monolithic Indian woman 6, 9

Nagaraju, S. 52n86
nāmakarana 104, 108, 114–16
Nath, V. 50, 64–6, 93n4, 93n5, 93n10
nāyaka 132, 162n37
niśkramana 104, 108, 116

occupational identity 35, 44, 127
Oldenberg, H. 120n8, 121n16
Ortner, Sherry 126, 130, 160n8, 162n35

Pandey, R.B. 120n2
Pargiter, F.E. 71, 94n36
patriarchy 15, 109, 130, 133, 148, 155–6, 161
patronage 23, 25, 35, 40, 43, 51, 50n13, 52n97, 95,
Patton, L. 122n86
Penzer, N.M. 134, 142–3, 158, 162n41, 163n51, 164n77
pillars, portrayal of men and women 44–8
Pollock, Sheldon 5, 16n10, 125, 160n3
polygyny 14, 144, 146–9
Prakrit 11, 23, 129
pregnancy 104–5, 109–14, 119
pumsavana 104, 108–11

Rājataraṅgiṇī 129, 142, 148, 150, 161n27, 164n74
Ram Gopal 107, 109, 120n13
Ramanujan, A.K. 126, 160n7, 163n53
Rangachari, Devika 6–9, 16, 124, 129, 160n1, 161n23
Rao, M. 53n130
Ṛgveda 4–5, 22, 66, 114
rites of passage 10, 13, 103–5, 120

sagotra marriages 5
samskāra(s) 10, 103–20
sangha 11, 22, 25, 27, 30, 39–41
Sanskrit 5–9, 11–13, 16, 30, 103, 110, 124–5, 129, 131, 143
Sanskrit *kāvya* tradition 6–9
Schopen, G. 29, 43, 51n55, 53n124
Shah, K.K. 64, 83, 93n2, 96n110
Shah, Shalini 6, 8–9, 16n17, 131, 162
Sharma, R.K. 76, 95n71, 97n122
Sharma, R.S. 34, 52n85
Sircar, D.C. 27, 50n14, 51n32, 94n86, 98n139
Shastri, A.M. 71, 94n35
Shrimali, K.M. 94n44, 94n52
sīmantonnayana 104, 108, 111–13
Smith, Vincent 83
Somadeva 124–6, 162n41
Stein, M.A. 161n27, 164n24

Stork, Helene 110, 121n31, 121n36, 122n84
Strīdhana 63
stūpa 11, 224, 27, 29, 37–9, 40–1, 43, 46–7, 49n1, 50n16
sūdra 2, 66, 116
Sugavaneswaran, A.V. 5, 16n13
Sutherland, Sally J. 163n59

Talbot, Cynthia 63, 68, 73, 93n1, 94n27, 95n54
Thapar, Romila 27, 50n7, 51n37, 52n97, 93n9, 107, 121n17, 126, 160n9
Trautmann, T.R. 34, 52n84
Trivedi, H.V. 82, 88, 96n107
Tyagi, Jaya 6–7, 9–10, 16n14, 106, 120, 121n18

Upreti, Kalpana 67, 93n24

Vākātaka(s) 13, 67, 69–78, 80–2, 84, 87, 90–1
van Gennep, Arnold 105, 120n7, 121n50
varṇa 7
Vedic age 2, 7

Warder, A.K. 160

www.ingramcontent.com/pod-product-compliance
Lightning Source LLC
Chambersburg PA
CBHW020341100426
42812CB00029B/3205/J
* 9 7 8 9 3 8 4 0 9 2 7 8 8 *

www.ingramcontent.com/pod-product-compliance
Lightning Source LLC
Chambersburg PA
CBHW020341100426
42812CB00029B/3205/J
* 9 7 8 9 3 8 4 0 9 2 7 8 8 *